AMERICAN VINTAGE

American Vintage

The Rise of American Wine

Paul Lukacs

HOUGHTON MIFFLIN COMPANY

Boston   New York

2000

Visit our Web site: www.houghtonmifflinbooks.com

Library of Congress Cataloging-in-Publication Data

Lukacs, Paul (Paul B.)
American vintage : the rise of American wine / Paul Lukacs.
p. cm.
Includes bibliographical references and index.
ISBN 0-395-91478-7
1. Wine and winemaking — United States — History.   I. Title.

TP557 .L87   2000
641.2'2'0973—dc21   00-040778

Book design by Anne Chalmers
Typefaces: Janson Text; Venetian 301 BT;
Type Embellishments Two, Altemus Borders Four

Printed in the United States of America

QUM 10 9 8 7 6 5 4 3 2 1

TO MY FATHER

CONTENTS

Acknowledgments

"Barbarian wines." That's what the man said, or at least what the translator speaking in my headphone said he said. I was attending a May 1997 symposium in Italy on the future of wine in the European Union, and the speaker, an aristocratic Tuscan wine producer, was complaining about wines from the United States. "Barbarian wines," he called them, and he urged his colleagues to man the ramparts against the invasion of this apparently undrinkable swill. Later that afternoon, the journalists in attendance were treated to a tasting of wines from various producers at the symposium. There, beaming with pride, was the same Tuscan *signor*, pouring glasses of his super-premium (and super-expensive) *vino da tavola*, a dark purple wine made from Cabernet Sauvignon grapes that tasted for all the world as if it came from the Napa Valley. That was the moment when I decided to write this book.

Back in the late 1970s, when I first became interested in wine, American producers openly imitated European models. Twenty years later, just the reverse was true, except now the imitation occurred on the sly. Yet all one had to do was taste — lush red Bordeaux, fruit-filled Burgundies, and Tuscan wines like this one — to realize that New World styles were profoundly influencing Old World winemaking. American wine, which in the aftermath of Prohibition surely had been barbaric, had become a world leader.

I decided that afternoon to tell the story of how this happened — the story of how American wine fell so low and then rose so high so quickly. I had been thinking about the subject for some time, and had written an article about it the year before for *American Heritage* magazine. Although a number of people suggested I expand the article into a book, I was reluctant to do so — first, because I was daunted by the prospect of writing a book; and second, because all that winter and spring I had been a candidate to become a dean at the college where I teach, and I knew that I couldn't tackle a book and a new job all at once. To make a long story short, I didn't get the job, and in fact during my trip to Italy was moping over having been rejected. But when I tasted that Tuscan Cabernet and remembered the earlier quip, I knew it was time to stop moping and start writing. The first person, then, whom I want to acknowledge is that aristocratic Italian producer, whose disingenuous condescension proved inspirational indeed.

I am even more grateful for the advice and assistance of many other people who helped me in many different ways. It is a cliché among wine writers that people in this business are uncommonly kind, but clichés only become clichés by being true. Whenever I needed some piece of information from a winery or a wine growers' association, the person on the other end of the phone or fax or e-mail line had the answer at the ready. A

[*x*]

number of people were especially helpful — hosting me during trips, helping arrange meetings or interviews, taking time to answer what must have seemed like silly questions, and in general giving of themselves without expectation of reward. To Jim Caudill, Nancy Light, Jan Mettler, Tim Puchta, Michael Rubin, Allison Simpson, Lisa Supple, and Phyllis Turner — many thanks. I would be woefully remiss if I did not also acknowledge Richard Slusser, my editor at the *Washington Times*. On the basis of a few sample articles, he took a chance six years ago and assigned me that newspaper's regular wine column. Having the opportunity to write (and learn) about wine on a weekly basis is the real origin of the ideas that led to this book.

I also want to thank those people who helped directly with this project: Richard Snow at *American Heritage*, who commissioned the original article; my agent, Georges Borchardt, who believed that a book based on that article had commercial potential; Marnie Cochran, my first editor at Houghton Mifflin; and Rux Martin, my current editor, who has guided the book (and me) with grace and charm. Closer to home, I want to thank my colleagues in the English department at Loyola College in Baltimore for putting up with my many distractions; Tom Scheye and John Hollwitz for helping me arrange for sabbatical leave; Gen Rafferty for all her kindness; and the interlibrary loan staff at the Loyola–Notre Dame Library for their help with my frequent requests. Even closer to home, my father, to whom this book is dedicated, has believed in me as an author for a long time, even when there was plenty of evidence to the contrary. I love and admire him greatly. My good friend and compatriot Michael Franz read the manuscript and, as with so much else over the years, gave me sage counsel. I am very appreciative. Finally, this book could not have been written without the help of two people who, at different stages of the project, provided much needed emotional as well as intellectual guidance. I would never have started it without the kind encouragement of Karen Lukacs, and I would never have finished it without the support and love of Marguerite Thomas. To them, and to everyone who helped me, I lift a glass of "barbarian wine" in toast.

Baltimore, Maryland
June, 2000

AMERICAN VINTAGE

Doubtless
As Good

W E IN AMERICA," declared Thomas Jefferson in 1808, can make wine "doubtless as good" as the great wines of Europe. No one in young America promoted wine more enthusiastically than Jefferson. As secretary of state, he selected the wines for President Washington's table. When he became president himself, he personally purchased an extensive cellar, and he later assisted both James Madison and James Monroe in keeping the White House well stocked with some of the world's great wines—claret and Champagne, Burgundy and Hermitage, hock, sherry, and Madeira. Jefferson considered wine to be both a mark of sophisticated taste and a democratic alternative to harsh spirits. "Good wine," he once said, "is a daily necessity."

But when it came to things American, Jefferson's enthusiasm often got the better of him. No domestic wines made in his lifetime were anywhere near as good as the fine European ones he imported to Washington and Monticello. Little changed for more than 150 years. Save for a fleeting period of glory in California in the 1880s and 1890s, American wine remained very much in the shadow of the great wines of the world. Even as recently as a generation ago, the United States was little more than an afterthought in terms of fine wine. The country certainly had a long history of grape growing, but that history hardly mattered. Nor did the wines themselves much matter. Large producers, led by E. & J. Gallo, made huge amounts of innocuous jug wine and cheap fortified tipple, but only a handful of small, largely unknown American wineries produced anything remotely resembling the famed European bottlings so sought after by connoisseurs. Then, seemingly overnight, American wine took a huge leap forward in quality and prestige. The nation that had been an afterthought suddenly became an obsession. All at once, Americans discovered that their country had the potential to make wines that could compete with the world's best. This book tells the story of that discovery —both why it took so long for the United States to produce truly great wine and how and why America was able to rise so quickly to its current position of prominence, if not preeminence, in the world of wine.

As with most discoveries, the story begins with a crucial moment of realization, an eye-opening instant filled with the awareness of new possibilities. In this case, the moment came in 1976, in Paris, where a young Englishman named Stephen Spurrier ran a small wine shop near the Place de la Concorde. His Académie du Vin had a loyal following, including a considerable number of Americans—foreign service officers from the nearby U.S. embassy, expatriates working abroad, and all sorts of tourists, including California wine producers making French pilgrimages. From time to time, these visitors brought along bottles from home. Spurrier drank and sold almost exclusively

French wines, because like connoisseurs everywhere at the time, he automatically assumed that France produced the world's most interesting and distinctive bottlings. Yet a few of the California wines he sampled seemed surprisingly, indeed shockingly, good. As he told his associate, Patricia Gallagher, they tasted "truly exceptional."

After visiting the vineyards of northern California in late 1975, Spurrier and Gallagher concluded that something significant was happening there. Virtually no one in France, though, knew anything about it. So they hatched a plan. They decided to organize a tasting of American wines and invite some of France's most esteemed wine professionals to serve as judges. The idea was to publicize the high quality of these wines by testing them against expert palates — and in the process to promote Spurrier's shop as *the* place in town where even a Frenchman might learn a thing or two. So on a warm May afternoon, they assembled a panel of nine eminent judges on the patio of the Inter-Continental Hotel to taste and evaluate twenty wines, ten whites made from Chardonnay and ten reds made primarily from Cabernet Sauvignon. Since Spurrier and Gallagher had promoted the event extensively, a crowd of spectators, including a number of journalists, came as well.

Of the twenty wines Spurrier poured that afternoon, twelve were American, all from northern California. The other eight were French. Spurrier thought it important to have some clear standard of comparison, so he made sure to choose some of the very best French wines — one grand cru and three premier cru white Burgundies, a first growth and three "super seconds" from Bordeaux. He had little doubt that the judges would prefer the Burgundies and Bordeaux, but he hoped that they also would be impressed by the overall high quality of the California wines, especially when tasted in such elite company. And because he knew that French gastronomes usually dismissed American wine out of hand, he decided to conduct the tasting blind—that is, with the labels hidden and the bottles unmarked. When the judges, led by Pierre Bréjoux, chief inspector of the Institut National des Appellations d'Origine took their seats, they knew only that some of the wines they would be tasting came from the United States and that the others were French.

The results of the 1976 Paris tasting shocked the wine world. When all twenty wines had been swirled and sniffed, savored, spat out, and scored, Spurrier removed the wrappings from the bottles. To everyone's surprise, including his own, the highest-rated wines turned out to be American—the red a Stag's Leap Wine Cellars 1973 Cabernet and the white a Chateau Montelena 1973 Chardonnay, both from the Napa Valley. (Two famous French wines finished in second place, Château Mouton-Rothschild 1970 and Domaine Roulot's 1973 Meursault-Charmes.) The press jumped on the story. In France, the reaction reflected anger and disbelief, but in America it was pure glee. Writing in the *New York Times*, Frank Prial noted that Europeans frequently had denigrated American wines by denigrating American tastes. "What," he asked rhetorically, "can they say now?" *Time* put the case more succinctly. In a story headlined "The Judgment of Paris," the magazine declared that the "unthinkable happened . . . California defeated all Gaul."

These statements were more expressions of chauvinism than objective reporting. Spurrier himself argued repeatedly that his tasting was less a competition than a vehicle for discovery—"an opportunity to acknowledge that a young vineyard area can produce top-quality wines, given the same love, interest, skill and money that has been lavished on European vineyards for centuries." The surprise, then, was not so much that some American wines received high scores. The real news was that, to a person, the experts had been unable to tell which wines came from which country. During the tasting, some of them had confidently announced that this or that wine was "definitely" or "certainly" or "unmistakably" a Bordeaux or a Burgundy, only to be repeatedly proven wrong. The wine that one judge said bespoke "the magnificence of France" turned out to be a Napa Cabernet, while another wine that a different judge dismissed as Californian because of its allegedly simple bouquet turned out to be a Burgundy. "Tender . . . a fine balanced wine," read one person's notes on the Stag's Leap Cabernet. "Fruity and elegant . . . *très complet,*" read another's on the Montelena Chardonnay. On it went. The egg on the judges' collective faces came from their inability to discern what until then everyone had assumed was obvious—namely, that the great French wines tasted better than other wines because they tasted, well, *French.*

The Paris tasting had far-reaching consequences. It demonstrated to Europeans and Americans alike that the United States (and possibly other New World countries) actually could produce world-class wines. In America it inspired the wine industry to raise its standards and to begin thinking of "world-class" as a goal, while in Europe it led winemakers to look at American wine with a new appreciation and respect. But most important, the realization that great wine could come from vineyards that did not have centuries of grape-growing history behind them suggested to people on both sides of the Atlantic that they had to rethink what great wine was all about. For generations people had assumed that quality was a function of history—the living, growing history of storied vintages from storied vineyards. The Paris tasting suggested that quality involved something else. Perhaps it came from the winemaking, perhaps from the vineyard, but in any case it was intrinsic, actually within the wine, no matter what was on the label. In short, Stephen Spurrier's publicity stunt woke everyone up. It presaged radical change, in the Old World as well as the New.

Plenty would change in Europe over the next quarter century, but the most radical development of all was the rise of American wine—in terms of intrinsic quality as well as influence and renown. The rise certainly was meteoric, as the United States quickly became one of the major winemaking countries in the world. It also was unexpected, particularly since American wine had experienced an equally great fall earlier in the century. In 1933, following the thirteen years of national Prohibition, wine in the United States was widely considered nothing more than an agent of intoxication. It remained perceived that way for nearly a generation. For centuries, men and women had distinguished wine from other alcoholic beverages—in part because of the sheer diversity of its flavors, in part because of its use at the table, and in part because of its historic role as a mark of refined culture and civilized taste. In post-Prohibition America, such distinctions were all but lost. Far from being a mark of sophistication, wine was viewed as a sign of destitution. In the mid 1960s, when the phoenix of American wine began to stir in its ashes, things could hardly have been worse.

How did everything change so quickly? The answer is paradoxically but quintessentially American. On the one hand, the winemaking entrepreneurs whose work inspired the rise advocated individual self-reliance. Like so many Americans in so many fields before them, they believed that their present success had little if anything to do with past accomplishment. Without a legacy of celebrated vintages and classified growths to define but also confine their efforts, they felt free to experiment with new approaches and technologies. They looked to science rather than tradition to tell them what to do, and they defined quality almost exclusively in terms of a wine's present composition. But on the other hand, those same winemakers wanted nothing more than to create a tradition and establish a legacy. They believed that no accomplishment was too great for American nature, and they considered it their mission to make history from the fruit of that nature—American wine from grapes grown in American vineyards.

The first stage in American wine's rise involved making premium wines that resembled the European classics as closely as possible. The ultimate accolade, as evidenced at Stephen Spurrier's Paris tasting, came when an American wine was mistaken for a European one. The second stage came when those successful handcrafted wines became models for less exclusive mass-produced ones, wines that in turn became models for improved *vin ordinaire* throughout the globe. If a great many of the world's wines, regardless of origin, taste similar these days, they do so in large measure because they are made to match a stylistic profile that used to be reserved for a handful of elite bottlings. American vintners were the first to emulate and then popularize that profile. But the third stage in American wine's rise has involved producing wines that can serve as touchstones with which to determine quality, thus complementing, and sometimes replacing, the European classics. In Italy and France, Spain, Portugal, and Germany, American wines today function as new classics, helping to define excellence at the highest level. For the first time in the seven-thousand-year history of wine growing, that level transcends regional and even national boundaries. Winemakers all over the world labor to make wines that are "doubtless as good" as the finest made in the United States—which does not mean wines that taste American, but wines that taste first and foremost of themselves. Perhaps the most important legacy of the rise of American wine has been the realization that inherent quality rather than reputation defines a classic. After all, quality is what gives any wine-growing country a tradition worth savoring.

Today the American wine industry is filled with people attempting to graft tradition onto what is still very much a new enterprise. The graft can take odd forms, as, for example, in the architecture of northern California's wine country, where faux Italian villas sit beside farmers' barns, or in the French names that some wineries put on their labels to make their wines sound sophisticated. Yet these oddities are only superficial manifestations of something more substantial: the realization on the part of winemakers and wine drinkers alike that American wine has at long last come of age. The proof can be found not just in a few successful bottles that trick tasters like those in Paris back in 1976, but rather in a series of wines from a series of vintages that themselves initiate a native tradition of quality. The finest wines in the world today are identified in terms of the grape in context—the context of the vineyard as well as the winery, the past as well as the present. In America, California is leading the way, but the lesson is being adopted in the Pacific Northwest, New York, Virginia, and wherever someone dreams Thomas Jefferson's old dream. That same lesson is also being learned at famed European estates and at wineries in other New World countries, since international rather than merely local standards now fuel winemaking ambitions the world over. The dawn of the twenty-first century is a truly golden age for wine, with vintners producing better wines than ever before in more places than ever before. This golden age is global, but both the improvement and the redefinition of quality elsewhere has been inspired in large measure by the success and the ongoing promise of American wine—its amazing rise from its equally amazing fall.

I

Eastern Dreams

He was a small man with big dreams. When twenty-one-year-old Nicholas Longworth hopped off the flatboat that brought him down the Ohio River to the frontier town of Cincinnati in the summer of 1803, he was virtually penniless. No one could have guessed that he would become the benevolent founding father of American wine. Longworth came to Cincinnati because his family estate back in New Jersey lay in ruins, his parents having remained loyal to the British crown during the American Revolution. Barely five feet tall, he was determined to succeed on his own and rid his name of royalist taint. So like many others of his generation, he went west, where over the next fifty years he realized the American rags-to-riches dream in spectacular fashion. Cincinnati in its infancy was a rough, often drunken place, a log village of some eight hundred inhabitants, many of them soldiers living in a military outpost. Longworth, flush with hope, ambition, and more than a little idealism, imagined turning it into a cultivated American garden—a community of men and women living off the land

and working together for the common good. He spent the remainder of his life trying to make that dream come true. When he died in 1863, he had become the city's leading citizen, a noted philanthropist, and a celebrated patron of the arts. He also was one of the wealthiest men in the United States. His money came almost entirely from real estate. Over the course of his career, he bought and sold thousands and thousands of acres of land. Some was in the city, but more lay in the surrounding countryside. And much of that was planted with wine grapes. Nicholas Longworth owned the first commercially successful winery in the United States, and his success provided American wine at large with its first taste of respectability. Before he cultivated his vineyards, almost no one in the young country drank domestic wine. What little existed was considered inferior to anything imported from Europe, and in truth most of it tasted very bad. Longworth, however, made wines that people actually liked to drink. They were enjoyed well beyond Cincinnati, earning praise and plaudits as far away as Europe.

For more than two centuries, in virtually every colony, state, and territory, from north to south and east to west, people had tried to make American wine from grapes grown in American soil. Here in Cincinnati, they finally succeeded. Longworth's accomplishments inspired a generation of grape growers, who in turn transformed the hills of southwestern Ohio from wilderness into a cultivated vineyard that became known as America's Rhineland. Their wines were recognized far and wide. Indeed, at midcentury they essentially *were* American wine. In the words of the official catalogue of the 1851 Great Exhibition in London, where Longworth's sparkling Catawba was displayed to considerable acclaim, Cincinnati had become "the chief seat of wine manufacture in the United States . . . attracting much attention, and growing in importance."

Sadly, that attention proved short-lived. An alarming number of the Cincinnati vines began to wither in the mid-1850s. By 1870, almost all of them had died. The growers did not understand what brought this blight to their vineyards. Nor did they know how to combat it. As a result, their industry itself soon died, and by 1880 Cincinnati wine existed only in memory. Nonetheless, Longworth's story—the story of why his vines failed, why for a short time they produced good wine, and most important, why he planted them in the first place—represents in microcosm much of the history of the first three hundred years of American wine.

Nicholas Longworth did not plant his vineyards to make money. Instead, being very much a man of his time, he was motivated by romantic, patriotic idealism. He envisioned western Ohio, and by extension all of the United States, becoming an agrarian republic. This was a widespread ideal during the first third of the nineteenth century. The notion that America should be a primarily agricultural society, one ruled by farmers rather than merchants or manufacturers, transcended virtually all differences of political party or faction. The common reasoning held that an agrarian life would provide cultural cohesion, as men and women of different geographic, religious, and ethnic origins became attached to their new homes by working the land. In such a young and undeveloped country, where immigration amid an already diverse populace threatened social stability, people's affection for their state and nation would develop naturally when they tilled the soil and cultivated their gardens. And where better to pursue such an ideal than on the unsettled and unspoiled frontier? As James Fenimore Cooper wrote in his 1823 novel, *The Pioneers*, the work of the first settlers on the frontier would be followed by "the permanent improvements of the yeoman," and every man would feel "a direct interest in the prosperity of a commonwealth of which he knows himself to form a part." Cooper was describing upstate New York, but Nicholas Longworth shared much the same vision for Cincinnati. To this son of politically and socially ostracized parents, western Ohio represented the possibility of a new beginning—specifically, the possibility of membership in an American "commonwealth." In turn, grape growing and winemaking would constitute his "permanent improvement."

But why grapes and wine? What would make anyone think that viticulture would improve living conditions on the frontier? The answer has to do with the conditions themselves. Although industrialization, urbanization, and sectional strife later would issue severe challenges to the dream of an agrarian American commonwealth, for someone actually living on the frontier in the early 1800s, a more immediate threat came from the bottle—or, more precisely, the jug, often filled with raw corn whiskey. Americans in the first half of the nineteenth century were notoriously hard drinkers. They consumed more alcohol per capita than ever before or since, and they drank mostly distilled spirits—rum from the West Indies, brandy from Europe, and whiskey made at home. There were many reasons for this, not the least being that in a town like Cincinnati there was not much else *to* drink, but such widespread consumption had one obvious consequence—equally widespread drunkenness, which in turn spawned sloth and violence, each in its own way threatening the agrarian ideal. To Longworth, wine and a culture of wine appreciation seemed the obvious alternative. He shared in the then popular belief that wine, as a fermented beverage, did not contain the same sort of dangerous alcohol as spirits. It was a natural gift from God, an agricultural product just like apples, corn, or wheat. In addition, he knew that the European countries with the lowest levels of alcoholism were those in which wine formed a part of daily life. When Longworth compared conditions in Cincinnati with those in rural France and Italy, he became convinced that America's scourge of drunkenness would decrease in direct proportion to an increase in table wine consumption. As his great-granddaughter wrote many years later, "He decided that the greatest service he could do his country would be to generalize [wine] production." Put simply, then, Nicholas Longworth planted his first vineyard and went on to become American wine's founding father, all in the name of temperance.

Although American grape growers or winemakers today do not campaign for temperance, many advocate much the same sort of reform that Longworth had in mind. They argue that wine, when considered as a food beverage, is fundamentally different from other alcoholic drinks — different because of how it is made (through natural fermentation, without any cooking or artificial manipulation), and more important, different because of how it is used (as part of a meal and familial or communal fellowship). This argument does not ignore the fact that wine contains alcohol. It contends, however, that wine historically has been Western culture's beverage of moderation, a mark of civilization because itself a civilized thing. In Robert Mondavi's words, printed for a time on the labels that carry his name, "Wine is part of our heritage, traditions, and the gracious way of life." That was precisely Nicholas Longworth's point.

He did not think it up on his own. Wine enjoyed a special status in much of the Western world during the nineteenth century. Especially in England, then the most powerful nation on earth, wine was appreciated and celebrated far more than other alcoholic beverages. This was in part because it offered a greater variety of styles and flavors than did whiskey, ale, or other drinks, and in part because the finest wines were relatively scarce and hence desirable. In the 1800s, fine wines, once the exclusive province of an aristocratic elite, became commodities available to anyone who could afford them. Middle-class people began to regard a taste for them as a mark of culture, much like a taste for fine books or fashion. In England, however, all wine was imported, the climate being inhospitable for viticulture. By contrast, in America, grapes grew wild and in profusion. Nicholas Longworth's goal was to democratize wine appreciation—to bring it within the ken of ordinary citizens by treating it as something refined and gracious and as part and parcel of America's agrarian ideal.

Making wine a democratic drink had been Thomas Jefferson's goal a generation earlier. Jefferson, the young country's most eloquent spokesman for the agrarian ideal, frequently argued that Americans needed to learn how to grow their own grapes and produce their own wines. "No nation is drunken where wine is cheap," he declared. Jefferson expressed "moral and physical preference [for] the agricultural, over the manufacturing, man," insisting that farming was "the employment of our first parents in Eden, the happiest we can follow, and the most important to our country." Wine, he contended, should be the natural drink of the temperate yeoman, much as it was in France, Italy, and the Rhineland. "Being among the earliest luxuries in which we indulge ourselves, it is desirable it should be made here," he said, adding that "we have every soil, aspect and climate of the best of wine countries." A renowned connoisseur who traveled extensively in European wine regions, Jefferson for a long time envisioned growing grapes and making wine at his home in Virginia, much as Longworth did later in Ohio. The significant difference between them is that Longworth realized that dream, while Jefferson never did.

The crucial thing separating these two men's attempts at viticulture was the specific grape variety Longworth used, the Catawba. He planted scores of other varieties, but this was the one that made the best wine. Jefferson's gardeners never planted it at Monticello because Catawba only became available commercially in 1823, almost a decade after Jefferson had abandoned any serious attempt at viticulture. After repeated efforts at considerable expense, he gave up wine growing because one of two things always happened: either the vines died or the wine turned out to be unpalatable. The first invariably occurred with imported European vines. The second took place when the vines were native Virginians. Although Longworth didn't know it, his Catawba belonged in neither of these categories. Instead, it was a native hybrid, an accidental cross (or, in all probability, a cross of a cross) between a European variety and an indigenous American one. It did not wither and die after only a few seasons, and it made palatable wine.

Botanists today know a great deal more about grape species and varieties than people did in the early nineteenth century, but both Jefferson and Longworth understood full well that native American grapes are quite different from European ones. All they or anyone else had to do was look. The plants have different leaves, produce different fruits, and grow on different roots. While the European grapes are all of one species, *Vitis vinifera*, the American ones divide into many species—*Vitis labrusca, rotundifolia, riparia, aestivalis,* and *cordifolia,* to name the primary ones. Most important, grapes thrive in the wild in North America, while virtually all European vines grow only as cultivated plants. Although grape growing now has become big business in many parts of the United States, no one in early nineteenth-century America grew grapes commercially. There was just no use for them. Thanks to refrigeration and pasteurization, today's grapes have become a common table fruit and a source of nonalcoholic juice as well as jelly. Grapes 150 years ago, however, were used only for wine or raisins. And native American vines did not yield either good wine or good raisins.

Although nearly half of the world's vine species are native to North America, they are for the most part poorly suited to winemaking. The problem, quite simply, is taste. Unlike the European *Vitis vinifera* grapes, native American varieties produce wines that taste overtly musky. The early settlers dubbed them "fox grapes" because of their "rank Taste when ripe, resembling the Smell of a Fox," according to Robert Beverley's 1705 *History and Present State of Virginia.* Fermentation only accentuates this offensive flavor, and the resulting wines prove extremely unpleasant—which may suggest why Native Americans never made any. The first colonists certainly made wine from these grapes. When the results proved undrinkable, they imported vines from Europe and tried to produce European-style wines from *vinifera* varieties. It stood to reason that a place in which so many grapes grew wild would be a place where other ones could be cultivated successfully. So it seemed, for example, to Lord Delaware, who in 1619 imported French growers and French vines to Virginia, where he planted a vineyard containing some ten thousand plants. To his chagrin, they all died. The same fate befell the three hundred acres planted in 1622 by Lord Charles Baltimore, son of the grantee of the Maryland territory. So too with the plots planted by Dutch settlers on the banks of the Hudson, and the vineyards started later in the century by French Huguenots near Charleston, South Carolina. In fact, the first generation of settlers in every colony tried to cultivate European *vinifera* grapes. And in all cases, from French Louisiana to Spanish Florida to English Massachusetts, the vines died.

Because there seemed to be no logical explanation for all this failure, the succeeding generations kept trying. Since *vinifera* grapes were a notoriously fickle crop even in Europe, perhaps the problem was just poor farming. So all through the Age of Reason, when enlightened men demanded that everything have a reason, colonial Americans planted vines and watched them die. Nowhere did people try harder than in Virginia, where the government encouraged numerous viticultural experiments. Jefferson's is the best remembered, but there were many others, vineyards and estates whose names have been long forgotten because they yielded only broken dreams. With the aid of hindsight and post-Darwinian biology, we now know why: European vines were defenseless against pests and diseases to which native American vines had developed immunity over centuries of evolution. A trinity of blight—black rot, downy mildew, and powdery mildew—devastated *vinifera* vineyards. If by chance a lucky plot avoided disease, parasites attacked—grape leafhoppers, berry moths, or phylloxera, a tiny plant louse that destroyed the roots and killed the vines within a few years. This, then, was American wine drinkers' great puzzle. They lived in a vineyard where they could not make drinkable wine.

Although all the American grapes produced poor wines, some clearly tasted worse (and some better) than others, leaving open the possibility that there somewhere might exist a native grape that would yield decent wine. Just such a grape was discovered, or believed to be discovered, growing in the woods beside the Schuylkill River just outside Philadelphia around 1740 by James Alexander, a gardener working for William Penn's son, Thomas. Alexander never tried to make wine from this new grape, but he did cultivate it, and some fifteen years later, Colonel Benjamin Tasker, Jr., planted a small vineyard with it near Annapolis, Maryland, where he produced a wine that he called Maryland Burgundy. According to a contemporary report, it was "much admired by all who tasted it," although it quickly lost color and turned so sour "that no person would touch it." A severe winter in 1760 destroyed Tasker's vineyard. More than twenty years passed before someone else attempted to make wine from this singular grape variety. Then a French immigrant named Pierre Legaux formed a company to make wine at Spring Mill near Philadelphia. Legaux, who was something of a schemer, changed his first name to Peter, sold shares in his Pennsylvania Vine Company before he planted anything, and advertised "the first vintage ever held in

America" well before he had produced a single bottle. Planning on a grand scale, he went on to plant some eighteen thousand vines, the vast majority of which he imported from France. They all died. The only variety that prospered was Alexander's, which Legaux called the Cape.

Legaux used that name because he refused to believe that this could be a native American grape. After all, by that point everyone knew that American grapes produced only foul, musky-tasting wines. Legaux had gotten a few cuttings from South African vineyards near the Cape of Good Hope along with his European imports, and he argued that this vine, so obviously different from the other *vinifera* plants, came from there. It remains uncertain whether he honestly believed this story or invented it in order to attract potential customers, but he clearly recognized that the grape was unlike all his others. It thrived while they died. By 1810 he had to confess that his company's only chance for success involved "pull[ing] out all the plants, and plant[ing] again with the Cape of Good Hope." Legaux ran out of money before he could replant, but in the meantime he sold some vines to a Swiss immigrant named John Dufour, who took them west—first to Kentucky and then to the Indiana Territory, where with his family and a small group of other Swiss settlers he built the town of Vevey in a region he nostalgically called New Switzerland. There, on the northern bank of the Ohio River, Dufour planted a vineyard consisting primarily of Cape grapes. Like Legaux, he argued that they had to be European in origin, declaring that he wanted to save the variety's reputation and character "from being merely wild." Both men were wrong, and growers soon named the grape Alexander, after its original discoverer.

The Alexander grape no longer exists, but in the first decades of the nineteenth century people planted it in many parts of the country. Some made wine from it with modest success. Dufour sent a few bottles to then President Jefferson, as did Major John Adlum, who was cultivating the grape in a Maryland vineyard. Adlum advertised it as a native variety, and Jefferson was so impressed that he urged other growers to "push the culture of that grape," confidently predicting that America's "first success will be from a native grape." But strictly speaking, the Alexander was not really native. Instead, it was an accidental hybrid—that is, an uncultivated cross between a native *labrusca* and an imported *vinifera*, most likely a European variety that William Penn had planted near where James Alexander made his discovery. No one knows the precise genetic ancestry of the Alexander, but it probably had much more *labrusca* than *vinifera* in it. Nonetheless, the presence of at least some European genetic material is what made for drinkable wine.

It would be almost fifty years before hybridization became widely understood and then exploited through intentional, cultivated crosses, and nearly a century before the principles of Mendelian genetics, which explain hybridization, became accepted. Still, hybrids would prove to be the key to the first commercially successful American wines. These wines came from another variety of John Adlum's vines, one that he planted from cuttings he had secured from a widow living in Montgomery County, Maryland. Her husband had grown grapes, but no one knew where he had gotten the vines. Someone told Adlum that they looked like grapes used to make Hungarian Tokay, and much like Legaux, he latched on to the idea that he was growing a *vinifera* variety. When he later discovered that the grape was not European, he resurrected the name that the Maryland widow had used, Catawba. Although most accounts indicate that his wines were not all that good, he propagated the vines. And in 1825 he sold some to a short, somewhat eccentric man from Ohio—Nicholas Longworth.

Twenty-two years after his arrival in Cincinnati, Longworth was a millionaire. Early on, he had hung up a lawyer's shingle, but he had not practiced law for almost a decade. Instead, his fortune came from buying and selling land with a Midas touch. Longworth acquired his first piece of property when as a young attorney he successfully defended a down-and-out client against a charge of horse stealing. The grateful client turned out not to have enough money to pay the bill, so he suggested as payment either the horse in question or a copper still. Longworth wanted neither. He suspected that his client may have lied and stolen the horse after all, and as an advocate of temperance, he did not drink whiskey. The still was housed in a local tavern, the owner of which offered to trade fourteen acres of land on the western edge of the city for it. Longworth made the deal reluctantly, but over the next few years he watched with amazement as the property's value skyrocketed. He then decided to sink virtually all his money into land speculation. Whether because of skill, luck, or both, he became extraordinarily successful. In the words of one contemporary, he was "shrewd, sagacious, quick-witted; with great common-sense and acquisitiveness." He also was somewhat odd. Short and spry, with a shock of gray hair and huge bushy eyebrows, Old

Nick, as the townspeople liked to call him, dressed only in black, spoke in cryptic phrases, and despite his ever-growing fortune lived a spartan personal life. Cincinnatians looked at him with a mixture of admiration and amusement. When he began planting vineyards, they regarded it as just another in a line of curious eccentricities.

Longworth first experimented with grape growing as early as 1813, but he did not devote himself seriously to it until around 1820. His first substantial vineyard was planted with vines acquired from the Swiss settlers in Vevey, but the results proved disappointing. In order to make a decent wine from Alexander grapes, he had to add sugar and brandy, fortifying it, so that the final result, which he considered "a tolerable imitation of Madeira," contained over 20 percent alcohol. This was far less than whiskey, but it wasn't what Longworth wanted. Dry table wine, with around 12 percent alcohol, was his goal, a goal that his neighbors long considered one of his peculiarities.

Because everything good had to be shipped across the Atlantic, Americans in the early nineteenth century drank very little wine. Most of what they did drink was fortified—port, sherry, and Madeira. This was to some degree because fortified wine would not spoil, but more because it contained so much alcohol. A public accustomed to rum and whiskey wanted strong wine if it wanted wine at all. Longworth had other ideas and other models in mind. He wanted to make table wine such as was produced in Germany, France, or Italy, countries with low levels of public drunkenness. By doing so, he hoped to encourage a culture of wine appreciation, a more egalitarian version of what was happening in England. He thought of wine as a natural and indeed providential drink, and he dreamed of its becoming part of American daily life. In this regard, it is important to remember that Longworth and his neighbors did not consume many of the beverages we drink regularly today. Not only were there few nonalcoholic juices (citrus fruits being unavailable and other fruits fermenting much like grapes), but coffee and tea were expensive, milk spoiled quickly, and water frequently was brackish and disease-ridden. Ironically, health and safety constituted the primary advantage of alcohol. Whiskey might make you drunk, but it would not make you sick. Too much wine could produce drunkenness also, but popular wisdom held that fermented beverages and distilled spirits had fundamentally different characters. Dr. Benjamin Rush made this argument in its most influential form in his 1784 *Inquiry into the Effects of Ardent Spirits upon the Human Body and Mind*, a work that Longworth knew well. Rush used a "moral and physical thermometer" to illustrate the different effects of temperance and intemperance. Among the latter he included "diseases" like jaundice, epilepsy, madness, and ultimately death, and "vices" such as fighting, lying, anarchy, murder, and suicide. By contrast, temperance's effects included "cheerfulness, strength, and nourishment." What produced intemperance? Rush listed toddy, grog, slings, morning drams, and peppered rum. And what produced temperance? Milk and water, beer, cider, and wine.

For a long time many people thought that wine might not really contain alcohol at all, or, at worst, a different, less harmful sort of alcohol. When chemists proved otherwise, people still insisted on distinguishing fermentation from distillation. In their view, distillation, being an artificial cooking process, produced alcohol that worked quickly and dangerously upon the body, while fermentation, being natural, produced alcohol that worked slowly and gradually. Longworth's son-in-law, W. J. Flagg, made the case as follows:

> When wine is drunk that is pure, its alcohol acts, not independently, but in combination; not abruptly, but gradually; and as it circulates, economizes and slowly distributes its power through every organ and member with an even, a balanced, and a mild effect, continuing long and disturbing little; exciting moderately but sustaining much. On the other hand, the alcohol of brandy, whiskey, and rum, escaping easily soon after entering the stomach, goes free and uncontrolled to work its will upon the tissues of the drinker; for which Nature is not responsible, but man, whose art has wrested the powerful fluid from its native envelopment, and man must bear both the consequences and the responsibility.

The crucial phrase here is "wine . . . that is pure." Longworth's goal (and Flagg's too, for Flagg succeeded him as head of the winery) was to make unfortified wine and thus promote the cause of temperance and public good.

It proved elusive. Most Cincinnatians had no interest in dry wine, and most of the wines Longworth produced lacked the sort of quality that might entice them. This was true even though he was making what in all likelihood was the finest wine yet produced in America. His Catawba tasted less foxy than wine made from any other non-*vinifera* grape, but it still had a distinctly musky character. Longworth observed that the taste of the grape skins was especially strong, so he decided to separate the clear juice from the dark skins before fermentation, thus producing a blush-colored white Catawba, somewhat akin to today's white Zinfandel. Although the wine did not excite most of his Anglo-Saxon neighbors, it did find a market in Cincinnati's growing German immigrant community. Longworth employed German laborers in his vineyards, sold them land on which to build their houses, and made wine for them to drink. "All the wine made at my vineyards," he wrote later, "was sold at our German coffee-houses, and drank in our city." White Catawba bore little resemblance to Mosel or Rhine Riesling, but the German immigrants who wanted a dry table wine had no other option. It was satisfactory enough, and they drank it up.

Longworth, though, wanted more. Not content to serve a minority population in one city, he dreamed of nothing less than changing America's drinking habits. Thus he experimented with literally hundreds of other varieties. Like all the would-be vintners before him, he tried to plant European grapes. He also tried different native grapes, including accidental hybrids. Some, like the Isabella, proved as good as Catawba, but none proved better, and as had happened countless times elsewhere, the European varieties all died quickly. He planted vineyard after vineyard and variety after variety all through the 1830s, but while his agricultural projects grew grander and more ambitious, his winemaking remained modest. The market remained very local.

The turning point came in 1842, when a batch of wine accidentally underwent a second fermentation, thus producing a sparkling wine. It tasted less foxy than Longworth's dry Catawba, and he determined to make more. Fortunately he had deep pockets. Longworth did not know how to make sparkling wine, so he hired French winemakers from Champagne. They introduced the expensive *méthode champenoise* in which, after the barely ripe grapes fermented and the resulting wine was bottled, the winemaker induced a second fermentation by adding a dollop of sugar. Then the bottles were turned, or "riddled," by hand to get rid of the dead yeast cells—a time-consuming and costly process. Adding to the expense, bottles kept exploding, the pressure of the second fermentation causing the glass to break. In one year alone, forty-two thousand bottles broke in the cellar. Since Longworth was not in the wine business to make a profit, he pressed on, buying new, thicker bottles, hiring new winemakers, and making more and more sparkling Catawba. For this pink, bubbly wine was good. People liked it—not only the Germans in their coffeehouses, but also other Cincinnatians and, soon enough, people from outside the region, even wealthy easterners who otherwise drank only European wines. Comparisons with Champagne were inevitable. Longworth never called his wine by that name, insisting always that it was a distinctly American product, but he had to be pleased when customers told him that his tasted as good as the French standard-bearer. Some even claimed that it tasted better. Most famously, Henry Wadsworth Longfellow celebrated it in rather treacly verse titled "Ode to Catawba Wine":

> For richest and best
> Is the wine of the West,
> That grows by the Beautiful River;
> Whose sweet perfume
> Fills all the room
> With a benison on the giver . . .

Very good in its way
Is the Verzenay
Or the Sillery soft and creamy;
But Catawba wine
Has a taste more divine,
More dulcet, delicious, and dreamy.

There grows no vine
By the haunted Rhine
By Danube or Guadalquivir,
Nor on island or cape
That bears such a grape
As grows by the Beautiful River.

At long last, after almost two hundred years of failure, someone had succeeded in making good wine in America.

Longworth's sparkling Catawba proved so popular that he could not help but make money from it. By the mid-1850s he was producing nearly 100,000 bottles annually and advertising his wine nationally. It even began to attract attention in Europe. Robert Browning drank it, as did the British journalist Charles Mackay, who reported in the *Illustrated London News* that an odd American grape with a strange name produced a wine that "transcends the Champagne of France." By then, other grape growers and winemakers had followed Longworth's lead. They planted vines across the river in Kentucky and down the river in Indiana as well as farther east in Ohio. In 1859, the region as a whole had more than two thousand acres under vine and was producing nearly 600,000 gallons of wine. Although Catawba accounted for almost all of it, much of the wine was still rather than sparkling. Only someone with lots of money could afford to make sparkling wine, and by this point people other than German immigrants had developed a taste for still wine. Although it never attained the renown enjoyed by the sparkler, "Cincinnati Hock" began to sell well. Longworth's neighbors, who initially had regarded his winemaking as a quirk, now looked upon it with considerable respect. "Everyone knows Nicholas Longworth," declared the *Cincinnati Commercial* in 1857, "the founder of wine culture in America, author of sparkling Catawba, the munificent and judicious patron of Art." He did not much care about fame, but being called the founder of American wine culture had to be for Nicholas Longworth the highest praise.

Yet while everyone knew Longworth, not everyone respected him. By midcentury, the American temperance movement had changed, its tactics becoming ever more coercive and radical. Increasingly, its goal came to be defined as prohibition rather than moderation. Although some people still held to the distinction between fermented and distilled alcohol, many others no longer accepted it. Most temperance advocates now saw all alcohol as equal, and equally evil. They began to fight for total abstinence, all in the name of social improvement. This first wave of prohibition reform was a middle-class and often nativist movement, and the reformers portrayed fermented beverages as something foreign and un-American. They pictured beer as low-class, immigrant swill and wine as something aristocratic—evil because both alcoholic and undemocratic. The prohibition movement enjoyed phenomenal success in the 1840s and 1850s, success the likes of which it would not see again until the turn of the century. In 1851, the state of Maine passed a law forbidding the manufacture and sale of all alcoholic beverages. Over the next four years, twelve other states and territories followed suit. The Ohio legislature soon forbade the sale of spirits in taverns, saloons, and restaurants, and a petition campaign garnered 145,000 signatures calling for a "Maine law" for the Buckeye State. Longworth's dream was being challenged and even ridiculed.

The most public voice of challenge belonged to Samuel Cary, a native Cincinnatian and the unquestioned leader of Ohio's temperance movement. In 1847 he had published a pamphlet entitled *Cary's Appeal to the People of Ohio* in which he threw down the proverbial gauntlet. "Traffic in intoxicating drinks [and] those who are engaged in it," he declared, "multiplies paupers, maniacs and criminals . . . endangers the security of life and property . . . perils the peace and quiet of neighborhoods, and furnishes schools of vice for the young." Such traffic should be made criminal, for "moral appliances alone cannot arrest [it]," and those who manufacture alcohol should be consigned "to the prisons now occupied by their ruined victims." Cary was thinking primarily about the whiskey distillers, but as a resident of the region increasingly known as America's Rhineland, he could not ignore the winemakers. Indeed, he had plenty of ire saved for them. He preached his gospel in the pages of the *Cincinnati Organ,* which declared the "most formidable enemies against the progress of temperance" to be those members of the city's "wine-drinking aristocracy" who think it "genteel and refined to have sideboard and tables loaded with costly decanters filled with the devil's drink." There could be little doubt about whom Cary and the other reformers had in mind.

The conflict between Cary and Longworth became public

in 1853, as prelude to the election in which Ohio's proposed "Maine law" would be put to a vote. Longworth, who despite his wealth and fame was a very private man, took what was for him the extreme step of writing an open letter to his fellow citizens. In it he made familiar arguments—that wine was itself a temperance beverage, that drunkenness did not abound where it was the principal drink, that wine was just as nutritious as other agricultural products. Cary responded two days later, scoffing at Longworth's claims. Wine contains alcohol just like whiskey, he insisted, with the same effects and no possible health or social value. To Longworth's claim that prohibition would harm Cincinnati economically, Cary responded coldly: "We protest against that wealth and splendor which are secured by the miseries, tears and blood of society." A flurry of letters and broadsides followed over the next few months, including conflicting medical reports, one declaring wine drinking to be beneficial, the other asserting just the opposite. Finally, on October 11, Ohio went to the polls. The prohibitionists lost, largely because Cincinnati and the surrounding counties voted so decisively against them. Cary was crushed. He angrily blamed just about everyone and everything in sight—distillers, winemakers, Longworth's money, the newspapers, and especially foreigners. "Take out the vote of the German wards," he claimed bitterly, and the prohibition ticket would have won.

Happily for Longworth and the other grape growers, the alcohol question, which dominated Ohio politics in the early 1850s, began to fade from public view, overwhelmed by the growing sectional crisis. Much the same thing happened in the rest of the country. No more "Maine laws" appeared on ballots, public agitation quieted, and by 1860 only three of the thirteen states that had legislated prohibition in the first part of the decade remained dry. Of course temperance agitation never went away. Reformers, led by the Woman's Christian Temperance Union, galvanized new and often unexpected support after the Civil War. Advocating a broad program of social reform, they integrated abstinence from alcohol with women's suffrage, labor rights, and most important, Protestant evangelization. Then, at the start of the twentieth century, the politically savvy Anti-Saloon League jump-started the drive for prohibition, this time at the national level. None of this much affected the Cincinnati wine business, for by 1860, Nicholas Longworth and his fellow growers were facing a far more immediate crisis. Their vines were dying in their vineyards.

The culprits were familiar: black rot and downy mildew. Catawba's partial *vinifera* ancestry, precisely that which made it successful as a wine grape, rendered it especially susceptible. Longworth easily recognized the problem because rot and mildew had been in his vineyards from the beginning. He just didn't know what to do about it. While dry weather inhibited the spread of disease in some years, nearly every one of his plants became infected in others. Because he could absorb the losses, he was able to endure such uncertainty. Other growers, however, could not afford that luxury. And the situation worsened each year as the vines grew older and the diseases became entrenched. No one understood what caused them, no one had a cure, and the decade of the 1850s saw only three good, dry vintages.

Although Longworth kept trying new grape varieties, he never found one better than Catawba — that is, one that would grow well, prove resistant to disease, and make good wine. Indeed, he was far more successful in his other endeavors—not only real estate, but also the arts. He became the patron of a number of distinguished American artists (including the sculptor Hiram Powers, who designed his grave), and conducted numerous other horticultural experiments, including the first commercial propagation of American strawberries. Nonetheless, grapes, wine, and temperance were his passion. After nearly fifty years experimenting with all sorts of grapes and all sorts of wines, Nicholas Longworth died in 1863. Among his last words was the fantasy of discovering "a new vine," one that "would neither mildew nor rot." As his son-in-law wrote mournfully, "He never found it in this world."

With Longworth's death, the Cincinnati wine industry lost both its leader and its inspiration. Farmers could grow other crops more profitably than grapes, and without Longworth's deep pockets to assist and promote them, they soon abandoned viticulture. A decade after their triumph over Cary, most of their vineyards lay fallow, and those that still produced a crop were riddled by blight. By 1870, the end had arrived. That year, Longworth's bottling plant, where he had perfected the production of sparkling Catawba, was purchased by a brewery.

The vines were gone, but the dream lived on. Over the next fifty years, men and women in almost every state east of the Rockies tried to make and sell wine. Most worked on a small scale, and many ended up abandoning the enterprise after a few bad harvests. Others were in it for the long haul, and some of them achieved considerable success. In Ohio, grape growing moved north, to the shores of Lake Erie and some of the islands in the lake, notably Middle Bass Island near Sandusky, where the Golden Eagle Winery, started by ex-Cincinnatians, grew to a capacity of a half million gallons. Catawba remained the grape of choice, but others, including the Delaware, Isabella, Iona, and Ives Seedling, were used as well. Farther west in Missouri, German immigrants worked primarily with a native red grape called Norton. Beginning near St. Louis, they produced wines to popular and critical acclaim, and the Show Me State soon passed Ohio in terms of both acres planted and bottles produced. In New York, a thriving industry developed in the Finger Lakes region, producing a large amount of sparkling wine from Catawba and Delaware grapes. By the turn of the century, "New York Champagne," made by firms such as Great Western and Gold Seal, had become synonymous with American bubbly. Around that time, "Virginia Dare," a wine made originally from southern Scuppernong grapes, also came into vogue. It was produced by Paul Garrett first in North Carolina, then in Virginia, and finally in New York, and in the two decades before Prohibition, it became one of America's best sellers.

Evidence suggests that many of these eastern wines were quite good. When the distinguished French scientist Jules-Émile Planchon toured American vineyards in 1873, he pronounced the sparkling Catawba from Middle Bass Island "*très agréable*," the Missouri Norton "excellent," and American wine in general far better than he had been led to expect. Its average quality, he confessed, was "superior to [French] *petits vins de consommation courante.*" Whether grown in New York or North Carolina, Missouri or Ohio, these successful late-nineteenth-century American wines constituted Nicholas Longworth's legacy. Wherever people east of the Sierra Nevadas planted grapes and bottled wine, they followed his lead. For in spirit at least, the eccentric visionary from Cincinnati was their mentor.

Longworth proved that good wine indeed could be made from American grapes. Moreover, he demonstrated that, if the wine was priced fairly, Americans would buy it. This was perhaps the key lesson to be learned from his work. Although it happened only locally in and around Cincinnati, and only for a short time, Longworth's wines had become part of daily life for a sizable portion of the population. Here and there as the nineteenth century drew to a close, in places like Hermann, Missouri, and Penn Yan, New York, the lesson was repeated and expanded upon. After all, it had been Nicholas Longworth's goal from the start—to temper the excesses of American social life with the world's most civilized and civilizing drink.

In order for Longworth's dream to be realized on a larger scale, what was needed above all else was a stable supply of better grapes. W. J. Flagg made this case convincingly in *Harper's Monthly Magazine* in 1870. Echoing what he had learned from his father-in-law, Flagg called wine "the natural and providential drink for civilized and refined humanity." He declared that drinking it served the true cause of temperance, and argued that the only way to increase consumption was to "grow our wines at home, and consume them as near to where produced as may be." Imported wines, he observed, "are only for the rich," while California wines "sell in the Atlantic cities even dearer than the French." Flagg's conclusion was inescapable. "The question of wine-drinking in America," he declared, "resolves itself into the question of grape-growing in America."

That question would be answered, and answered affirmatively, over the next half century. One of the most important developments was the identification of phylloxera, the tiny yellow louse that feeds on the roots of *vinifera* vines. Phylloxera made its way from America to Europe in the 1850s, perhaps as a stowaway aboard a shipment of nursery stock, perhaps in the mud on someone's boots. No matter how it got there, this unwanted import soon made itself right at home. Beginning in southern France, it immediately started eating roots and destroying vines—so much so that, over the next forty years, it went on to devastate all of the continent's vineyards, causing an agricultural crisis matched in nineteenth-century Europe only by the Irish potato famine. At first, phylloxera proved difficult to identify. Because it ate roots, not leaves, people did not understand what was happening to their vines. When a farmer dug up a dead plant, the villains already had left to feed on another. Only in 1868 did Jules-Émile Planchon lead a group of researchers who discovered the cause of the mysterious plague. They dug up sick rather than dead vines and found tiny insects, individually almost microscopic but swarming in such numbers that the roots appeared to be painted yellow. "An elegant little aphid," marveled Planchon in his notebook, "that could bring about the destruction of even the most vigorous of vines." Once it had been identified, the next problem was how to combat it. Planchon and his team knew that native American vines were in effect phylloxera-proof, and they wondered what would happen if *vinifera* vines were grafted onto American roots. In 1869 and 1873 Planchon exchanged visits with Charles Riley, a leading entomologist from Missouri. Together the two men proved both that the graft would take and that the essential character of the grapes would be unchanged. Over the next two decades,

Riley helped organize the shipment of millions of American cuttings and vines to France, the majority of which came from vineyards in eastern Missouri.

Phylloxera is native to the eastern United States, which is why native American vines evolved a resistance to it. *Vinifera* vines, with no resistance, die from the roots up. Many European growers, especially in France, were initially reluctant to graft their *vinifera* vines onto American rootstock for fear that the flavor of the resulting wine would be compromised. In Burgundy, for instance, grafting was outlawed until as late as 1887, since no one wanted Chardonnay or Pinot Noir to taste foxy. Planchon and Riley insisted that a new rootstock would not alter the taste of the grapes. Gradually, their findings became widely accepted. So in the end, though an American pest caused the crisis, American vines saved the day. It would be nearly a century before American wines could claim to be the equal of the finest French ones, but all during that time, when French wines were touted as the world's best, they came from vines growing on American roots.

Although phylloxera did not infect eastern American vineyards, its identification, along with the discovery of the "cure" offered by American rootstock, had significant consequences for eastern viticulture. One was the realization that if American roots could support *vinifera* plants in France, Italy, and Germany, they might also be able to do so in New York, Ohio, or Virginia. The most promising development along these lines took place in the grape-breeding program at the New York State Agricultural Experiment Station in Geneva. The emphasis here was on native grapes, but as early as 1890 the program included some experimental *vinifera* plantings. The vines struggled, but some survived, and in 1911 the station started what its historian called "a real experiment," concentrating exclusively on *vinifera*. More than one hundred different varieties were planted, and a 1917 report indicated that *vinifera* vines on phylloxera-resistant roots might have sufficient vigor to combat winter damage and summer disease. It seemed only a matter of time, and a short time at that, before there would be sufficient stock to begin commercial production. The old dream of growing European vines and making European-style wines in the East might at long last be about to come true.

Another consequence of the phylloxera crisis was the discovery of fungicides that could effectively control the diseases that long had plagued eastern vineyards. Downy mildew accompanied the Missouri vines that were shipped to France in the 1870s. It took only four years for French scientists to come up with a cure: the colorful "Bordeaux mixture" of lime and copper sulphate that stains everything it touches bright blue. Powdery mildew, or oidium, already was under control, sulfur dust or powders having been discovered a bit earlier. Black rot proved more troublesome, but the Bordeaux mixture helped, and by the turn of the century, American grape growers were fairly confident that they could check the diseases that had dashed so many of their forebears' dreams.

These scientific advances enabled more Americans to grow more grapes than ever before, and the last decades of the nineteenth century saw a virtual grape boom in the eastern United States. American wine consumption increased from a little more than three-tenths of a gallon per capita in 1870 to nearly half a gallon in 1890—small numbers when compared with those of European wine-producing countries, but a real increase nonetheless. Still, the American palate much preferred whiskey or beer, and wine remained largely a local product. What, then, were all the new grapes used for? It may seem obvious today, but it was entirely new back then: Americans were growing and selling grapes as table fruit and using them to make bottled juice.

Although people had eaten grapes since time immemorial, they almost always had cultivated them for wine or raisins. At least they had done so with *vinifera*. Yet while cultivated native American grapes were too foxy for wine and lacked sufficient sugar for raisins, they often made excellent eating. By the turn of the century, these had become a regular part of the American fruit market. This shift in gastronomic fashion reflected a change in how grapes were cultivated. For centuries, growers had propagated vines with cuttings rather than seeds. They knew that cuttings produce a younger version of the parent plant, while seeds produce a similar but different plant. A *vigneron* in Burgundy whose Pinot Noir fetched a high price wanted to perpetuate it, so he never bothered with seeds or seedlings. Of course, growers also knew that chance seedlings could produce new and interesting grape varieties—the Alexander or Catawba, for instance. But because they cared primarily about propagation, they rarely experimented with cross-fertilization and hybridization.

Not until the mid-nineteenth century did agriculturists devote serious attention to breeding grapes and creating new varieties. Once they started, however, they hardly stopped, and the second half of the century saw the creation of a profusion of new grape varieties. Professional nurserymen and amateur horticulturists alike crossed grape with grape with grape—sometimes native with native, sometimes native with *vinifera*, and later hybrid with hybrid. Close to two thousand new varieties came to be offered for sale, everything from one named the Ada to another named the Zoe. Some were used for wine, even more for fruit, and new vineyards sprouted up just about everywhere. By 1890, grape growing had emerged as a profitable business in many parts of the country, most notably in western New York and Pennsylvania. Four-fifths of the fruit grown there that year was for table use—more than sixty thousand tons.

The most important new variety of the era was a cultivated native *labrusca* grape, the Concord. Developed in Concord, Massachusetts, by one Ephraim Bull, a goldsmith with a passion for gardening, it quickly became America's most successful commercial grape variety. Bull first offered it for sale in 1854, and the catalogue from the Boston nursery of Hovey and Company summarizes what made it so popular. "This remarkably fine new American variety," read the description, "is sufficiently hardy to withstand the coldest climate, and early enough to mature its fruit . . . a most vigorous growing vine, perfectly hardy . . . the berries have never been known to mildew, rot, and drop off, under any circumstances during the five years since it has first borne fruit." As the repeated use of the word "hardy" makes clear, Concord's great advantage came in its ability to grow and indeed thrive virtually everywhere it was planted. And it soon was planted just about everywhere—New England, of course, but also New York, Pennsylvania, Ohio, Michigan, even Missouri, and all this just in the six years before the Civil War. After the war, Horace Greeley, ever the promoter, offered a prize of $100 to the man who produced the best grape for America's future. Bull won with his Concord, dubbed by Greeley "the grape for the millions." This was in 1866, when most of Nicholas Longworth's Catawba vines already had died.

Ephraim Bull, a teetotaler himself, thought of Concord as a wine grape. After all, even as late as 1854, wine essentially was all that grapes were used for. "I venture to predict," he wrote, that New England soon will be "supplying herself with native wines, and even exporting them." People did make wine from Concord. Some still do. The problem is that the wine tends to taste sappy because it needs to retain a fair amount of grape sugar—both to make it less bitter, the skin being very astringent, and to soften the inevitably foxy *labrusca* flavor. The resulting quality is not high, especially when the wine is paired with food, and Concord never achieved wide use as a wine grape. Nor did it really catch on as a table fruit, for its skin is barely edible. Concord is ideal, however, for jams and jellies, candies and desserts, and its commercial success came largely from what could be done with it on a stove or in a kitchen. This is what a New Jersey dentist named Thomas Bramwell Welch discovered when, beginning in 1869, he invented an entirely new product—unfermented, nonalcoholic grape juice.

Something of a jack-of-all-trades, Thomas Welch had worked as a Methodist preacher in upstate New York and then as a physician in Minnesota before he took up dentistry and in 1868 moved to the appropriately named community of Vineland, New Jersey. An inveterate tinkerer, he concocted a syrup for soothing stomachaches, published a variety of magazines, made and marketed dental alloys, and even invented a system for simplifying spelling, replete with a new dictionary. He also was an avid gardener who, like so many Americans at the time, tried his hand at growing grapes. Not surprisingly, he planted Concord. Welch had read about the esteemed French scientist Louis Pasteur's discoveries concerning fermentation and the process that we now know as pasteurization—heating a liquid to a specific temperature for a specific length of time in order to kill yeasts or other microorganisms that can cause disease, spoilage, or unwanted fermentation. In the fall of 1869, he decided to experiment and see if he could pasteurize grape juice. With his son, Charles, at his side, he picked several baskets of grapes, crushed them, squeezed the juice through cloth bags, and filtered the liquid into bottles, which he then corked and sealed before immersing them in boiling water. He left them there for what he hoped would be a sufficient period to destroy the yeast and prevent fermentation. It worked, and beginning the next year he offered the first bottles of what he called Dr. Welch's Unfermented Wine for sale.

Although grape juice and wine come from the same fruit, they have little else in common. One is modern, the other ancient. One is cooked, the other left alone. One requires human artifice so as not to turn naturally into the other. Juice and wine belong to different contexts and different situations. Commercial fruit juice did not exist in Nicholas Longworth's day, but there can be little doubt that he would have welcomed it. After all, the primary cause of the drunkenness that so disturbed him was the absence of safe, healthy things to drink, including unspoiled milk, juice, and water. At the same time, it is difficult to imagine Longworth or anyone else claiming that sweet, sappy Concord grape juice should be considered a mark of Western civilization or be thought of as part of an especially gracious way of life. Yet Thomas Welch clearly thought of his invention as a substitute for wine. An ardent prohibitionist, he experimented with pasteurization only because, in his role as the communion steward at the local Methodist church in Vineland, he objected to alcohol's being part of the sacrament. At first, many members of the congregation thought he was going too far. A sip of wine at church on Sunday, they said, could not be considered sinful. Others argued, quite logically, that the Bible specified wine, not juice. Welch, adaptable, even changeable in so many other aspects of his life, would not yield. Alcohol, he insisted, was evil, and wine just another version of the devil's drink. To the question of why Christ drank wine and even changed water into wine, he insisted (against all evidence except that of his faith) that the wine in the Bible had to have been nonalcoholic. "Dr. Welch's Unfermented Wine," read one early advertisement, "the kind that was used in Galilee . . . not one particle of alcohol . . . write us for prices." Although the Vineland Methodist Church decided not to use Welch's invention, the thin, white-bearded dentist never changed his mind. He stopped making his juice for almost ten years, starting again only at Charles's insistence, but he remained devoted to the cause of temperance, which he defined as complete and total abstinence.

By 1900, Nicholas Longworth's understanding of "temperance" had been largely forgotten. Many Americans advocated moderate drinking, and some even claimed a special place for wine, but few considered themselves, or were considered by others, to be supporters of temperance. A century before, Benjamin Franklin had placed temperance first among his list of virtues, defining it with a pithy maxim: "Eat not to dullness. Drink not to elevation." This meaning of the word went back to the early sixteenth century, when people first began to think of it specifically in terms of food and drink. "Surfetes do kyll many men," declared an English Renaissance *Dyetary*, "and temporaunce doth prolonge the lyfe." Only in the mid-nineteenth century, around the time when Samuel Cary's harangues were echoing through the Cincinnati streets, did a new meaning emerge—not moderation but abstinence. For a host of reasons, this meaning found greater acceptance in America than just about anywhere else, and by the final third of the century, temperance as abstinence or prohibition once again had become a mass, grassroots reform movement.

Dr. Thomas Welch may appear to be an extremist today, but in his time he was very much part of the mainstream. The crusade against drink belonged to a slew of programs and causes embraced by Americans convinced of the inevitability of social and indeed moral progress. For reformers who advocated the liberation of women or workers, allegiance to the temperance cause came easy. It was all of a piece—the attempt, in whatever guise, to free the individual from exploitation and dependency. The call for national Prohibition, first made in 1876, presented itself not only as morally right but also as democratic, something that would allow men and women to control their own destinies. It claimed to serve the interests of both God and man, and hence of America's future. And it became increasingly coercive. For Welch, as for many of his generation, there was no doubt about the justice and ultimate triumph of this cause. Thus Welch organized a Temperance League in Vineland—not to bring prohibition to the town, which already was dry, but to spread the prohibitionist gospel to surrounding communities. He worked with the police to help track down moonshiners and prosecute tavern owners. He even enlisted in a vigilante group called the Law and Order Society, whose sole purpose was, in his words, "ferreting out and bringing to justice saloon keepers who violated their license." It is hard to picture this God-fearing dentist storming a saloon, ax or pistol in hand. In his mind, however, temperance as moderation belonged to the distant past.

Grapes had become an important cash crop in many eastern states by the turn of the century, but the production of jam, jelly, and juice was more important (and more profitable) than the production of wine. Charles Welch changed the name of the product his father had invented when he incorporated the family company in 1897. Much more than Thomas, he was responsible for making grape juice a standard product and Welch's a household name. That took time, but by 1900 the Welch Grape Juice Company, having relocated to western New York, was selling fifty thousand gallons annually, with sales more than doubling just about every year.

Viticulture and winemaking had gone hand in hand for thousands of years. In early-twentieth-century America, they became separate enterprises for the first time in history. The irony is that the obstacles that for three centuries had prevented the growth of a healthy wine industry had been surmounted at long last. Modern science in both the vineyard and the winery promised that the profitable production of fine eastern wine was just around the corner. Fungicides protected the vines from powdery mildew, downy mildew, and black rot; the controlled use of yeasts during fermentation prevented spoilage and unnecessary lot variations; hybridization created new, hardier grape varieties; and phylloxera was under control. Best of all, *vinifera* varieties were being grown successfully, if only experimentally. "There are reasons why grape growers may now succeed," wrote U. P. Hedricks, probably the era's most knowledgeable student of American grapes and viticulture, "even though those of one, two, or three centuries ago failed. We know now how to control the insects and fungi that attack the vine." But then Prohibition arrived, and the promise went unfulfilled. It would take more than two generations for eastern wine to recover. Not until the late twentieth century did Nicholas Longworth's dream again begin to come true.

The prohibition movement, coupled with the dominance of Concord and the invention of pasteurized grape juice, certainly hindered eastern wine growing in the first decades of the new century. But equally important was the fact that by 1900, wine from California had become widely available in the eastern market. As demand for it grew, production rose steadily. The Golden State produced 18 million gallons of wine in 1895, 23 million in 1900, 31 million in 1905, and 45 million in 1910. California vintners enjoyed a huge advantage over their eastern compatriots, as *vinifera* vines flourished in their dry, temperate vineyards. This hardly mattered back when Longworth made his sparkling Catawba, since California wine shipped overland by wagon and stagecoach often spoiled, and wine shipped by boat around Cape Horn ended up costing more than most European imports. But by the turn of the century, transcontinental rail lines made shipping wine east extremely profitable. By far the largest group of customers were European immigrants, and California wines, being wholly *vinifera*, tasted much more like the wines they remembered from home than did anything made in the East.

In 1894, seven of the largest California wine merchants banded together to form a monopoly, or trust, to satisfy the growing demand for their wines. The California Wine Association (CWA) made and sold wine both under its own label and under the various labels of wineries it purchased. At one point it operated fifty-two wineries in addition to its own facilities, brands that in the public eye competed with one another but that in truth sent all profits back into one central coffer. CWA wine was sold nationally and overseas. The 1906 earthquake in San Francisco damaged stock and hurt profits, but the trust rebounded quickly, building a cavernous storage facility named Winehaven near Richmond, beside the shipping docks and next to the railroad tracks. During the next decade, the CWA came to control some 80 percent of the state's wine trade. It owned warehouses in all the important eastern cities, and exerted its influence near and far.

The CWA sold a mass-produced product with which few eastern wineries could compete. Large-scale immigration and urbanization had changed the market. A bottle of wine now was much more likely to be found on a supper table in the city than on the farm, and Nicholas Longworth's old agrarian dream seemed increasingly out of touch with the realities of modern life. That dream had started to fade into the soft mist of nostalgia after the Civil War, when the twin forces of urbanization and industrialization began to transform the country from a predominantly agricultural society into a commercial world power. Longworth, like Jefferson before him, had wanted wine to become part of daily life in a country composed primarily of farmers. It never occurred to him that the nation's growth would take place in cities. American wine consumption increased in the second half of the nineteenth century, but the people who drank wine regularly tended not to live on farms. They were mainly central and southern European immigrants who settled in the urban East, where they worked in the factories whose output provided the gold to gild the age. Although some of the wine they drank came from eastern vineyards, more and more of it came from California.

California became the country's leading wine-producing state sometime in the 1870s, and then increased production at a rate far above that of all the other wine states put together. By the turn of the century, Golden State grape growing and winemaking, led by the CWA, had become big business. It made money for growers, winemakers, and shippers, and it helped foster the emergence of an isolated but genuine wine culture in immigrant neighborhoods in New York, Chicago, and other large American cities. Yet there was a downside as well. Because producers and consumers alike increasingly viewed wine as a manufactured commodity, its essential identity as an agricultural product began to be ignored. No such problem existed in Europe, where wine was equally at home in the country and the city. Wine growing there had a long history, and prohibitionist sentiment was at most a minor annoyance. But in America, where there was little tradition of wine appreciation, a bottle of wine became just as suspect as a bottle of whiskey or rum. Ironically, those harboring the most suspicions tended to use the rhetoric of agrarianism. They idealized rural ways that themselves were becoming anachronisms, and they considered all alcohol an impediment to the pursuit of pastoral American happiness.

Temperance as abstinence enjoyed widespread public sup-

port across the political spectrum. Its advocates included capi-
talists who wanted to increase workers' productivity as well as
socialists who wanted a new economic system, women agitating
for a voice in the political arena, and evangelists crusading for
Christian morality. "Drys" like Dr. Welch often quoted Scrip-
ture to bolster their arguments, but they also cited scientific
data, medical reports, and sociological studies. Many different
forces fueled the drive for prohibition, but the cause was
nowhere more popular than in rural America, where "King Alcohol" was associated with the sort of urban vice and corrup-
tion that many thought was threatening a distinctly American
way of life. The Anti-Saloon League led the drive for national
Prohibition, and the name is revealing. The saloon, symbol of
corrupt morals and politics, was a fundamentally urban institution, and a great deal of prohibitionist rhetoric was directed not
only at the bottle but also at the city and the changing character
of American society. "What [happens] if the saloon controls the
city," a popular temperance writer asked rhetorically in 1911,
and "the city controls the state and nation?" This was in many
ways the great fear. The city was home to the machine, whether
represented by the automobile, the factory, or the political
boss, all of which allegedly was lubricated by the "whiskey ring"
or "liquor trust." Filled with prostitutes and thieves, bosses and
immigrants, the city threatened an idealized home and country
— precisely what the advocates of temperance as abstinence set
out to defend. "We confront a foe that has ill-gotten wealth,"
declared Purley Baker, the general superintendent of the Anti-
Saloon League in 1912. "Love for country, human character,
domestic happiness, personal reputation, have no place in its
code of warfare." The evangelist Billy Sunday put it more

bluntly. "If you don't fight the saloon," he told his audience, "I will say that you are not an American citizen."

The Anti-Saloon League defended the ideals of a rural America that no longer existed, if indeed it ever had. The irony, though, is that this was the same America, or the same vision of America, that had inspired Nicholas Longworth to plant his first vineyard. Longworth believed passionately in the agrarian ideal. He never conceived of wine as an elitist, aristocratic beverage, let alone an urban one. Instead, he thought of it as an agricultural product, literally the fruit of the earth. Wine, he argued, is fundamentally different from whiskey or other spirits precisely because it is pure—that is, not cooked or manipulated by any machine. Wine, he insisted, should be America's antidote to "demon rum." On December 17, 1917, the House of Representatives concluded debate on the proposed Eighteenth Amendment to the Constitution. Twenty-seven states already had gone dry, so if the measure passed the House with a two-thirds majority, only a handful more would have to follow in order for prohibition to become the law of the land. The final tally read 282 to 128, with one of the minority votes belonging to Old Nick's grandson, an Ohio congressman. According to the United States government, wine then became just another form of liquor, and all liquor became illegal. Longworth must have shuddered in his grave.

2

California
Gold

CALIFORNIA WINE began to become big business in the
1880s. Up until then, production had been mostly local, the
vast majority of wines consumed where the grapes were grown.
The advent of transcontinental rail shipping, coupled with the
expanding immigrant market back east, changed everything.
What one California grower prophesied as "halcyon days for
everyone possessed of a vineyard" led hundreds of entrepreneurs who previously had no interest in wine to buy land
and plant grapes—some in southern California, but even more
in the counties north and east of the San Francisco Bay. From a
base of roughly four million gallons per year in the mid-1870s,
production boomed to well over twenty million by the early
1900s. The growth was not always easy, as the new production
at first outpaced consumer demand, and from time to time
prices plummeted, leaving growers in economic depressions
despite the increasing popularity of their products. "Wine Is
Too Cheap," declared an 1886 *San Francisco Examiner* banner
headline during one particularly severe slump, adding in
smaller print, "A California Industry [Is] Threatened with De-

structive Low Prices." Opinions differed on how to regulate supply and demand. Some people urged better cooperation between wineries and growers, while others advocated replanting with different crops. Still others advanced the idea of increasing demand by using the excess wine to make brandy.

Three men in particular embodied the controversies of the era. George Husmann, Eugene Hilgard, and Percy Morgan each thought of wine and the 1886 grape crisis differently. Husmann, a Missouri viticulturist and the leader of that state's wine industry, went west after he helped organize the shipment of Missouri vines to phylloxera-plagued France. Widely regarded as the most expert American wine grower of the day, Husmann argued that the solution to California's grape surplus lay in increased home consumption. Like Nicholas Longworth before him, he considered wine an antidote to whiskey, so wanted it to find a place on American supper tables—especially in small towns and on farms, the agrarian America he knew and loved. Hilgard too had moved to California from the Midwest, specifically from Michigan, where he had taught geology and natural history at the state university. An appointment as the first professor of agriculture at the University of California brought him to Berkeley, and in that role he promoted improved wine quality. In his view, the wine industry's problems came from there being too much cheap, flawed wine on the market, and the *Examiner* soon printed a long letter from him in which he outlined how quality control in vineyards and wineries would lead to better wines sold at higher prices. Percy Morgan, also a newcomer, saw the surplus as a way to make money. An accountant and would-be financier from England, Morgan argued that the solution to depressed prices was the creation of a monopolistic organization that could control supply and thus stabilize prices. It took time, but eight years later he became the director of the California Wine Association. As he acknowledged, this "combination" existed simply to "raise the selling price of wines." Morgan did not much care who drank the wines, or what kind of wines they drank. His goal above all else was profit, and he clearly realized it. Much as happened with other American industries at the time, the CWA monopolized production.

The emergence of the CWA reflects the radical changes that transformed forever California wine growing, taking it from a collection of small, mostly individual agricultural enterprises to a mercantile industry, from a local concern to a national and even an international one. The different roles played by Husmann, Hilgard, and Morgan illustrate both what was lost and what was gained in the transformation. In no other state of the Union before the 1880s was the vision of wine at home on the farm more widely accepted and widely realized than in California. This was in part a legacy of Spanish settlement and in part a result of the gold rush's having left the state with an ethnically diverse populace, many members of which had brought a taste for wine with them. It also came from California's being the one place in the country where people grew *vinifera* grapes successfully. Twenty years later, even though the state's vintners were producing more wine than ever before, less and less of it was being drunk on the farm. California wine, often in CWA bottles, now belonged primarily in the city—San Francisco, Los Angeles, and more to the point, even larger cities like Chicago, Philadelphia, and New York back east. Big business it certainly was.

Before moving to California, George Husmann had worked with American grapes for more than forty years, beginning as a boy after his family emigrated from Bremen to become shareholders in the new German community of Hermann, Missouri. The settlers there, refugees from the European political upheavals of 1830, had been attracted by America's pastoral promise, romantically envisioning life in the open fields of the Midwest as a bucolic alternative to their mercantile northern German homes. Largely men of education, they read Goethe more than Jefferson, but they also felt the lure of the agrarian ideal. Wine growing became one of their principal activities not because many of them had any experience with it, but because they understood it to be an integral part of an agrarian life. In the words of Friedrich Muench, one of the community's leaders, "the vine-dresser, free, lord of his own possessions, [is] in daily intercourse with peaceful nature." Husmann devoted his career to the realization of just that ideal. A small, almost elfin man, he brought boundless energy to the promotion of a "new viticulture" for a new world. "This," he declared after visiting California, is "*the* great *Vineland* . . . now only in its first stage of development, destined to overshadow all others."

Much like Longworth a generation earlier, Husmann thought of grape growing and winemaking as noble, patriotic work. He too preached the gospel of wine as "the *best* agent" of "true temperance." Longworth, shy and eccentric, often had been reluctant to speak publicly. Husmann had no such reservations. His mission, as he saw it, was not just to grow grapes and make wine, but also to lead others to do the same. So in addition to lecturing widely, he provided lasting leadership in print—in articles in newspapers, essays in horticultural journals, and in a series of successful books designed to popularize wine growing. In all this work, Husmann combined visionary zeal with literally down-to-earth advice and information, offering his own experience as a model to be emulated. He supported and advised plenty of commercial winemakers, but he always reserved his most ardent enthusiasm for individual wine growers. "I have never for a moment lost sight of the interests of those, who, like myself, have to commence at the lowest rung of the ladder," he wrote near the end of his life. "There is not an operation in the vineyard, from the clearing of the unbroken forest and prairie, to the finishing touch given to the wine at its last racking, which I have not performed and am not thoroughly familiar with, and I can, therefore, fully sympathize with the poor laborer, who has nothing but his industrious hands, and an honest intention to succeed."

By 1880, Husmann had developed a considerable national reputation. Although he lacked any formal education, he had been appointed professor of horticulture at the University of Missouri at Columbia, where he managed an experimental vineyard containing more than 130 grape varieties. Successful and respected, the head of a large and happy family, with a son (also named George) who was set to follow him in his life's work, he seemed ready to slow down and leisurely sip the fermented fruit of his labor. Then he made his first trip west. Only a few months later he packed up family and belongings and moved to a farm in Carneros in southern Napa County. He was fifty-three years old, and he thought he had seen the future— "*the* great *Vineland*" where families could drink their own home-grown temperance. Yet when he moved, George Husmann did not realize that the luster of California's gold would come as much from lucre as from ripe grapes on the vine. His essentially agrarian vision was not able to encompass the new commercial realities of the California wine industry. So while his story neatly embodies American wine's movement from east to west, it is symbolic in a still more important respect, as it illustrates the separation of California from the rest of viticultural America. That separation began in the vineyard and extended to the finished wine in the bottle, wine that often was shipped east and consumed not only at home but also in the saloon.

Eugene Hilgard had little interest in the sort of wine served in saloons — heady, often fortified tipple that people drank primarily, if not exclusively, for its inebriating effect. He cared only about premium table wines, and for nearly twenty years he fought a running battle with the leaders of California's commercial wine industry on behalf of improved quality. Although his position eventually carried the day, it did not do so in his lifetime. Instead, California wine achieved unprecedented popularity by becoming a standardized product, "wine for the masses." It remained as such through and especially after Prohibition. Hilgard's argument that high quality was the industry's only guarantee of long-term success fell largely on deaf ears. It would not be renewed on anything but an idiosyncratic basis until the 1960s.

Much like Husmann, Hilgard came to the United States from Germany as a boy, settling with his family on a farm in southern Illinois, where his father grew a wine called Hilgardsberger. At age sixteen, he returned to Germany, where he enrolled in the university at Heidelberg. He stayed abroad for six years, earning a doctoral degree in geology and soil science. Back in America, he spent the first half of his professional career studying the soils of the Deep South, serving as the Mississippi state geologist and as a professor at the University of Mississippi in Oxford. Then, after a sojourn in Ann Arbor, he went to California, where he concentrated on problems of irrigation, plant nutrition, and alkaline soils. Geology was always his main field of expertise, with wine never more than a sideline. (His entry in the *Dictionary of National Biography* does not even mention his involvement with it.) But as professor of agriculture, Hilgard took it upon himself to promote the application of scientific principles to practical farming. He arrived in California just as wine growing was becoming an important part of the state's economy, and he considered working to improve California wine an important part of his job.

A progressive thinker, Hilgard envisioned California wine becoming a world leader, arguing that modern science could make it such. In this regard, he was the antithesis of Husmann, whose views were much more parochial. Everything the Missourian knew about grapes and wine came from his own experience, and his experience with native or native-based hybrid grapes had little to do with California viticulture. By contrast, Eugene Hilgard was the quintessential nineteenth-century scientist, emphasizing controlled experimentation, systematic analysis, and statistically verifiable inquiry. He promoted what he called "rational winery practice" and was quick to apply European research, especially research involving the use of pure yeasts and cool fermentation, to California. While Husmann came to California to help the individual farmer, Hilgard issued hundreds of bulletins and reports for an entire industry. No matter that the pre-Prohibition industry often ignored him, Hilgard's insistence on high quality, coupled with all the scientific literature issued under his supervision, made him one of the fathers of today's world-class California wines.

Percy Morgan also helped father contemporary California wine, though few people today even recognize his name. He was the first person to realize that the wine business had to act like a business, meaning that in the economically depressed early 1890s it needed to develop new markets and, just as important, new strategies for reaching those markets. Hungry in his ambition, Morgan was in tune with the rapacious business dealings of the age. Although he had come to San Francisco with only a few dollars to his name, he quickly gained a reputation as a shrewd financial speculator. The vintner firm of S. Lachman & Company was one of his clients, and it was when he was auditing the firm's books that he hatched his scheme for the "wine trust." Like John Pierpont Morgan, with whom he shared a fiercely capitalistic vision as well as a surname (but no family relation), he advanced the notion of a "community of interests" to justify the creation of a monopoly. J. P. Morgan's community became U.S. Steel. Percy Morgan's became the CWA, which, like the steel trust, so dominated the business that it effectively eliminated competition. In 1900 he persuaded some of the state's wealthiest bankers, most prominently Isaias Hellman, to invest in the CWA, and this infusion of capital allowed him to acquire a controlling interest in most of the commercially significant California wineries. The following year the CWA produced two-thirds of the wine in the state.

As director of the CWA, Percy Morgan became very rich. He retired in 1911 to an Elizabethan-style mansion in the Los

Altos hills, and devoted much of the rest of his life to collecting art. His legacy was the introduction of wine as a manufactured commercial product, one with a consistent character and a brand identity in the marketplace. Before the CWA, most California wine left the winery in bulk—in cask, barrel, or puncheon. Wholesalers, retailers, and saloon keepers would bottle it as they saw fit, meaning that the same lot of wine likely would taste very different depending on the circumstances in which it was consumed. The CWA changed all that, as Morgan oversaw not only vineyards and wineries but also massive storage facilities where the wines were blended. Most of the wines were bottled in glass in San Francisco, so what a customer purchased in Chicago would taste identical to what another customer purchased in New Orleans. The only problem was that Morgan and the bankers who served on the board of directors did not much care about wine. The majority of the CWA's production was red and white table wine, but the proportion of heady, sweet, fortified wines under its label increased steadily until Prohibition. Outside immigrant neighborhoods, these were becoming increasingly popular. At the same time, they were what the temperance movement stridently opposed. The presence of the CWA's new manufactured product made wine appear to many people to be much like whiskey or rum, which only helped them ignore the historic distinction between wine and spirits. In addition, because the CWA did not emphasize high quality, connoisseurs who treated fine wine as a mark of fine living had little use for its products. So while it would be grossly unfair to say that Morgan and the CWA's directors helped bring on Prohibition, they did help sow the seeds of their own destruction. For they made California and by extension American wine something very different—and to many people, something very suspect—from what it had ever been before.

The first *vinifera* grapes were brought to California by Franciscan priests. Beginning in 1769 at San Diego, the padres moved north from Mexico as part of their effort to convert the natives up and down the Pacific Coast. Although some historians cite that date as the start of California viticulture, the first vines probably were not planted until 1788 at San Juan Capistrano, with the initial vintage coming three or four years later. Over the next fifty years, the Franciscans grew grapes at almost all their missions, failing only when, as at Mission Dolores in San Francisco, the climate proved inhospitable. They used the wine primarily to celebrate mass, and they made it from a grape they sometimes called Criolla and sometimes just Mission. The vines came from vineyards in Baja California and New Mexico, which in turn had been planted with cuttings taken from older vineyards farther south, perhaps as far away as Peru. Its genetic origin uncertain, this Mission grape probably was brought to the New World as a seedling on a Spanish galleon in the sixteenth century, and thus surely had crossbred many times before its arrival in California. In any case, it was a true *vinifera* grape—the first and for a long time the only one to be cultivated successfully in what would become the United States.

Healthy, hardy *vinifera* vines thrived in California (and even earlier in Spanish New Mexico) for a number of reasons. Winter temperatures never fell too low, while summer humidity never went too high. Fungal diseases, while not unknown, posed only minor and infrequent problems. And phylloxera was not native west of the Rockies. Because a dry, hot growing season free from endemic disease resembled conditions in *vinifera*'s Mediterranean home, vines that died back east could flourish here. For a long time, however, no one in the East knew anything about them. California was first Spanish, then Mexican territory, and not until the Mexican-American War did people in the United States care much about it. Then gold was discovered at Sutter's Mill, and everything changed. In 1848, California had some fourteen thousand inhabitants. Four years later, the population neared a quarter of a million. The lure of wealth drew people from all over the world, but more often the agreeable climate and fertile terrain induced them to stay. Much the same things made *vinifera* grape growing possible, and the first efforts at commercial winemaking took off as soon as the gold fever hit. They were centered down south, near Los Angeles, and their patriarch was a Frenchman with the delightful name of Vignes—Jean Louis Vignes, California's first professional winemaker.

Vignes came to Los Angeles in the early 1830s after a career in Bordeaux as a cooper and a distiller, and he soon began to make wine and brandy. For a long time, the market for his products was isolated and local. When American troops occupied the area in early 1847, they sampled something they had not known existed—"the truly delicious . . . wine of the country," as one officer wrote in his diary. Demand increased with the gold rush, and in 1855 Vignes, now seventy-six, sold his estate to his nephews, Pierre and Jean Louis Sainsevain, who immediately decided to expand the business. The Sainsevains continued to use Vignes's fruit but also purchased grapes from other growers, and they marketed the resulting Sainsevain

Brothers wines and brandies throughout the state—125,000 gallons in 1858, much of which they shipped north and sold in their newly opened San Francisco store. So too with their chief competitor, the firm of Kohler & Frohling, which both owned vineyards and purchased grapes, and which sold wine far afield. At this point, California wine came mainly from grapes grown in Los Angeles, but it was drunk in San Francisco and, admittedly in very small measure, even in New York.

These southern California growers and winemakers used Mission grapes almost exclusively. Vignes had imported some other varieties, but many did not survive the long voyage around Cape Horn. The Mission, by contrast, vigorous and productive, yielded good enough wine—especially if it was vinified sweet or, as came to be the fashion under the name "angelica," barely fermented and then fortified with brandy so as to retain grape sugar. Yet because the Mission is high in sugar and low in acid, it never produced distinctive dry table wine, particularly when planted in the hot, desertlike climate of Los Angeles. Consequently, the better southern California wines, whether made in Los Angeles or later Anaheim and San Gabriel, remained sweet. That was not the case up north—in Sonoma and Napa Counties above San Francisco Bay, in Santa Clara and Livermore to the east, even in El Dorado and the rest of the gold country in the Sierra foothills. Almost as soon as commercial grape growing came to these regions, the search was on for grapes that would produce better dry wines. At first people tried what worked back east, notably Catawba shipped from Cincinnati, but they soon began to experiment with other varieties of *vinifera*. These growers almost always were European immigrants who had drunk (and sometimes made) fine wines at home. Antoine Delmas, Charles Lefranc, and Pierre

Pellier in Santa Clara, Jacob Knauth in the Sierra foothills, Charles Krug and Jacob Schram in Napa—these and others became northern California's viticultural pioneers. Unlike their counterparts back east, they were inspired by recollection in addition to a vision of an idealistic, pastoral future. Put simply, they wanted to make wines the likes of which they remembered.

The most famous member of California's pioneering generation was a Hungarian who settled in Sonoma County after earlier stops in Wisconsin, San Diego, and San Francisco, all places where he had tried with little luck to grow grapes and make wine. Agoston Haraszthy had a genius for self-promotion, and his fame came more from what he said than what he did. A gold speculator sued for embezzlement, a political activist rebuked by his legislative colleagues, a landowner who ended up bankrupt—Haraszthy's career was a series of often flamboyant failures. What almost never failed, however, was his belief in himself, as well as his ability to persuade others to believe in him. Investors and all sorts of hangers-on flocked to him, seduced by his extravagant schemes. By the mid-1850s, these centered almost exclusively on grapes. The California Horticultural Society had declared wine growing to be "as valuable and as feasible a mine of wealth to us as our mines of gold," and Haraszthy set out to work it for all its worth. Over the next few years, no one promoted California's viticultural gold more powerfully or more persuasively. He did so in two ways: first by developing America's (he claimed the world's) largest wine estate, and second by insisting loudly and often that northern California needed only more and better grapes to become a truly world-class wine-producing region.

Haraszthy's estate lay north of the town of Sonoma where

General Mariano Vallejo, after overseeing the secularization of the Franciscan mission in 1835, had taken over the mission vineyard and started commercial winemaking on a small scale. Haraszthy, though, never did anything on a small scale. He began with 560 acres in 1856, and only a few years later owned more than 5,000. Much of it was pastureland, but he cultivated nearly half a million grape vines, some of which he sold to other growers, more of which he used to make wine. Chinese laborers dug tunnels two hundred feet long in a hillside to serve as cellars, built a stone winery and a brandy distillery, and helped with the construction of the owner's manor house, an Italianate villa crowned with a series of statues. Haraszthy called the estate Buena Vista, and in 1859, only three years after he started developing it, Buena Vista's wines won first prize at the California state fair.

Haraszthy chafed, however, at the limited supply of grape varieties available to him. Although he was importing anything and everything he could find, over 90 percent of his vineyard was planted with Mission vines. "If we make such good wines already from one quality [or variety]," he asked rhetorically, "how much better wines will we make when we have differently flavored varieties?" He was convinced "that California will produce as noble wines as any part of Europe . . . [only] when it will have the proper varieties of grapes." In early 1861, the state legislature authorized the creation of a commission to "promote the improvement and growth of the grape vine in California." It had three members, each with distinct responsibilities. One traveled around the state surveying current viticulture; another went to Mexico and South America to see the quality of Mission and other wines there; and the third, Haraszthy, went to Europe. That no one bothered to look east suggests that even at this early stage, people recognized the significant differences that existed between viticulture in California and wine growing elsewhere in America.

Haraszthy, armed with all sorts of official documents and letters of introduction, spent about six months in Europe—in Burgundy, Bordeaux, and the Rheingau, then in Piedmont, Tuscany, and Spain—inspecting vineyards, purchasing plants, and undoubtedly making quite an impression on his hosts. It remains unclear how much he learned as opposed to postured. Certainly very few of the 100,000 vines he ordered ever got planted in California, for his fortunes fell dramatically upon his return. First he petitioned the state legislature to reimburse his expenses, even though reimbursement had not been part of the original commission. Not surprisingly, the legislature refused. Haraszthy, running out of money, then turned Buena Vista into a corporation, with the financier William Ralston signing on as the primary investor. A few years later, with rumors of extravagances circulating, Ralston pulled out, compelling Haraszthy in turn to resign as manager. In 1868 Agoston Haraszthy left California for good. Trailing debts, he moved to Nicaragua, where he persuaded the authorities to let him run a sugar plantation. He died a year later, legend has it eaten by an alligator. Clearly, his actual accomplishments pale next to his renown, which was largely of his own making. Clearly too, his contributions to the advancement of California viticulture were nowhere near what he (and later his son, Arpad) made them out to be. Nonetheless, all his public posturing and quasi-official pronouncements had one long-lasting effect. After Haraszthy, no one in northern California who wanted to make first-class wine—that is, wine on the European model—could take the Mission grape seriously.

The shift to different, better grape varieties happened nowhere more rapidly than in the Napa Valley, which by 1880 had established itself as California's premier wine-growing region. Commercial winemaking came to Napa after Sonoma, with the first wines offered for sale (by one John Patchett) in 1857. These were made with Mission grapes, but three years later a physician turned grape grower, George Belden Crane, planted a few acres of what he called "foreign vines"—German varietals, primarily White Riesling and Sylvaner, obtained from a nursery down in Santa Clara. It remains unclear whether Crane was motivated by visionary genius or frustration. He had planted twelve acres of Mission vines two years earlier, half of which had died, so he may well just have been looking for healthier plants. Whatever his reasoning, his wines proved to be a revelation. Newspapers declared them to be the best yet from Napa, perhaps the best in all of California. His neighbors agreed. Led by Charles Krug, they soon began replanting themselves.

Krug, born Karl in Westphalia, had immigrated to Philadelphia in 1847, gone back to Germany to fight for republican unification, and then returned to America for good in 1852, ending up this time in San Francisco, where he edited the local German-language newspaper, the *California Staats Zeitung*. There he met another immigrant full of grandiose plans. Like many others, Krug fell under the spell, and he soon followed Agoston Haraszthy to Sonoma. In 1858 he borrowed a small press and crossed the mountains to help some of the early Napa settlers make wine. He moved there permanently three years later, largely because marriage to Caroline Bale, a great-niece of General Vallejo and the daughter of one of Napa's first landowners, brought him her dowry of 540 acres. Krug started with Mission grapes, but inspired by Crane, he soon began replanting, first with German varieties, later with French ones. After a slow start, business boomed. His production went from 20,000 to 50,000 gallons in just two years, and in 1872 he built a cellar with a storage capacity of some 250,000. Krug's success was based on quality production, which came in large measure from his choice of grapes. A widely admired and truly visionary man, he more than anyone else led Napa as it became synonymous with high standards—not only because of his own success, but also because of the leadership he provided for others.

Krug indeed soon was accompanied or followed by plenty of others—wine growers who shared his commitment to quality. Hamilton Crabb came to Napa from Ohio in 1865. Caught up in the grape-breeding frenzy that was erupting back east, he immediately began experimenting with different grapes. Within a decade, he had nearly two hundred varieties growing on his estate, which he named To Kalon, or "most beautiful." Jacob Schram, an immigrant from the Rheinhessen, planted his first vines in 1863. He used some Mission vines at first, but as he acquired acreage he planted only "foreign" varieties— mostly White Riesling, Burger, and Palomino for white wines, and Zinfandel for reds. His wines drew praise far and wide, winning awards at a host of competitions, and leading Robert Louis Stevenson, who visited Napa in 1880, to wax rhapsodic. "Here," Stevenson wrote later, "earth's cream was being skimmed and garnered," as Schram produced "bottled poetry."

Another German immigrant, Gottlieb Groezinger, purchased twenty acres of vineyard land in the late 1860s and immediately grafted the existing Mission vines to White Riesling and Zinfandel. He soon owned two hundred acres, and kept buying more. Still another German, Jacob Beringer from Mainz, came to Napa in 1869, where he worked as Charles Krug's foreman for eight years. Then, with the help of his brother, Frederick, he started his own winery, devoted to European-style wines. There certainly was a great deal of the agrarian spirit here, no matter that the old Jeffersonian ideal had inspired few of the original wine growers. As much as any place in the country, the Napa Valley of the 1860s and 1870s was home to men and women who lived in harmony with nature in a peaceful commonwealth dedicated to the pursuit of pastoral happiness. Nicholas Longworth would have been delighted to see that grapes and wine were an integral part of the Edenic scene.

By 1880, Napa had approximately eleven thousand acres under vine. What Mission grapes remained were used primarily for brandy. Although all sorts of other varieties were growing, the most common had a Germanic heritage. Indeed, the valley itself was quite Germanic. As Charles Sullivan details in his *Napa Wine: A History*, the county was home to two German brass bands, picnics at the Habermehl Union Gardens, and high school dramatic productions in the mother tongue—including Schiller's *Die Rauber*, "quite a feat, since the play is difficult even for Germans to understand." No wonder George Husmann felt at home when he made his first trip west in the summer of 1881.

Hamilton Crabb first contacted Husmann sometime in the mid-1870s, to inquire about purchasing vines from his nursery. The two men soon corresponded regularly, and in time Husmann invited Crabb to contribute a chapter on the Napa Valley to his book *American Grape Growing and Wine Making*. As an author, Crabb could not have been more enthusiastic. He praised Napa's climate and soils, noted how many different *vinifera* varieties he was growing, and concluded that Napa in particular, and California in general, "with her golden shores, her sunny clime, her vine-clad hills and plains," was poised to become "the Vineland of the world." Husmann, however, harbored doubts. "I have tried a great many [California] wines," he wrote as late as 1879, "and although there is a vast improvement perceptible lately in the quality of their products, yet they are all too heavy to suit the palate of the true connoisseur." Then he made his visit. Two things changed his mind. First, he saw for himself that northern California possessed ideal soils and an ideal climate for viticulture. Second, he discovered that its vineyards, just beginning to evince their great potential, were under siege. The root louse phylloxera had arrived to despoil the garden. Husmann had been working closely with Charles Riley to supply many of the cuttings shipped to phylloxera-plagued France. Since no one knew more about American grapes, he believed that his expertise could save the day.

Phylloxera probably first came to California in a shipment of eastern vines sometime in the late 1860s. Unlike in Europe, where the bug seemed to travel miles in minutes, here it moved slowly, appearing, as some farmers put it, "lazy." No one identified it positively until 1873. The louse's sluggish pace, combined with the fact that the decline in French production was helping to increase consumer demand for American wines, led many growers to dismiss its threat. Some went so far as to talk about phylloxera as a friend, suggesting that it was a different type than the European foe. Even Charles Krug thought it only a minor problem, reporting in 1882 that "the fear of further spread and any serious damage has vanished."

Yet phylloxera was no friend. It moved slowly because it sometimes failed to develop a winged form as it had in Europe, but once in a vineyard, it destroyed grapevines just as eagerly as it did in France. Husmann recognized as much when he visited in the summer of 1881. This, he thought, is "*the* great disaster." Some growers had suggested drowning the insects. Others, including John Wheeler, the secretary of the Board of State Viticultural Commissioners, urged disinfecting vines with carbon bisulfide. Still others buried their heads in their vineyard sands and hoped that the whole mess would go away. Husmann knew it wouldn't. An inspection of the southern Napa vineyards, where the infection was especially acute, convinced him that while California had the potential to be America's, indeed the world's, greatest wine producer, its vineyards were in grave danger. "It is worse than useless to try to ignore [phylloxera], as has been done in some sections of the State," he wrote. "It will make itself seen and felt, and no mechanical or chemical means have as yet been found that are of real practical value. All the insecticides that have so far been tried, have proved too costly and impractical in their application; and we must resort at last to the only practical preventative, now recognized by all nations to be their salvation, *viz.*, American resistant vines."

Husmann moved to California in order to help save American wine's golden land. No one's voice was raised more loudly in support of what indeed was a painful but necessary remedy —replanting on native rootstock. Others advanced similar arguments, but his became the most persuasive, since he had so much experience working with native vines. Yet when it came to the specifics of replanting, Husmann's expertise, which seemed so formidable in Missouri, turned out to be largely irrelevant in California. For one thing, he had no experience growing *vinifera*. He certainly knew native American grapes, but any advice he might offer concerning which *vinifera* variety to graft onto which native rootstock was at best conjecture. Because not all native stock proved equally resistant or vigorous, no one could be sure what to plant—a problem exacerbated by wine growing being a long-term venture, with only one harvest each year and a product—the bottled wine—only available for analysis and assessment years after that. For another, California winemaking was well on its way to becoming a commercial enterprise on a scale that far surpassed anything back east. A big company had needs that were different from an individual grower's, and Husmann was slow to adapt. He tried to bridge American wine's continental divide, but he was forced to admit before long that California had little in common with Missouri, Ohio, New York, or the other eastern wine-growing states. Winemakers here worked in what he called "an entirely different field."

In order to combat phylloxera, Husmann promoted varieties of rootstock he knew from home, especially the Herbemont, which he called "the most valuable." Herbemont, however, turned out to be largely useless. Meanwhile, Eugene Hilgard advocated using the native vine *Vitis californica*, reasoning that there would be no question of adaptation with such a hardy and abundant plant. Back in the 1850s, Charles Lefranc had grafted French varieties onto wild vines in his Santa Clara vineyard, and they were still bearing fruit. Yet that had been before the phylloxera infestation, and *Vitis californica* turned out not to be resistant after all. Hilgard and the other researchers at Berkeley then began to experiment with new rootstocks. They based their work on research conducted by French scientists who by necessity had investigated hundreds of different types of rootstock. Much as in France, the California researchers soon discovered that *Vitis riparia* and *rupestris* worked best, but it took them years to identify which varieties within those species were the most resistant. In 1896, a young Berkeley scientist, Arthur Hayne, went to France, met with French researchers, and returned convinced that a relatively obscure variety called the St. George du Lot would provide the best all-around rootstock for use in California's vineyards. Hilgard, always willing to trust good, sound scientific evidence, agreed. Husmann did not. The old man from Missouri argued that laboratories and research stations were no substitute for a lifetime of experience in actual vineyards, and in a series of public letters called Hayne an "incompetent" for suggesting otherwise. But no one much listened. By then, Husmann's was a voice from the past, one that could not speak to the realities of commercial California grape growing and winemaking. The forward-thinking university scientists advised using the St. George, and soon tens of thousands of California vineyards were replanted with *vinifera* varieties grafted onto this *rupestris* rootstock.

For nearly twenty years, Hilgard and the other university

researchers considered phylloxera their most urgent challenge. So in addition to researching the resistance of different root-stocks, they surveyed the state's vineyards for evidence of infestation and studied the life cycle of the insect itself. They even planted a small vineyard in Berkeley, replete with infected vines, in order to conduct field experiments. That led to trouble. When the state legislature had funded the creation of the University of California's viticulture department, it also had established the Board of State Viticultural Commissioners, an appointed body charged with "promot[ing] the viticultural industries of the state." At first, the board and the university worked together. Soon, however, the board's members, led by its chief officer, Charles Wetmore, and the university scientists, especially Hilgard, began fighting. Much of the conflict was political, as each side accused the other of trying to run its affairs. Some was financial, since the same legislative appropriation funded both enterprises, and some surely was no more (and no less) than a monumental clash of egos. A public battle, fought mainly in the newspapers, erupted over the issue of Hilgard's experimental vineyard. Phylloxera had not yet infected nearby vineyards, and some growers worried that the Berkeley campus now posed the "danger of contagion." Wetmore, who owned property in the neighboring Livermore Valley, declared that research should be conducted only in areas already infested, and he urged university officials to destroy the experimental vineyard. Hilgard was furious. He insisted that research required a controlled environment, that the campus vineyard posed no threat to anyone, and that scientific experiments could not be left to amateurs. Wetmore responded in turn, arguing that it was senseless to conduct research that endangered other men's livelihoods. Hilgard and his assistant, Frederick Morse, had begun studying the winged form of phylloxera. "So far as that infected spot on the university being of service to the state," Wetmore declared contemptuously, "[all] it has accomplished [is that] it has taught Mr. Morse how to find the winged phylloxera . . . If we are to have state institutions maintaining pests for the purpose of educating the professors and their assistants . . . our university is working on a very small plane."

Hilgard's feud with Wetmore lasted for nearly fifteen years, coming to an end only when the legislature finally decommissioned the board. George Husmann did not support or belong to either side. His reticence may at first seem odd, given his otherwise exuberant character, but it suggests the most important reason why his Missouri expertise proved irrelevant in California. Hilgard and Wetmore both worked in service of a growing business. Indeed, wine industry leaders were the ones who had petitioned the legislature to fund both the viticulture department and the viticultural board. But wine as a commercial industry was never Husmann's concern. He remained committed to the old agrarian ideal of the self-sufficient farmer, "grow[ing] his own grapes, and mak[ing] his barrel or two of wine." Husmann saw California as the "promised land" because in his mind it was the place "where every one [can] sit 'under his own vine and fig tree.'" Here, he believed, man and nature could be in harmony. "I intend," he wrote, to "talk as the plain, practical farmer to his co-laborers, and confine myself to simple facts, gathered from my own daily practice."

Yet the golden land of California viticulture had little to do with small, self-sufficient farms. By the 1880s, as the United States entered its gilded age, American agriculture at large had become a commercial enterprise, one that served and increasingly depended upon an industrial, urban market. In turn, the vision of an agrarian commonwealth had entered the realm of myth. The myth still resonated in the national consciousness, but with each passing year it did so more as a form of nostalgia than as something that actually could be realized. As even the *Prairie Farmer* editorialized: "The old rule that a farmer should produce all that he required, and that the surplus represented his gains, is part of the past. Agriculture, like all other business, is better for its subdivisions." When it became big business, American agriculture also became speculative, mobile, and capitalistic—in the words of the historian Richard Hofstadter, "thoroughly imbued with the commercial spirit." So too, it became a form of science, mechanized and systemized, attempting to control rather than be controlled by nature. It is hard to imagine any crop or agricultural product better illustrating this change than California wine, especially as embodied by Eugene Hilgard. And with all this, George Husmann was out of step.

For twenty years, Hilgard promoted the use of superior grape varieties, issuing numerous reports on the soils and climates of California's wine-growing regions in order to assist growers in deciding what to plant. He and his university colleagues examined virtually every variety in California, and they constructed a model winery on the Berkeley campus where they produced small lots of wines made from grapes grown all over the state. They then published a detailed series of papers, filled with scientific analysis as well as tasting notes, on the wines they made. In 1880, the Mission was still the dominant wine grape in the state, but by 1900 it had faded into obscurity. The same sort of enthusiasm for grape growing that back east led to the cultivation of new hybrids led to experiments with imported varieties in California. "New" grapes, such as Cabernet Sauvignon, Cabernet Franc, Petite Sirah, and Zinfandel (for reds), and Semillon, Sauvignon Blanc, Traminer, and Green Hungarian (for whites), yielded better and better wines. Some of them could be found, in small quantities, in private clubs and choice restaurants as far away as England.

Despite the phylloxera crisis, the 1880s and 1890s constituted California wine's first golden age. The wines seemed to improve every year, and demand for them increased steadily. Low-priced, everyday wines, many produced from grapes grown in central and southern California, often were flawed, but the top wines from the North Coast counties near the San Francisco Bay merited considerable acclaim. These were the wines that Eugene Hilgard held up as harbingers of a prosperous future. "Now is your golden opportunity," he told a meeting of wine growers in 1880. He urged them to emphasize quality rather than quantity, to rip out their Mission vineyards so they could replant with better varieties, and to make wines that could compete with the finest imports. Hilgard opposed what he called the "old style" of wine—highly alcoholic, frequently oxidized plonk that he thought should be "consigned to the rubbish pile." California wine, he said, was good enough to "show its own face in the best of company."

By all accounts, the finest California wines could do just that. They won medals and awards at numerous international fairs, including Antwerp in 1885, London in 1887, Paris in 1889, and Bordeaux in 1895. They were exhibited to admiring reviews at the 1893 Columbian Exposition in Chicago and the 1894 Midwinter Exposition in San Francisco. World-class California wine came from Alameda, Sonoma, and Napa Counties, with Napa wines fetching the highest prices and winning the most awards. In her 1889 book, *Wines and Vines of California*, Frona Eunice Wait called Napa "the banner wine-making county." In doing so, she singled out one estate for particular praise—Gustave Niebaum's Inglenook.

A Finnish sea captain who had made a fortune in the Alaska fur trade, Niebaum purchased Inglenook in 1880. Mission grapes first had been planted there by a Scotsman, William Watson, who ran the place as a sort of rural retreat. Niebaum kept the odd name, which means cozy chimney corner, but little else. When he grafted Watson's vines to better varieties, he also transformed the property from a pastoral hideaway into an efficient, modern winery, the Napa Valley's grandest. His wines soon acquired an image and a reputation above those of virtually any other California producer. A number of things distinguished Inglenook. First and foremost came Niebaum's philosophy to make the best wines possible, regardless of cost. In this he had a great advantage over most of his neighbors, for whom wine growing constituted the primary source of income. Niebaum's money came from the fur trade, so he could afford to weather the vagaries of the market. He also could afford to hire expert vineyard and winery managers, and to give them free rein in their respective fields. The result was superior wine —according to Wait, "the most celebrated in the state." Inglenook also distinguished itself by producing some of the first commercial California wines to be estate bottled. Most other wines were shipped to San Francisco and then blended and sold in bulk. Niebaum had read about the practice of bottling wines at several elite Bordeaux chateaux. Since he was making wines to compete with the best from France, he followed suit—imprinting corks with his estate's name, using labels with a distinctive diamond-shaped design, and, in order to prevent fraud, placing a wire hood around the capsule, replete with a seal that had to be broken before the bottle could be opened. Niebaum also paid considerable attention to marketing, hiring agents on both coasts to introduce the wines to high society, and making sure that newspapers reported who was drinking Inglenook where. His goal was not just to make world-class wines, but as important, to make wines that people thought of as world class. He succeeded. Inglenook wines won awards at numerous international expositions. They also were served at exclusive clubs and private soirées in Philadelphia, New York, and Newport.

By 1889, Inglenook was producing four red wines (labeled as Zinfandel, Extra Fine Claret, Burgundy, and Medoc Type) and five whites (Sauterne, Chasselas, Hock, Burger, and Riesling). As that list suggests, premium California wines sometimes were identified by grape variety and sometimes by type— the type being a European wine or, more accurately, an imagined European wine. As the list also suggests, premium wines sometimes came as single varietals and sometimes as blends— Inglenook's Hock, for instance, being made solely with Gewürztraminer, while its Medoc Type included Cabernet Sauvignon, Cabernet Franc, and Malbec. By this point, Napa's best wines were being made on French as well as German models, with the French focus becoming more and more important. The valley had developed a reputation as "claret country," and its most celebrated wines tended to be red. By contrast, the Livermore Valley had a reputation for premium whites—many

Germanic, but others made in a French, particularly a Bordeaux, style. Sonoma's best wines came in both colors. They included whites from Jacob Gundlach's Rhinefarm, reds from Isaac de Turk's Santa Rosa estate, and sparkling "champagnes" made by the brothers Korbel. The "science" of matching grape with location continued apace. Given the time-consuming process of planting vines, waiting for them to bear fruit, and then making and aging the wine, advances came slowly. Nonetheless, by the turn of the century certain areas had proven themselves with certain grapes and certain wines—a necessary step in the evolution of any fine wine–growing region.

Award-winning premium wines represented only a small fraction of California's total production. Eugene Hilgard thought that their success would help raise quality overall, but most industry leaders disagreed. They saw premium and bulk wine as two entirely separate products. American "Lafites and Chambertins" should be left to "chance or future generations," argued Arpad Haraszthy at an 1887 meeting of the state viticultural board. "For now, we must content ourselves in securing abundant yields of really good table wines with satisfactory moneyed returns." This debate continued through the first decades of the new century, stopped with Prohibition, and then resumed decades later, in the 1960s and 1970s, when California wine began its renaissance. The issue was simply put. What would best help the United States begin to develop a genuine wine culture—more sound, inexpensive wines, or more premium, world-class ones? If Americans did not drink wine because they thought it cost too much or lacked quality, or because they regarded it as effete and pretentious, then the industry position made good sense. But if Americans did not appreciate wine because they did not know anything about really good wine, then Hilgard's position made even better sense. Although the debate never has been completely resolved, Hilgard's position came to carry the day during California's late-twentieth-century revival. It did not earlier, as the industry, led by Percy Morgan's California Wine Association, focused its efforts primarily on producing wine for mass consumption. But perhaps the most compelling evidence of California wine's success in the late nineteenth century is the fact that the debate was being conducted at all. Producers large and small made both sound everyday wines and first-class premium ones, and each category competed in quality (though not always in reputation) with European imports.

The biggest challenge for the commercial wine industry, especially after grape prices fell in 1886, came with bulk wine. Knowledgeable tasters judged the average quality of California wine to be comparable to that of European imports, but the market, especially in the East, did not agree. Beyond the state's border, everyday California wine lacked prestige. Merchants and consumers alike generally regarded it as inferior to wine from Europe, so except for Inglenook and a few other premium labels, the only California wines available in New York, Philadelphia, and Chicago were cheap, undistinguished blends. At least these were the only wines identified as Californian. Plenty of others were sold under false labels—some fictitious, all fraudulent. Robert Louis Stevenson tells of visiting a prominent San Francisco wine dealer who showed him drawers full of "French" and "Spanish" labels, Château This and Bodega

That, many sporting the names of characters in novels, all ready to be slapped onto bottles of California wine. And Fiona Eunice Wait contended that the only genuine part of a prominent merchant's wine list was the menu of European names — classified-growth Bordeaux, famed Burgundies, and the like. The wines themselves came from grapes grown in California. Wait thought the situation absurd. "If our wines are of good enough quality to masquerade as celebrated foreign importations," she declared, "they are good enough to sell on their own merits at reasonable prices." The challenge, then, did not simply involve questions of quality. It also was a matter of marketing and sales, image, perception, and prestige.

Morgan and the California Wine Association met the challenge head on. The CWA's size enabled it to control how California wine was sold. Massive quantities of wines from vineyards all across the state were blended and stored in central facilities, then bottled and shipped around the country. This meant that small lots of truly first-rate wine inevitably were blended with larger lots of cargo wine. But it also meant that the CWA produced sound, reliable products on an unprecedented scale. Its flagship Calwa brand included red and white table wines, sparklers, brandies, and a growing number of fortified dessert wines. These were sold throughout the country, the biggest markets being cities like New Orleans, Chicago, and New York. Eastern consumers who had tended to regard California wine with suspicion before the CWA's arrival now began to accept it as their own — American wine for Americans to drink. Although there were plenty of New York, Missouri, and other eastern wines available in local markets during the last decades before Prohibition, California wine now dominated

national production. To many people, it was becoming synonymous with American wine. And the specific California wines
they knew likely came from the CWA.

Although the CWA eventually became so big that it eliminated most serious competition, it was not the only large winemaking enterprise in California. Agoston Haraszthy's Buena
Vista had been designed on a grand scale back in the 1850s, but
financial troubles had prevented Haraszthy from realizing his
ambitions. Others were more fortunate. In the Central Valley
near Fresno, a former mining engineer named Robert Barton
built "a princely domain" that eventually had a capacity of
500,000 gallons. Along with the Eggers and Fresno Vineyard
Companies, the Barton Estate Company dominated Central
Valley production. Because only irrigated farming was possible
in this otherwise arid region, and because digging ditches,
dikes, and drains required a substantial investment, viticulture
here always took place on a large scale. Almost all Central Valley wines were sweet, many fortified, and the vast majority
ended up being shipped to San Francisco for blending. Plenty
of sweet wines came from the southern part of the state as well.
Leonard Rose's Sunny Slope, J. de Barth Shorb's San Gabriel
Wine Company, and the Cucamonga Vineyard (owned in part
by Isaias Hellman, who later helped finance the CWA) all produced enormous quantities. But southern California wine
growing was dealt a near fatal blow when the extensive vineyards in and around Anaheim began to wither and die, victims
of a mysterious blight. At first no one could identify the disease.
Then in 1891, the U.S. Department of Agriculture sent a
young scientist, Newton Pierce, to the Santa Ana Valley to investigate. Pierce's careful studies proved that this disease had no

known remedy. His reward was to have it named after him. Agriculture in Anaheim and the neighboring valleys only began to recover when farmers replaced grapes with oranges and other fruits.

Farther north, former California Governor Leland Stanford's Vina Ranch dwarfed every other wine-growing enterprise in California. Stanford may have been first inspired to go into the wine business by Agoston Haraszthy, who had reported to him following Haraszthy's trip to Europe to find better grapes. He dabbled in wine off and on for a while, and then in 1881, with the market booming, decided to invest heavily in it —at least in part, he said, because wine growing served the interest of temperance. Stanford purchased a huge piece of property in Tehama County, a largely untested area north of Sacramento, and over the span of a decade planted about four thousand acres with varieties such as Zinfandel, Charbono, and Burger, as well as sweet grapes for angelica, sherry, and other fortified wines. He then built a massive winery with a nearly two-million-gallon capacity. Stanford dreamed of making premium table wine, but Tehama turned out to be a poor location, and virtually all his grapes ended up having to be distilled into brandy—an ironic turn of events given his initial motivation. By 1890, Vina had become one of the world's largest distilleries, with Sanford's commitment to the temperance cause long forgotten. Before his death in 1893, he included the property in the endowment of the university he founded in honor of his deceased son. Over the next twenty years, the Stanford trustees sold it piecemeal, with the final vintage of wine coming from a small lot in 1915.

The Italian Swiss Agricultural Colony in northern

Sonoma County was a more successful large-scale enterprise. Andrea Sbarboro, originally from Genoa, founded it in 1881 as a cooperative experiment, his initial idea being to help Italian and Italian-Swiss immigrants earn money for housing by employing them in a profit-sharing arrangement. Based on the model of a building-and-loan society, the agricultural colony would deduct a portion of each worker's earnings and reinvest it in the company (the original plan called for five out of a monthly wage of thirty-five dollars), until eventually the worker would own sufficient stock to purchase land and build a house. The plan never really got going, because the immigrants were suspicious of the very notion of payroll deduction, and Italian Swiss ("Agricultural" was quickly dropped from the name) soon evolved into a regular corporation with moneyed investors. By dint of keen management and plenty of hard work, it proved a great success. By the turn of the century, the original Italian Swiss vineyards in Sonoma had become the largest single source of table wine in the country. Following the purchase of extensive vineyards in the Central Valley, Italian Swiss Colony could boast a storage capacity of more than fourteen million gallons. The company produced all sorts of wine, including red, white, and sparkling, with its most commonly recognized single label being Tipo, sold in faux Chianti straw baskets. Pietro Rossi, from Turin, served as president and general manager, and he and Sbarboro promoted their wines tirelessly. They won numerous awards and exported their wines to Europe, Asia, and South America. A network of offices and storage vaults allowed them to sell wine directly to eastern customers, and the growing Italian immigrant population provided them with a ready domestic market. By 1910, the company's stock, originally valued at around $150,000, was worth more than $3 million.

By then, though, Italian Swiss was part of the expanding CWA empire, having been swallowed up by the trust in 1900. As he did with other brands, Percy Morgan sold Italian Swiss under its own label. Consumers may not have known that Italian Swiss (or Lachman & Jacoby, C. Schilling, and many others) were CWA wines, but all bookkeeping was done at the trust's San Francisco headquarters, and all revenue went into a central bank account. Pietro Rossi and Andrea Sbarboro certainly had not wanted to join the CWA. Back in 1894, when Morgan first formed the trust, they had responded by organizing a group of fellow growers and winery owners into a cooperative in an effort to compel the merchants to pay a fair price. At first these two entities worked together. In 1895, the merchants purchased four million gallons of wine from the growers' cooperative, with an agreement to buy five million each year for the next five years. But as soon as Morgan cultivated other sources, things soured. First the CWA reneged on the agreement, refusing to buy the cooperative's wine. Then Morgan cut prices, selling CWA wines in the lucrative East Coast markets far below what any of his competitors could afford to charge. The press dubbed this the Wine War, and Morgan's business tactics competed in the headlines with the growing threat of a real war with Spain. In 1899, the growers' group disbanded, their tanks and barrels full of wine they could not sell. Morgan had won the Wine War, and his victory was what persuaded Isaias Hellman and the other financiers to invest in the association. The monopoly was born.

For the next twenty years, the CWA's only sizable commercial California rivals were located in San Bernardino County east of Los Angeles. The biggest was Secondo Guasti's Italian Vineyard Company. Guasti had emigrated from Piedmont via Mexico, worked for a while as a coal miner and then a cook, all the time dreaming, like many Italians of his generation, of making wine. He persuaded a group of investors to join him, and in 1900 bought an eight-mile tract in the Cucamonga desert where he began planting grapes. The vines flourished, the only problem being a plague of jackrabbits. Guasti organized massive hunts, spent a small fortune on fencing, and watched his company grow and grow. By 1915, four thousand acres were under vine. Guasti imported whole families from Italy to farm the land, and he even built a town for them— which he named after himself—replete with school, inn, post office, and Catholic church, San Secondo d'Asti. Guasti was not the only wine grower in Cucamonga, an infertile-looking expanse of arid land that had damp subsoil beneath its sandy surface. In 1911, Captain Paul Garrett purchased two thousand acres for Virginia Dare, state prohibition laws having exiled him from North Carolina and Virginia. Consumers may have thought that Virginia Dare came wholly from the East, but a significant amount was grown in the West. By 1920, when Prohibition came, San Bernardino County had twenty thousand acres of vineyards, twice as many as Napa. The vast majority of the wines, whether Guasti's, Garrett's, or those made by growers controlled by the CWA, were sweet and heady.

In the two decades before Prohibition, the CWA's operations increasingly came under the control of bankers, financiers, and other moneymen, as opposed to the wine merchants who along with Percy Morgan had formed the original board of directors. The businessmen prudently left the actual winemaking and blending to men with long experience, notably Henry Lachman and Albert Morrow. At the same time, the quest for profit, more than anything else, dictated what sort of wine they sold and how they sold it. Wine in California became a standardized, even homogenized business. Its average quality probably had never been better, but most experts agreed that the best wines made a generation earlier were superior. Something had been lost. Producers such as Inglenook continued making premium, high-class wines, but they toiled in the CWA's long shadow. So too did the men (and occasionally women) who grew grapes in order to make their own wine on the farm—George Husmann's old agrarian ideal, the yeoman sitting beneath his or her vine, drinking the fruit of homegrown temperance. The march of industrial progress, represented by the omnipresent Calwa label, which showed a young Bacchus standing in the prow of a ship, helped destroy that ideal. The CWA offered a readily available bottled product, made to a uniform standard, so there was little reason for a noncommercial farmer to go to the trouble of growing grapes and making wine. What had been lost, then, was the connection between the wine and its origin, the grape and the vineyard. More and more American wine drinkers wanted the sort of consistent and affordable product that the CWA could give them. What was new in all this was the very notion of wine as a mass-produced product. Large-scale commercial winemaking obscured wine's essential identity, making it appear to many Americans to be but another form of liquor.

George Husmann died in 1902, just as the CWA became truly dominant. By then, his nearly half-century advocacy of

American wine had been rendered largely obsolete—not by the CWA itself, but by the changing market that the CWA served so effectively. Eugene Hilgard retired from Berkeley two years later, his days of advocating wine quality and combating what he thought of as a nearsighted industry long behind him. During the remaining years before Prohibition, American wine became even more of an urban phenomenon. It was poured in restaurants and clubs, taverns and saloons, where it became further removed in public perception from its agricultural origins. *What* was in the bottle stayed pretty much the same, but *how* it was used did not. Although dry table wines still constituted the majority of California's production, the proportion of sweet, fortified wines rose steadily. At least some of this heady tipple found its way into saloons, where it was consumed much like whiskey—or like California brandy.

The CWA did nothing to disassociate itself from the liquor trade. (It was the sole sales agent, for example, for Leland Stanford's Vina brandy.) Wine's historic difference came in the context in which it was consumed—the dinner table rather than the bar, with food rather than alone as an intoxicant—but the financiers who controlled California's wine industry cared little about any of that. American wine growing had changed. Like other forms of agriculture, it served the country's growing urban population. During the Jazz Age of the coming decade, the myth of an agrarian republic would recede still further into nostalgic fantasy. The Volstead Act, which put Prohibition into actual practice, allowed Americans to make wine for their own, noncommercial use. Many people did just that, but few did so in vineyards and cellars. Instead, living in Baltimore or Boston, Chicago or Cleveland, they made wine in their basements.

Hence another irony. With the advent of Prohibition, American wine came home. Its home, however, was not the bucolic paradise that Husmann had envisioned. Nor was the wine of the quality that Hilgard had championed. Instead, its home was the city, where, during the 1920s, American wine became booze, under the influence and often the control of mobsters.

3

Wine
As Booze

IN THE EARLY YEARS of what would become the American Century, the wealth and power of the United States began to exert unprecedented influence on cultural tastes the world over. From a distance, the prospects for American wine must have appeared bright. In the East, hardy disease-resistant vines were yielding better grapes than ever before, while in California commercial production had established itself as an integral part of the state's economy. Wines from both East and West received international acclaim. Some forty different American wines won medals at the 1900 Paris Exposition—the majority from California, but some from New Jersey, New York, Ohio, and Virginia. An expanding consumer base, along with a growing export market, seemed to promise golden days ahead. American art, music, and fashion were beginning to turn heads abroad. Why not wine too? But then came national Prohibition, and with it American wine's great fall. The extreme "drys," who contended that drinking alcohol of any sort led to eternal damnation, had carried the day—first in community after community, and then in state after state, including states with significant wine production.

The fortunes of Paul Garrett, whose Virginia Dare was one of the country's best-known wines, illustrate the darkening horizon at home. Garrett first made Virginia Dare from southern Scuppernong grapes in his native North Carolina. When the state went dry in 1903, he was forced to move his operation to Virginia, which adopted prohibition nine years later. Garrett then moved to the Finger Lakes in New York, and Virginia Dare became a blend of juice from grapes grown all over the country. By 1919 Garrett owned wineries in New York, Ohio, Missouri, and California, with a total capacity of some ten million gallons. National Prohibition arrived the following year to shut them all down. Garrett then tried to sell a nonalcoholic wine and a cola-flavored grape drink, but he lost millions. Although he resumed selling Virginia Dare after Repeal, there were few Scuppernong vineyards left, and his wine lost its distinctive character. Many vineyards east of the Rockies had been converted to other crops, and the ongoing Great Depression made replanting untenable. Wineries throughout the country lay abandoned or in ruins, and state legislatures passed laws making it difficult if not illegal for farmers to sell wine from grapes that they grew. Indeed, much of the country remained legally dry, local prohibition laws taking precedence over national Repeal. For Paul Garrett, as for so many American winemakers, the fall proved devastatingly deep.

The fall of American wine clearly involved production, since most commercial winemaking became illegal during Prohibition, when a bottle of wine was contraband goods. But the even greater crisis involved confidence — the shattered confidence of grape growers and winemakers in wine as a natural product with an honored and historic place at the table. Even during the years when the prospect of making fine American wine had appeared dim, the people who toiled in the vineyards and labored in the cellars kept faith in the value of their work. No matter whether motivated by agrarian ideals or commercial realities, they insisted that wine was a healthy part of civilized life and that its becoming a component of American culture would signal national maturity. With Prohibition, however, consumers and producers alike came to view American wine solely as a source of alcohol. Back in 1818, Thomas Jefferson had called wine "the only antidote" to the nation's "bane of whiskey." Over the years, men as different as Eugene Hilgard, George Husmann, and Nicholas Longworth had advanced similar claims, urging their countrymen to drink wine at home rather than whiskey at the saloon. Prohibition undid virtually all their efforts. By midcentury, when American styles in film, art, music, architecture, and more had come to influence and often dictate tastes around the world, no one paid much attention to American wine anymore. It had become just booze.

National Prohibition lasted only fourteen years, but its legacy lingered much longer. Brewers and distillers recovered fairly quickly, but serious wine growers did not really begin to rebound until the 1960s and 1970s, a full half century after the initial fall. When recovery finally came, it involved building almost completely anew. The nineteenth-century achievements of men such as Longworth, Husmann, and Hilgard ended up being ignored if not forgotten, as America's pre-Prohibition heritage became ancient history, largely unconnected to modern reality. As Matt Kramer perceptively argues in his *Making*

Sense of California Wine, America's original fine wine ambitions are almost totally lost to us, the connections between contemporary and past accomplishments being at best a matter of archeological curiosity. "We know that others passed this way before," writes Kramer, "but the path—if discernible at all—leads nowhere." Today, at the dawn of a new century, American wine has indeed become a world leader. Yet the United States is conspicuous among the great wine-producing countries for its near total lack of tradition. This is not because American wine, or even world-class American wine, is something new. Instead, it is because Prohibition effectively severed the links between past and present. People wanting to make fine wine in America after Prohibition (or more precisely, after Prohibition's long legacy had begun to wane) had to reinvent the proverbial wheel. They might use historical names on their labels, but what they did in their vineyards and wineries had little if anything to do with tradition or history. They were at battle with a strange new obstacle—the post-Prohibition history of American wine itself, both its image and its reality.

The story of American wine in the first two-thirds of the twentieth century, the years of Prohibition and its legacy, is the story of its gradual but steady cheapening—not so much in terms of price or even overall quality, as in terms of reputation and renown. Plenty of people can share the blame. Self-righteous teetotalers, progressive zealots, government regulators, and corporate distillers all contributed in different ways. But so did the wine industry itself. Even before ratification of the Eighteenth Amendment, the moneymen like Percy Morgan who ran the California Wine Association and some of the large East Coast wineries had abandoned their historic mission to promote wine as a civilizing force. Fearing Prohibition, they sacrificed long-term interests for short-term gains. Then after Prohibition, when they discovered that the notion of drinking wine for any reason other than intoxication pretty much had been lost, they chose to profit from what they euphemistically called wine's "stimulant property." As a result, America's wine culture became divided against itself—West versus East, sweet versus dry, high alcohol versus low alcohol, bulk versus premium. Ironically enough, wine increasingly became associated in the public eye with drunkenness, while spirit-based cocktails acquired a chic and sophisticated reputation. The few people who cared at all about good wine thought that it had to come from Europe. They knew that domestic wine had no place in middle-class dining rooms or fine restaurants. Instead, it belonged in paper bags on skid row. There the men drinking it were known as winos—a revealing Americanism that first entered the national lexicon around 1910.

The cheapening of American wine began well before Prohibition, with commercial producers who deliberately confused attitudes and blurred popular perceptions concerning wine's identity, use, and cultural role. After George Husmann's death, Andrea Sbarboro of Italian Swiss Colony became American wine's most prominent advocate. During the years before the First World War, when the bellows of progressive rhetoric were inflaming the fires of prohibitionist reform, he campaigned to distinguish wine from beer and spirits in the public mind. Yet his words, while eloquent, had little effect, in large measure because the wine industry itself was so divided. On the one hand, wine men tried to win a special place for their product. On the other hand, they wanted to protect the status quo and preserve their profits, almost half of which came from the sale of high-alcohol, fortified wines and brandies. Even Sbarboro was divided. He opposed what he called "the evil of drunkenness," arguing that if Americans drank wine rather than whiskey, "our people, especially our working classes, [would] then be as happy and sober as they are in all the large grape-growing countries of the world." Yet while he recommended "the use of the healthy beverage of American wine on every American table," he insisted that he "[would] not condemn the use of any other beverage." Italian Swiss regularly produced large quantities of both brandy and grappa in addition to the spirits it distilled in order to make sweet, fortified wines. It sold a sizable percentage of those products in roadhouses and saloons, and Sbarboro, his company part of the California Wine Association empire, had to watch the bottom line.

Although many leading politicians, including President Woodrow Wilson, privately supported an exemption for wine, the wine industry's fight against Prohibition proved wholly ineffective. At first, grape growers and winemakers opposed any and all dry initiatives. Savvy wine men like Napa County's Theodore Bell tried to get the industry to disassociate itself from the liquor interests, but most producers refused. After all, their fortified wines and brandies were sold in saloons, many of which were owned and operated by large distillers. Even after the election of 1916, when the increased number of dry votes in Congress made a prohibition amendment seem likely, the wine industry bungled its efforts.

Andrea Sbarboro's California Grape Protective Association launched a last-gasp campaign on wine's behalf in 1917. Yet the association insisted that anything labeled "wine," no matter its alcohol content and no matter where and when it was consumed, had to be given the same legal protection. Sbarboro supported a state bill prohibiting the sale of distilled liquors while permitting the sale of 21-percent-alcohol wine for "home use." Otherwise sympathetic observers were unimpressed. The influential progressive newspaperman and politician Chester Rowell at first supported the exemption for wine, but then became so irritated by the association's disingenuous tactics that he ended up opposing it. "There never has been any excuse for [fortified wines] except a booze excuse," Rowell declared, echoing the sentiments of many moderate voters. "Logically they should be stopped whenever whiskey is stopped." His wish came true soon enough. In 1918 Congress passed wartime prohibition legislation. Early the next year, the last states ratified the new constitutional amendment. Wines of every type then became illegal, precisely because they were viewed by voters, politicians, and often by many in the industry itself, as forms of liquor.

To be fair, no one could have stopped Prohibition. With its origins deep in the country's history, this attempt to regulate private life through public action signaled the simultaneous triumph and decline of the populist-progressive movement that had dominated American politics for more than a generation. It marked that movement's triumph because it was a genuine grassroots effort at reform, but it signaled decline because it was marked by self-righteousness and hypocrisy. Table wine had little to do with what the Anti-Saloon League or the Woman's Christian Temperance Union wanted to change. Nonetheless, because table wine producers made distilled spirits and fortified wines, and because wine in whatever guise was increasingly associated with liquor, any hope of exempting it was dashed against the hard rock of moral reform. The wine industry's ineffective response came in part from shortsightedness and greed. But it also came from wine's not having become a regular part of American life, at least not as that life was popularly defined and imagined. To many Americans—especially to Yankee Protestants like William Jennings Bryan, who upheld the outdated but still powerful agrarian ideal as progressive reform's restorative goal—wine seemed foreign and dangerous. It was not part of their tradition, but instead belonged to the two segments of the urban population that they distrusted most: wealthy aristocrats and ignorant immigrants. Andrea Sbarboro could talk until he was blue in the face, but his claim that "the home is the natural and rightful drinking place" simply did not make sense to millions of Americans. To them, wine was just another form of demon drink, and demon drink most definitely did not belong in the progressive American home.

Sbarboro died in 1923, a defeated man. The cooperative agricultural colony that he had founded so idealistically some forty years earlier had been gobbled up by the California Wine Association, which was itself now in near total disarray, the financiers having abandoned it for more lucrative enterprises. The next year, Sbarboro's former partner's sons, Edmund and Robert Rossi, bought back the company's original property at Asti, in northern Sonoma County. For a time, they sold grapes there as the Asti Grape Products Company, while saving the name Italian Swiss Colony for the day when they again could sell wine. That would not come for another decade. Meanwhile, they profited from one of the great paradoxes of Prohibition, as they helped American wine come home.

Prohibition drove most drinking underground, where bootleggers controlled production and gangsters oversaw distribution. Such was the case with imported alcohol smuggled from abroad as well as with domestic spirits. Grape growers, however, never had to go underground. Their product, fresh fruit, was perfectly legal, and more grapes were sold in America during Prohibition than at any time before. As odd as it may seem, American per capita wine consumption rose significantly during the period. Very little of the wine people consumed came from commercial wineries. Instead, Americans drank wine that they made at home. Section 29 of the Volstead Act permitted each head of household to manufacture up to two hundred gallons a year of "nonintoxicating cider and fruit juices exclusively for use in [the] home." Although too much wine obviously can prove intoxicating, the Internal Revenue Service, which was in charge of enforcement, had no intention of pursuing home winemakers. The statute read "nonintoxicating," not "nonalcoholic," and what happened in private homes was private business. The IRS agents cared much more about the hard liquor traffic, specifically the illicit revenue generated by the sale and transportation of whiskey, gin, and rum. No law prohibited people from selling and shipping grapes, and no one imagined huge profits coming from the manufacture of wine in basements. As a result, home winemaking became widely accepted. In many city neighborhoods, it was standard practice.

Because the first thing any home winemaker needed was grapes, demand for hardy fruit quickly outpaced supply, causing prices to escalate rapidly. Growers who in 1918 had received $10 for a ton of grapes found buyers offering them more than $100 two years later. The boom continued until 1926, when a surplus drove prices back down, but even then, growers had no difficulty finding a market. East Coast growers sold Concord and other native varieties, but the demand was especially strong for California *vinifera* grapes, which were shipped all over the country by railroad. In 1919, about 300,000 acres were under vine in California. Seven years later, the acreage had doubled. Not surprisingly, many growers, their wallets bulging, concluded that Prohibition was not such a bad thing after all.

The important markets for wine grapes were the big eastern and midwestern cities, along with San Francisco and, to a lesser extent, Los Angeles. Most growers sold their produce to shippers, who in turn sold grapes by the boxcar to local dealers. Home winemakers, bringing wheelbarrows and baby buggies to the railyards, then purchased crates of grapes, as did bootleggers, who made wine for restaurants and speakeasies. Growers quickly recognized that there was an important difference between the fruit that a winery located a few miles down the road might purchase and grapes that had to travel thousands of miles before the final customer even saw them. The husbands or wives who purchased a crate or two knew little about the fine points of winemaking. They usually decided what to buy on the basis of how the fruit looked. So the new home market demanded above all that grapes be pretty. This meant big bunches and fat berries, along with thick skins to prevent rot and premature breakage. Color also mattered. Since the boom was almost completely in red wine, dark grapes suggested deep flavor, while lighter ones looked as though they might taste watery.

With the grape market expanding, virtually all new California plantings during Prohibition involved varieties whose chief virtue was how pretty they looked in a boxcar, not how well they made wine. And growers soon saw that the classic *vinifera* grape varieties did not look particularly good, especially after a couple of weeks in a train. The bunches and berries often were small. Most were delicate and had fairly thin skins, which made them susceptible to mold and rot soon after they were picked. By contrast, raisin and table grapes such as Thompson Seedless, Flame Tokay, and Emperor looked great. So did dark-skinned but inferior *vinifera* varieties such as Alicante Bouschet. Consequently, thousands of California acres soon were either planted or grafted to red table grapes and to Alicante. Because the juice was so dark, these grapes could be pressed and repressed several times. The final batch barely qualified as wine, but with the addition of sugar and water, it certainly contained alcohol.

By 1925, the overwhelming majority of America's vineyards were planted with inferior wine grapes — native varieties in the East and hardy, heavy-bearing shipping grapes in the West. Many of these grapes, especially in the East, were used for unfermented juice, for jams, jellies, and syrups, even for paper products. Others, particularly out west, were pressed into hard "winebricks." These were sold with instructions indicating how much water to add, as well as a warning that read: "This beverage should be consumed within five days; otherwise in summer temperature it might ferment and become alcoholic." In many American basements, summer lasted all year long.

The Rossi brothers in Asti were fairly typical large-scale grape growers. They sold juice, grapes, and various grape products all across the country. Although they had little control over what happened to the fruit they shipped east, they made sure to take a hands-on approach with the grapes they sold closer to home. In San Francisco, their biggest single market, they employed "service men" who would come to a customer's house, crush the grapes, and then put the juice in kegs. If it happened to ferment, well, that was the homeowner's business. In 1929, the Rossis joined with a number of other large California growers as well as with Paul Garrett to form a new organization, Fruit Industries, Ltd., which took this notion of service to a new level. Since many big-city railyards and marketing terminals had come under gangster control, people were afraid to go there and buy grapes. Fruit Industries solved the problem by selling a packaged grape concentrate called Vine-Glo directly to consumers at home. It came in nine varieties: Port, Virginia Dare, Muscat, Angelica, Tokay, Sauterne, Riesling, Claret, and Burgundy. Customers ordered five- or ten-gallon barrels, which a service man brought to their homes. Two months later, the service man returned and bottled the finished wine. The growers who formed Fruit Industries pledged support for the Eighteenth Amendment. Vine-Glo, they assured customers, was legal. "You take absolutely no chance when you order your home supply," one advertisement read. "Section 29 of the National Prohibition Act permits you." Of course, this wasn't really true, and when the Justice Department threatened suit in 1932, Fruit Industries halted sales. Nonetheless, Vine-Glo had proved profitable, so much so that Al Capone complained that its sales hurt his rum-running business.

That was the problem. American wine had become like rum. It had entered millions of homes, but it had betrayed its traditional identity in order to do so. Vine-Glo, like most homemade wine, had only one thing to recommend it—alcohol. No one thought of it as a mark of culture or as an antidote to drunkenness. No one believed that it made the United States a more mature country. It just was a cheap, easily available, and seemingly legal form of booze. Especially for many new drinkers, wine's sole virtue was the effect it produced. And to get that effect, one had to drink a fair amount. Hence another casualty of the Prohibition years—the notion of wine as an agent of temperance defined as moderation. The 1920s saw little moderation in America. It was a decade of paradoxes—the hedonistic Jazz Age coupled with the inhibitions of Main Street, rising hem lines with rising fundamentalism. The paradox for American wine came as its history got flipped upside down. The beverage of temperance fast became the drink of excess.

Not all Prohibition-era wine was consumed because of the effect it produced. For the many immigrant families who continued to drink it with meals, wine remained a form of food. Yet even for them, American wine changed during the dry years. Being homemade rather than commercially produced, it became heavier and headier, with a high level of alcohol. This shift went along with the developing tastes of the millions of new American wine drinkers. They knew wine primarily as something served in a speakeasy or consumed before, after, but rarely with dinner, and they wanted it strong. As a result, when Prohibition ended in 1933 and commercial winemaking resumed, some two-thirds of the wine sold in the United States contained over 20 percent alcohol (as opposed to the roughly 12 percent in most table wine). Fortified by the addition of brandy or neutral spirits, some of it was dry, more sweet, but it all packed a wallop.

Consumer preference for this sort of high-alcohol wine continued for thirty-five years, reaching a peak immediately after the Second World War, when three out of every four bottles produced in the United States were fortified. These wines came to be thought of by many people as drunkards' swill, their only reason for existence being the buzz they provided. Whether inferior forms of sherry or port, or whether so-called dessert wines such as muscatel, they only strengthened the broad public perception of American wine as something shabby and cheap.

Prohibition cheapened American wine in one other important way. Because selling grapes proved profitable (at least until the inevitable surplus developed), and because most commercial wine production was illegal, the balance of power and influence between growers and winemakers shifted subtly but significantly. Before Prohibition, growers tended to plant the varieties that wineries wanted to buy, and the best grapes in any given region usually fetched the highest prices. But at Repeal, most growers had no intention of replanting their vineyards. Their grapes had sold well enough for more than a decade, and Americans willingly drank wine made from them. What was the point of changing? The country was in the midst of the Great Depression. Few growers had money to replant, especially so long as wineries could not afford to pay much more for one container of grapes than for another. Yes, Cabernet Sauvignon would produce better wine than would Alicante Bouschet, but in 1934 a ton of Cabernet and a ton of Alicante sold for about the same price—$15 in northern California. Until wineries could pay more for better grapes, growers had no incentive to replant. And wineries would not be able to do that until consumers valued wine for something other than its alcohol. It was a vicious circle. The growers controlled wine's raw material. Thirty years earlier, the best of that material, premium wine grapes, had greater value than ordinary grapes, all because consumers wanted the wines made from them. From a grower's point of view, if alcohol now was all that wine grapes were good for, what possible difference could such things as variety, yield, or location make? Put simply, grapes were grapes and wine was wine. Only fools and snobs cared about anything else.

Before Prohibition, there had been more than 1,000 commercial wineries in the United States. At Repeal, in December 1933, only slightly more than 150 remained—some 130 in California and a couple of dozen others scattered about Ohio, New York, and the eastern seaboard states. These had survived largely by making specialized wines under government permit —medicinal "tonics" that could be prescribed by doctors, salted wines for cooking, and sacramental wines for rabbis and priests. Almost all of the survivors were in bad shape. The cheapening of wine had shrunk profits, and few producers had been able to afford to replace worn equipment. Matters were worse at wineries whose doors had been shut for the past fourteen years. They were filled with rotted casks, rusted presses, and stocks of old wine that had turned into vinegar. Repeal brought an infusion of energy and optimism but, because the Depression was in full swing, little money. Speculators, many with no experience in the wine business, bought abandoned wineries on the cheap, and then rushed into production. The wines that they hurried onto the market in 1934 may well have been the worst commercial American wines ever produced. Some, still fermenting when first shipped, literally blew up on store shelves. Others, made of fresh wine blended with old stock, proved barely drinkable. Still others turned out to be spoiled, and the California Department of Public Health soon condemned several million gallons. Fresh beer and legal whiskey became available at the same time, with quality on the whole far superior to what had been bootlegged during Prohibition. So when it at last became legal, wine's reputation continued to fall while that of other forms of alcohol improved. American wine had not just become booze. It had become cheap, bad booze.

Things only got worse. Although the Twenty-first Amendment ended national Prohibition, it permitted individual states to stay dry. Nineteen did, and many stayed that way for a long time, Mississippi being the last to pass a repeal law — in 1966. Equally problematic, the amendment effectively removed alcoholic beverages from the protection of the Commerce Clause, so that individual states began to impose their own taxes, license fees, and regulations. No two states had identical systems of control, making the shipment of wine a logistical and bureaucratic nightmare, especially for small producers. Seventeen states created state or municipal monopolies for the sale of liquor, and only a few permitted wine to be sold in grocery stores alongside other foodstuffs. In addition, most legislatures passed laws that discouraged and in effect prevented individual farmers from growing grapes and making wine. In Kentucky, for example, a grower could not sell more than one bottle of wine to any one person each year. And in

Georgia, it was illegal for a farmer to sell wine to a wholesaler, even though all retailers and restaurants had to purchase wine from state-licensed wholesalers. In much of the country, then, government regulations made wine growing difficult if not impossible.

For a brief moment, the Roosevelt administration tried to help. Assistant Secretary of Agriculture Rexford Tugwell proposed that wine be exempted from federal taxation in order to help reduce the consumption of hard liquor. He also authorized the construction of two model wineries to assist grape growers and winemakers with scientific research. But his proposal died, and the two wineries never crushed a grape, all because the House Appropriations Committee, chaired by Missouri's Clarence Cannon, a lifelong prohibitionist, refused to go along. For the next thirty years, until Cannon's death in 1964, the very word "wine" was essentially stricken from Department of Agriculture publications. The department conducted research to assist table, juice, and raisin grape growers, but it would have nothing to do with wine grapes. For all practical purposes, as far as the U.S. government was concerned, wine was no longer considered an agricultural product.

This, then, was the state of American wine after the "noble experiment" of Prohibition had come to a close. Government at all levels regarded wine with distrust. So did all those American citizens who did not drink it, and who increasingly associated those who did with poverty and alcoholism. To make matters worse, inferior grape varieties in the vineyards, along with shoddy equipment and inexperienced winemaking in the wineries, produced very poor wines. Winemakers made much more fortified wine than table wine. And fortified wine, precisely because it was high in alcohol and relatively inexpensive, became the drink of choice on skid row. In short, Repeal in no sense ended the fall brought on by Prohibition. American wine was legal again, but it no longer merited respect.

The challenge for the wine industry—growers, winemakers, and owners alike—was clear enough: to teach Americans about wine's traditional use at the table and thus regain more than two decades' worth of lost ground. Over the next thirty years, a number of visionary individuals tried to do so. They worked, in very different ways and often in isolation, to make table wine a respectable part of American daily life. Yet the majority of the industry shunned the challenge. Most growers were happy enough with the status quo, and most winemakers lacked the means, financial and otherwise, to change it. So too, most owners cared about their profits far more than about their product. As the author, publicist, and long-time wine enthusiast Leon Adams reminisced later, the fundamental problem was that "most of the big people in the industry . . . lacked respect for [wine]." They too "thought of [it] as the skid-row beverage." The speculators who got into the business because they expected a wine boom knew little about wine, and the bankers who financed them knew even less. According to Adams, many of them never drank the stuff, looking down on it as something less sophisticated than cocktails. Bankers and financiers paid virtually no attention to the quality differences between grape varieties or vineyard locations. They viewed grapes as a generic commodity. Wine was just one use of that commodity, and a rather tawdry one at that.

In 1934, Leon Adams and A. P. Giannini, head of the Bank of America, led a drive to organize California's wineries through a cohesive association they later named the Wine Institute. A forum for the exchange of ideas and a vehicle for government lobbying, the institute served as a publicity board for an otherwise fragmented industry. Nearly all of the state's large wine growers eventually became members. In 1938, the Wine Institute sponsored a nationwide advertising campaign urging Americans to drink more wine. Although consumption did go up, almost all of the increase came in the fortified or so-called dessert category, and the growers soon started bickering among themselves. Many thought that any attempt to promote table wine and mealtime drinking was a waste of money. Adams, who dreamed of the day when table wine would become a staple of the American diet, was actually told, "in open meeting protest —'That's not what we're selling. We're selling sweet wine to skid-row.'" The Wine Institute remained intact, but its campaign to educate Americans to drink wine with food soon fizzled out. So long as table wine remained an afterthought to many producers, all the leaflets and advertisements in the world made little difference. The industry as a whole remained divided against itself.

Quality remained a primary source of the division. Table wines were supposed to be the civilized beverage, and fortifieds just drunkards' swill, but taken as a whole, fortified wines ironically offered higher quality in the late 1930s. The choice of grape variety and vineyard location mattered far less to fortified producers, many of whom were located in or purchased fruit from California's Central and San Joaquin Valleys, areas that at the time did not grow premium table grapes. The addition of brandy or other spirits covered up defects, and American ports or sherries, while a far cry from their European namesakes, usually were sound. The same could not be said for most table wine. Part of the problem was that the majority of California wine once again was being sold in bulk. Shipped from San Francisco by rail, it either was bottled back east and packaged under local labels or made available to restaurants and retailers in small barrels with spigots, allowing customers or bartenders to fill their own bottles or glasses. But unlike fortified wine, table wine in a half empty barrel will spoil quickly. Consequently, much of the commercial table wine sold in post-Prohibition America went bad. According to Ernest Gallo, "Back then, table wines were heavy, very dry, high in tannin, usually oxidized, coarse, harsh, and often sour." Not surprisingly, they received a cool public reception. The country's few connoisseurs bought European wines, while many first- and second-generation immigrants who wanted to drink wine with meals continued to make their own—according to estimates, around twenty million gallons a year.

Some large producers tried to take a stand for better quality, or at least for unspoiled, drinkable wines. Edmund and Robert Rossi led the way, and Italian Swiss Colony soon began bottling and labeling its own wines. Other companies, including Cresta Blanca and Roma, did so as well. Their attempt to upgrade their wines proved expensive. These wineries spent much of the money that bulk producers pocketed as profit on equipment, labor, and promotion. With their names on the labels, however, they hoped to become well known in many different markets. And since they were compelled to stand behind what they sold, the overall quality of their wines did get better. The Rossis thought that Italian Swiss's history gave them a special responsibility to produce sound everyday wines and thus help wean Americans from whiskey and other spirits. Even before Repeal, they had organized a group of old-time wine growers into something called the Grape Growers League, which later became part of the Wine Institute. In the late 1930s, as members of the institute, they lobbied hard for advertising campaigns to focus primarily on wine as a food beverage, and they became leading advocates of table wine. Italian Swiss Colony did well financially, becoming the third-largest wine company in the nation, and the only large commercial producer to be located in California's North Coast, the historic home of premium vineyards and premium wines. Yet despite their commitment to table wine, the Rossis were businessmen who knew what the market wanted. Fortified wine constituted a majority of their production, as it did for virtually every winery of significant size. So when at the end of the decade Italian Swiss purchased new property, the Rossis went shopping for land in the San Joaquin Valley, not in Sonoma.

In 1942, the liquor giant National Distillers offered Edmund and Robert Rossi $3.7 million for Italian Swiss Colony, the properties in Asti and Fresno, and the company name. It was an offer the Rossis could not refuse, and the family business that had started as an idealistic agricultural venture became corporately owned. National's purchase of Italian Swiss constituted an advance in what came to be called "the whiskey invasion" of the war years. During the first half of the 1940s, large distillers purchased vineyard after vineyard and winery after winery, until by 1945 they owned approximately half of the nation's stock of commercial wine. Four companies—Schenley, Hiram Walker, Seagram, and National—did almost all the buying. These companies became interested in wine only when the government ordered them to convert their own alcohol production to munitions and other nonbeverage wartime uses. They still were making money, but with Washington as their only customer, their distribution network had ground to a halt. So led by Schenley, which bought the big Roma Wine Company to become for a time the country's largest wine organization, they purchased wineries in large measure to give their sales force something to do. When the war ended, they left the wine business and went back to what they knew best—making, marketing, and selling spirits to a country that, following wartime deprivation, was thirstier than ever for them.

Although the whiskey invasion lasted only about a decade, it profoundly marked American wine. On the positive side, the distillers, flush with money, supplied needed capital to what was still very much a struggling industry. On the negative side, they forged the first actual connection between wine and whiskey, providing a foundation to what previously had been a misperception, that wine was much the same as liquor. Over the next half century, the big spirits companies would continue to move in and out of wine, buying when it looked as though consumption would go up, selling when profits proved disappointing. In the process, they changed the industry. After the war, winery owners looked jealously at the kind of money the distillers made, and many decided to follow their lead. "Bigger is better" became the mantra of the day, and large companies increasingly came to dominate American wine. In 1936, at the height of post-Repeal speculation, some 1,300 bonded wineries operated in the United States. By 1960, only 271 remained. Big is not necessarily bad, but in the case of wine, it often was. American consumers by and large still distrusted wine, especially table wine, and the challenge of educating them about the benefits of moderate wine consumption remained unmet. The big companies, whose shared goal was to become ever bigger, had little interest in it. Like the distillers they so admired, they wanted above all to sell more booze.

The biggest eastern wineries were located in the Finger Lakes region of New York. They produced wines made mainly from native or hybrid grapes, including America's best-known sparkling wines. The Pleasant Valley winery on Keuka Lake was home to Great Western "champagne," a bubbly blend of primarily Delaware and Catawba grapes. Founded in 1860, Pleasant Valley's first winemakers, Joseph and Jules Masson, had worked for Nicholas Longworth in Cincinnati. When a Boston connoisseur proclaimed Jules's first sparkler "the great champagne of the West," the company's owners came up with what may seem an odd name for an eastern wine made from eastern grapes. Also on Keuka Lake, the Urbana Wine Company made Gold Seal "champagne," using both native and hybrid grapes. Charles Fournier, formerly the chief winemaker at Champagne Veuve Clicquot in Rheims, oversaw production, and his wines won numerous awards. Both Pleasant Valley and Urbana produced still wine as well, as did the region's other big producer, Taylor, a family-run company that specialized in what Fred Taylor liked to call "uncomplicated wines." Made primarily from *labrusca* grapes, some of these were designed to be drunk with food, while others were fortified—New York ports, sherries, and other proprietary blends. During the 1940s and 1950s, Taylor became the state's biggest winery by increasing the production of these cheap wines, many of which found their way onto skid row. So too with the wines made by

Canandaigua Industries. Using almost exclusively bulk wine, Canandaigua's biggest seller was a pink, *labrusca*-flavored blend called Richard's Wild Irish Rose. The wine came in both table and fortified strengths, with the 20 percent version far out-selling the 12 percent one. In eastern slums, "the Rose" became an extremely popular, because cheap, buzz. Canandaigua reaped a considerable profit, and the company grew ever larger.

California was home to even larger companies. The two biggest were E. & J. Gallo and United Vintners, which throughout the 1950s dueled in what the trade press called "the battle of the giants." The companies could not have been more different. United Vintners was the marketing arm of a huge co-operative, Allied Grape Growers, owned by Louis Petri, whose father had been a successful wine merchant before Prohibition. After the Second World War, Petri set out to become America's "wine king," and by the late 1950s, he controlled two dozen different brands, nearly a quarter of all the wine consumed in the United States. His talent lay more in marketing and selling wine than in making it, and his various wineries remained distinct, separate enterprises. By contrast, the Gallo brothers made all their own wine. They too sold it under different labels, but everything came from their ever-expanding facility in Modesto. Ernest Gallo's confessed goal was to become "the Campbell's Soup Company of the wine industry"—that is, to supply America with mass-produced wines under instantly recognizable names. Like Louis Petri, he wanted more than anything else to be number one.

Petri's big coup came in 1953 when he purchased Italian Swiss Colony. The reason, rumor had it, was that he wanted "to beat Ernie Gallo to the punch." Even though Italian Swiss still produced plenty of fortified wines, it was one of the few national brands that had a reputation for quality table wines priced for everyday use. Petri thought that table wine sales were bound to increase, and his strategy was to try to control the table wine market. Italian Swiss under his direction came to dominate the category. The Gallos tried to match him in market after market. Italian Swiss's best-selling table wine was its Vin Rosé, promoted on radio and later television by "the little old winemaker" of advertising fame and the slogan, "You can't miss with Italian Swiss." The Gallos competed with a rosé of their own, which they advertised as the "light, bright" wine for "people who don't normally like wine." "Try it chilled," urged the announcer, "over ice, or tall, cool, pink, with your favorite mixer." As that copy indicates, even table wine was not necessarily for the table in the 1950s. Especially for new drinkers, it often became a cocktail beverage.

Sales of table wines did increase during the decade, but not as much as Louis Petri hoped. In 1951, Americans drank some 33 million gallons of table wine. By 1957, this figure had risen to almost 41 million. During the same period, however, consumption of fortified wines went from 84 to nearly 94 million gallons. Ernest and Julio Gallo were not blind to these numbers. They realized that the way to beat Louis Petri was with fortifieds, and here Gallo already was a major player. Its white port, sherry, and muscatel sold well, particularly in low-income neighborhoods, what some people called "the misery market." The challenge was to come up with something new. As Julio Gallo said, "New products . . . mean new customers."

To that end, the Gallos persuaded the Wine Institute to lobby for a change in federal regulations that would allow wine

Nicholas Longworth, American wine's founding father, dreamed of making wine part of daily life in the young agrarian republic. Using Catawba grapes grown near Cincinnati in vineyards dubbed "America's Rhineland," he began producing the country's first successful commercial wines in the 1840s. *Portrait by Robert S. Duncanson, 1858. University of Cincinnati Fine Arts Collection*

Samuel Carey, a strident advocate of temperance defined as prohibition, insisted that wine was no different from "demon" whiskey or rum. Carey fought a public battle with Longworth during the 1850s. Two generations later, prohibition became the law of the land. *Cincinnati Museum Center Archives*

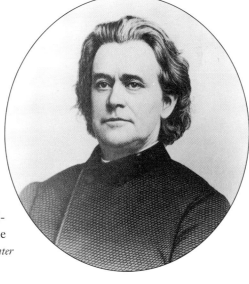

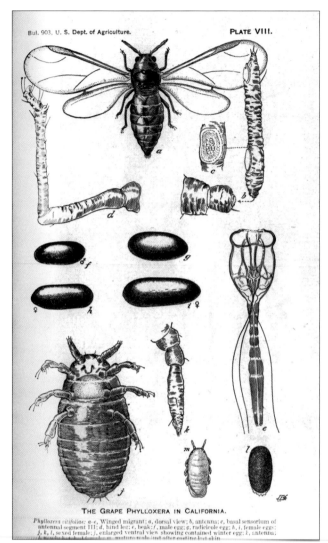

Bul. 903, U. S. Dept. of Agriculture.

PLATE VIII.

THE GRAPE PHYLLOXERA IN CALIFORNIA.

Phylloxera vitifoliae: a–e, Winged migrant; *a,* dorsal view; *b,* antenna; *c,* basal sensorium of antennal segment III; *d,* hind leg; *e,* beak; *f,* male egg; *g,* radicicole egg; *h, i,* female eggs; *j, k, l,* sexed female; *j,* enlarged ventral view showing contained winter egg; *k,* antenna; *l, m,* mature male just after casting last skin

Phylloxera, a microscopic root louse native to eastern North America, devasted *Vitis vinifera* vineyards first in Europe and then in California in the last quarter of the nineteenth century. In both places, the only solution was to graft the vines onto resistant native American rootstock. *Courtesy of the Wine Institute*

Agoston Haraszthy traveled to Europe in 1861 on behalf of the State of California to research grape varieties. Although few of the vines he ordered actually were planted in California, his findings persuaded the industry as a whole to improve wine quality by planting better grapes. *Courtesy of the Wine Institute*

Eugene Hilgard, the first professor of agriculture at the University of California, championed quality wine production in the Golden State during the last decades of the nineteenth century. He argued that California wine should be good enough to "show its face in the best of company." *Courtesy of the Wine Institute*

George Husmann came to California after nearly a lifetime in the vineyards of Missouri. The nineteenth century's most ardent popularizer of American wine, he saw California as "*the* great *Vineland* . . . destined to overshadow all others."

Percy Morgan came to California from England as a young man. An accountant, he conceived the idea of organizing the state's wine merchants into a "community of interests," or trust, the California Wine Association. As a result, American wine became big business for the first time. *Courtesy of Ernest P. Peninou and Gail Unzelman*

In 1907, the California Wine Association constructed a massive storage facility on the shore of San Francisco Bay at Richmond. Called Winehaven, it held more than ten million gallons of wine, which the association shipped by rail across the country and by boat around the world. *Courtesy of the Wine Institute*

Andrea Sbarboro, the founder of Italian Swiss Colony, campaigned to distinguish wine from spirits in the public mind. But because the California wine industry produced brandy and high-alcohol fortified wines in addition to table wines, his words, while eloquent, had little effect. With the passage of the Eighteenth Amendment and the advent of national Prohibition, wine in America became booze. *Courtesy of the Wine Institute*

In the dark decades following Prohibition, when American wine was widely viewed as belonging on skid row, a few visionary individuals tried to bring it home to the supper table. Philip Wagner did so in eastern vineyards, pioneering the use of French-American hybrid grapes that produced "wines that taste like wine." *Courtesy of Boordy Vineyard*

Dr. Konstantin Frank came to the United States from Ukraine after the Second World War. He proved that *vinifera* vines could grow and produce high-quality wines in New York's Finger Lakes region. Eastern wine growing was changed forever. *Courtesy of Dr. Konstantin Frank's Vinifera Wine Cellars*

Two of the grand old men of American wine, André Tchelistcheff (left) and Dr. Konstantin Frank, are shown here near the end of their careers. After the war, Tchelistcheff in California and Frank in New York shared a vision of premium American wine competing with the world's best. *Courtesy of Dr. Konstantin Frank's Vinifera Wine Cellars*

Ernest (right) and Julio Gallo as young boys in California. Their memories of a difficult childhood and a painful young adulthood would profoundly affect their future business decisions. *Courtesy of E. & J. Gallo Winery. All rights reserved*

Cesare Mondavi, shown here with his two sons, Peter (right) and Robert, was the family patriarch, a man of few words whose sons knew that his word was law. *Courtesy of Robert Mondavi*

Peter (right) and Robert Mondavi ran the Charles Krug Winery in the Napa Valley for more than twenty years, with Peter making the wines and Robert marketing them. It was, both brothers acknowledge, a successful combination. *Courtesy of Robert Mondavi*

Heads turned when Robert Mondavi began constructing his winery in 1966, the first completely new facility to be built in Napa since Prohibition. *Courtesy of Robert Mondavi*

Above: Julio Gallo (right) promised to make all the wine that Ernest could sell, while Ernest pledged to sell all that his brother made. Here the Gallo brothers are toasting their success in 1967, the year after their winery had become the country's largest. *Courtesy of E. & J. Gallo Winery. *

Louis Petri of United Vintners became America's "wine king" after the Second World War, marketing and selling mostly cheap, often fortified wines throughout the country. He dueled with Ernest Gallo for two decades in what the trade press called "the battle of the giants." *Courtesy of the Wine Institute*

Maynard Amerine, professor of enology at the University of California at Davis, helped revitalize American winemaking by insisting on scientific standards. "If you don't know biochemistry," he insisted, "you don't know anything about wine." *Courtesy of the Wine Institute*

Jess Jackson pioneered a new category of wine, the "fighting varietal," when he introduced Kendall-Jackson Chardonnay in 1983. A blend of wines made from grapes grown all over California, it expressed a stylistic recipe rather than a particular vineyard or region, and quickly became phenomenally popular. *Courtesy of Kendall-Jackson Wine Estates*

Bob Trinchero (left) of Sutter Home, shown here with his brother Roger, invented what in the 1980s became America's most popular varietal wine, white Zinfandel. It was an entirely new product, a *vinifera* wine without any European model. *Courtesy of Trinchero Family Estates*

Demanding and difficult, Martin Ray made some of America's finest wines in the 1940s and 1950s on Table Mountain. A generation later, a new breed of boutique winemakers would follow his lead, viewing winemaking more as an art than a business. *Courtesy of the Ray Family Trust / Barbara Marinacci*

Warren Winiarski, at his new
Stag's Leap property in 1972, came to
California in search of both better wine
and a better life. His Cabernet Sauvignon triumphed in Paris in 1976, sig-
naling that American wine was coming
of age. *Courtesy of Stag's Leap Wine Cellars*

Miljenko (Mike) Grgich, a Croatian
émigré, made the Chateau Montelena
Chardonnay that astonished the wine
world in Paris in 1976. The next year,
he started a winery of his own, Grgich
Hills. "That's why I came to America,"
he explains. "I felt a little artistic blood
in my veins . . . I wanted to do it my
own way." *Photo by Lindy Lindquist, courtesy
of Grgich Hills Cellar*

Dr. Walter Clore brought *vinifera* wine growing to Washington State. As the horticulturist at the state research station in Prosser, he planted more than three hundred grape varieties, proving conclusively that quality wine grapes could be grown successfully in the Columbia River Valley. *Courtesy of the Washington Wine Commission*

David Lett of Eyrie Vineyards pioneered wine growing in Oregon. He is shown here in 1966, holding the first *vinifera* rootings to be planted in the Willamette Valley. *Courtesy of Eyrie Vineyards*

Betty and Jim Held were corn and hog farmers who knew little about wine when they purchased the old Stone Hill Winery in Herman, Missouri, in 1965. In the years since then, they have played a leading role in the revitalization of grape growing and winemaking throughout the Midwest. *Courtesy of the Held family of Stone Hill Winery*

Beginning in the mid-1960s, Julia Child, here pictured on the set of *The French Chef*, brought a new awareness of food and cooking into American homes. She inspired the rise of American cuisine that accompanied the rise of American wine. *Photograph by Paul Child, courtesy of Julia Child's Kitchen*

Alice Waters at Chez Panisse in Berkeley, California, gave new spirit and vision to American restaurant dining. Her insistence on using the freshest and finest ingredients and cooking them so as to highlight their natural flavors became a hallmark of the new American cuisine. *Courtesy of Robert Messick*

In the late 1990s, an emphasis on *terroir,* or vineyard location, became all the rage with American vintners. But it was nothing new. Paul Draper at Ridge Vineyards had been making wines that expressed their *terroir* for nearly thirty years. *Courtesy Ridge Vineyards*

Robert M. Parker is the world's most influential wine critic. His reviews and ratings have helped change wine styles worldwide and, whether he intended it or not, have promoted wine's internationalization. *Courtesy of Robert M. Parker, Jr.*

to be made with the addition of natural flavorings. The new regulations went into effect in 1955, and two years later the Gallos launched their new product, a 21-percent-alcohol white port flavored with concentrated lemon juice. They came up with the idea after observing that many inner-city liquor stores sold lemon juice or lemon Kool-Aid with white port as a sort of package. Customers, particularly African Americans, would mix the two. The Gallos' idea was to do the mixing for them. They named the result Thunderbird, and it took the country by storm. Although Ernest Gallo claimed later that he thought of Thunderbird as a "lower-alcohol alternative to the evening cocktail," it became popular precisely because it contained so much alcohol. At sixty cents a quart, it provided a cheap, fast high, and it soon became America's best-selling single wine— *the* brand of choice in the ghetto and on skid row.

Louis Petri and Italian Swiss Colony quickly entered the flavored-fortified market with something called Silver Satin. Edmund Rossi, Jr., had followed his father and grandfather at Asti, and he understood well the success of these new wines: they provided half the proof of whiskey for about a quarter the price. Silver Satin never became as popular as Thunderbird, but Italian Swiss kept trying. Over the next few years, Rossi's staff produced a slew of fortifieds flavored with everything from coffee to pineapple juice, with names such as Ariba, Golden Spur, Red Showboat, and Zombe. None had sales anywhere close to Thunderbird's, and the Gallos slowly but steadily gained on Petri. Within a decade after inventing Thunderbird, they caught him. In 1967, Gallo became what it remains today —the world's biggest winery.

By then, however, things were beginning to change. The

1960s saw at long last a real increase in consumer demand for table wines and a slow but steady decline in the sale of cheap fortifieds. What Leon Adams predicted would be America's "wine revolution" finally had begun. The seeds of that revolution had been planted earlier, by iconoclastic visionaries like Adams himself who, during the dark decades after Repeal, labored to promote American wine as a mealtime beverage. Their efforts had long-term benefits but few immediate results. For with the arrival of Thunderbird and the other flavored fortifieds, American wine hit rock bottom. Wineries like Gallo and Italian Swiss Colony now had the resources and the know-how to produce high-quality table wines. But the market was small, and rather than work to build it, they chose to devote much of their effort to the production of wines whose only reason for being was the fact that they gave poor drunks what Edmund Rossi, Jr., called "the most alcohol for the money."

The visionaries and mavericks who worked during the decades following Prohibition to make American wine something more than booze often did so in isolation and with little hope of reward. Whether in the East or the West, their advocacy of American wine's potential fell largely on deaf ears. For example, in Baltimore, Maryland, a newspaperman and amateur wine grower named Philip Wagner helped change the course of eastern viticulture, although for a long time hardly anyone else in the mid-Atlantic states much cared. Wagner, whose father had been a professor of romance languages at the University of Michigan, grew up drinking European wines with meals. Then, like many Americans, he was forced to make home wine out of

California grapes during Prohibition. Wagner found that he enjoyed winemaking, and it became his hobby. After Repeal, when the supply of Alicante grapes began to dry up, he tried using native varieties. Not surprisingly, his *vinifera*-trained palate did not much like the results. Rather than give up the hobby, he decided to look for better grapes. He knew that the classic European varieties probably would not grow in Maryland, but he wondered about some of the French-American hybrids that had been created back in the 1880s and 1890s in response to the phylloxera plague. These grapes supposedly combined the hardiness and pest resistance of American vines with the accepted wine quality of French ones. Although French regulations discouraged the presence of hybrids in the most famous appellations, about a third of France's *vin de pays* vineyards were planted with them. Wagner wrote to France for vines, acquired others from American compatriots, and in 1936 made his first batch of hybrid wine. He was delighted with the results. This wine did not taste foxy like wines made from native grapes, and it seemed just about as good as anything he had made during Prohibition. He soon became convinced that French-American hybrid varieties could resurrect wine growing in the East. They would make it possible for vintners to produce "wines that taste like wine." So in 1945, he took his hobby to a new level. Now an editor at the *Baltimore Sun*, he started commercial production at the first post-Prohibition bonded Maryland winery, Boordy Vineyard, in Riderwood, a prosperous suburb north of the city.

Philip Wagner worked at the *Sun* for another twenty years, and Boordy always remained a small operation. His wines developed a loyal following, but few consumers outside the Baltimore-Washington corridor knew much about them. His significance thus came less from the wines he produced than from the knowledge he imparted—through books and lectures as well as through the vines he grew at Boordy. He supplied cuttings and rootstock to both commercial wineries and amateur wine growers throughout the East and Midwest. At the same time, in books such as *American Wines and Wine-Making* and *A Wine-Grower's Guide*, he provided professionals and amateurs alike with much needed guidance. Wagner never claimed that his French-American hybrids produced great wines. He argued, though, that they made solid, everyday wines as good if not better than nine-tenths of the world's *vinifera*. "They nourish," he explained. "They taste good and make other foods taste better. The list of elements they contribute to the diet is almost as formidable as those lists of 'minimum daily requirements' on boxes of breakfast food. Better than any pill they ease tension and replace it with a sense of well-being. They bring good cheer and merriment." As those sentences suggest, Wagner was in many ways a latter-day George Husmann, promoting American wine as a healthy, civilized, unpretentious mealtime beverage. Wine, he insisted, while harmful in excess, was beneficial in moderation. Like Husmann, he especially encouraged the planting of small, domestic vineyards for family use. He envisioned table wine becoming an essential part of American daily life. To that end, he wanted grapes to be grown throughout the country, and good, everyday wines to be made from them. People would only begin to drink wine regularly, he thought, when it became a local product, much as it was in France and Italy. By the time of his death in 1996, many of the better eastern and midwestern wines came from grapes he introduced, varieties such as Baco Noir and Chambourcin (for reds) and Seyval and Vidal Blanc (for whites). These and others like them were being grown in vineyards throughout the East, bringing quality table wine as a local product within reach of millions of Americans for the first time in history.

Not everyone shared Wagner's view that eastern growers should plant French-American hybrid grapes. Plenty of farmers still grew native varieties, including the ever-popular Concord, and plenty of Americans still drank wine made from them. Most of it was sweet, and much was fortified. Quality table wine had to come from something else, and of course the world's best wines had always come from *vinifera*. It took another visionary, Dr. Konstantin Frank, to prove that it was possible to grow *vinifera* grapes commercially in the East. A Ukrainian émigré who had studied viticulture and organized a collective farm near Odessa before the Second World War, Frank came to America in 1951. Unable at first to speak English and without any money to his name, he supported his family by doing menial jobs such as washing dishes in restaurants and working as a field laborer at the New York State Agricultural Experiment Station at Geneva. There he observed that the nearby Finger Lakes growers planted mostly native grapes. Why not *vinifera?* he asked. When he was given the standard answer, that the climate would prove too severe, he was baffled. In the Ukraine, where temperatures fell so low that his "spit froze before it hit the ground," his *vinifera* vines had not died. The American problem, he argued, had to be bad rootstock and bad care, not excessive cold.

Frank's arguments soon came to the attention of Charles Fournier at Urbana. Fournier remembered snow-covered vineyards and undamaged vines from his years making Champagne at Veuve Clicquot. So although everyone else thought that Frank was talking nonsense, Fournier hired him to experiment with *vinifera*. Frank grafted Riesling, Chardonnay, and other vines onto rootstock he acquired from the coldest vineyards he could find, including one at a convent near Quebec where a monk told him that a few vines of uncertain origin bore fruit one out of every three or four years. The crucial moment came one night in February 1957, when temperatures fell to 25 degrees below zero. Some native *labrusca* vines died. Many others suffered severe damage, as did the French-American hybrids in nearby vineyards. But Frank's *vinifera* vines showed very little damage, and they produced full, ripe crops the following fall. He felt triumphant, going so far as to proclaim his accomplishment "the second discovery of America."

Konstantin Frank soon purchased property and built his own winery, which he named Vinifera Wine Cellars. His wines, especially those made from German varieties, attracted the attention of connoisseurs and collectors, with one of his first releases, a Trockenbeerenauslese Riesling, being served at the White House. Other growers soon followed his lead and planted experimental vineyards, but for a long time Frank's was the only eastern winery to produce wines made wholly from *vinifera* varieties. The scientists at the Geneva Station continued to maintain that *vinifera* was too risky to be grown successfully, and commercial producers were unwilling to take the gamble. Frank battled the "Genevans" for years, and not until the late 1980s did a significant number of eastern wineries begin to devote serious attention to *vinifera* varieties.

No one much cared when Philip Wagner first planted his

French hybrids in the 1930s, but twenty-five years later, most serious eastern wine growers followed his lead. Similarly, when Konstantin Frank first grew *vinifera* vines successfully, no one dared follow him. Today, some forty years later, almost all the best eastern wines come from *vinifera*. Working separately and in many ways at odds, these two men thus changed the face of eastern grape growing and winemaking. Frank aimed to produce premium, world-class wines. Wagner wanted to make solid, everyday table wines. Despite their different ambitions, they both demonstrated that Thomas Jefferson's and Nicholas Longworth's eastern dreams finally could come true. These wines could be as good as European imports.

Another Russian émigré played an equally important role in California, but as with Wagner and Frank, it would take decades for the significance of his work to be appreciated widely and fully. André Tchelistcheff, born in Moscow and educated in Czechoslovakia and France after serving in the czarist army, came to California in 1938 via the French Institut National Agronomique. He was hired by Georges de Latour to take over winemaking at Beaulieu Vineyard in the Napa Valley. Beaulieu, founded by de Latour in 1900, had been one of the few Napa wineries to stay open throughout Prohibition, San Francisco's Roman Catholic diocese having purchased its wines for sacramental use. Georges de Latour had plenty of ambition, and unlike most of his competitors at Repeal, he had money to spend. But in 1937, just when his long-time winemaker retired, a good portion of the Beaulieu wines turned out to have microbiological problems. He desperately needed a new winemaker, someone who knew his way around a laboratory as well as a cellar. In Tchelistcheff, he got all that and more.

This wiry little man was a perfectionist. Tasting a sample of Cabernet Sauvignon from the 1936 vintage convinced him of Beaulieu's (and by extension Napa's and America's) potential to produce great wines. But while Tchelistcheff was impressed by the Beaulieu estate and de Latour's rather aristocratic life-style, he was chagrined by the state of the vineyards and the winery. He saw that many of the vineyards were planted with the wrong grape varieties, and he found the winemaking facili-ties in near disrepair. Much of the cooperage was dirty and filled with bacteria; the cast-iron pipes and pumps were rusted; the copper filters had corroded. Tchelistcheff began to clean things up. He quickly corrected the technical problems that had caused difficulties the year before, and then turned his at-tention to long-term improvements. He scrubbed and washed the storage casks, replaced the antiquated presses and pumps, and slowly purchased new equipment, including new barrels in which to age the best red wines. He also gradually introduced new procedures, such as cold-temperature fermentation for white wines and sterile bottling. In 1940 Georges de Latour died. The next year Tchelistcheff and Beaulieu released the 1936 Cabernet that had tasted so impressive in cask. At the sug-gestion of de Latour's widow, it carried a new label, Georges de Latour Private Reserve. For the next thirty years, it would reign as America's most honored red wine.

André Tchelistcheff cared first and foremost about quality, no matter the cost. By contrast, Madame de Latour and later her daughter, Hélène de Pins, considered Beaulieu a source of family income, and thus looked to maximize profits rather than reinvest in new equipment or replanting. Not surprisingly, their relationship with the tough-minded winemaker fre-quently proved contentious. Yet despite the sometimes difficult conditions under which he had to work, Tchelistcheff stayed at Beaulieu for thirty-five years, during which time his best wines helped define what constituted quality in Napa and beyond. His concern with cleanliness and technical precision in the winery set a standard for other producers in Napa and all of California. But his most important accomplishment may well have come from his obsession with planting the right grapes in the right places. Tchelistcheff was one of the first people to re-alize that even the small Napa Valley possesses a range of quite different climates. Not all vineyards are the same here, he kept telling anyone who would listen. In large measure because of his guidance, the varietal composition of the valley's vineyards began to change, with cooler-climate varieties like Chardonnay and Pinot Noir planted in the south—where the San Pablo Bay has a moderating influence on temperatures—and warmer-cli-mate varieties such as Cabernet planted farther north, where the mercury is apt to soar. After retiring from Beaulieu, Tche-listcheff worked for another two decades as a consultant to wineries in California, Oregon, and Washington. By the 1970s, he was recognized widely as the dean of American winemakers.

Back in the 1940s and 1950s, however, only other Califor-nia winemakers knew André Tchelistcheff's work. Even in the Napa Valley, America's best-known wine district, premium table wine took a back seat to other wines—sweet fortifieds, of course, but also generic blends. Beaulieu produced a wide range of such wines, even though Tchelistcheff kept urging management to narrow its focus and concentrate primarily on a smaller number of wines made from only the top grapes. "With thirty wines to take care of," he said, "I am producing little star-lets, when I should produce only great stars."

Concentrating on individual varietals was the hobbyhorse

of another of the era's viticultural visionaries, the author and wine merchant Frank Schoonmaker. Soon after Repeal, Schoonmaker coauthored *The Complete Wine Book* with Tom Marvel. In it, he lambasted the state of the American industry —its devotion to fortified wines, the overall poor quality of its products, and its use of generic labels and invented names. American producers, especially in California, came to consider Schoonmaker an enemy, an eastern snob with a prejudice in favor of anything French. They particularly objected to his demand that American wines eschew generic or fictitious nomenclature in favor of specific information concerning grape varieties and geographic origin—"Sonoma Pinot Noir," for instance, rather than "California Burgundy." Schoonmaker argued that generic names confused consumers and excused poor quality. "[That] 'Burgundy,'" he wrote, "can be *any* red wine, from whatever wine district, out of whatever kind of grapes." Such names perpetuated what he called "wine hokum." Their existence allowed growers to justify growing poor or inappropriate grape varieties, and winemakers to continue to make sterile, innocuous wines. Producers accused him of bias and pretentiousness. But when Schoonmaker began buying wine to ship back east and sell alongside the European wines in his catalogue, a few began to change their tune—and their labels. Promoted under the slogan "American Names for American Wines," vintage-dated, varietal-specific wines from Wente Brothers in Livermore, Paul Masson in Saratoga, Fountain Grove and Korbel in Sonoma, and Inglenook, Larkmead, and L. M. Martini in Napa began to show up in wine shops and on restaurant lists in New York, Boston, Philadelphia, and the other important eastern markets. Schoonmaker advertised in

Town and Country and *The New Yorker*, and his name on a selection came to carry a certain cachet. It would take nearly forty years, however, for the American wine industry as a whole to adopt varietal and geographic labeling. During that time, America's best-selling wines would still be the Thunderbirds and Silver Satins, its most popular table wines the different forms of "chablis" and the like. Schoonmaker, idealistic and ahead of his time, did not greatly change public tastes. But for those few producers who had ambitions to make wines of higher quality, he was a pioneer who helped them see the way.

Another man who never wavered in his devotion to high quality was John Daniel, the grandnephew of Gustave Niebaum at Inglenook. Virtually alone among American wine producers in the 1940s and 1950s, Daniel worked to make wines that would uphold a tradition of excellence. He saw it as his duty to resurrect the standards established by the Finnish sea captain in the 1880s when Inglenook became America's most renowned label. For Daniel, this meant that all Inglenook wines would be labeled by variety and origin, and that all would be bottled on the estate where the grapes were grown. The other Napa wineries that produced premium table wines— Beaulieu, Larkmead, and Martini, later Christian Brothers and Charles Krug—made a range of inexpensive generic wines to support their shaky premium lines. Daniel refused to do the same, feeling that generics and fortifieds would besmirch the Inglenook legacy. André Tchelistcheff, for one, was impressed. "The philosophical position of Captain Niebaum remained in [Daniel's] mind," he recalled years later, adding that Inglenook, not Beaulieu, was "properly speaking" America's only true premium wine estate in the 1950s.

John Daniel and André Tchelistcheff, Philip Wagner and Konstantin Frank, Leon Adams and Frank Schoonmaker— these six iconoclasts kept faith in American wine during the long, dark years of its fall. The icon they sought to overthrow was the popular image of wine as a form of booze, an image largely of the American wine industry's own making. Working in different ways and in different places, these six men shared a belief that wine someday could become a respected and respectable part of American life and culture. They had little on which to base that belief save for their own palates and convictions, for table wine occupied a place only on the fringe of America's cultural fabric. That would change in the 1970s and 1980s, the years of American wine's meteoric rise. But the fall had been very deep.

Nothing better illustrates how deep than the sad conclusion of John Daniel's story. Inglenook was both Daniel's duty and his love. It had been the foundation upon which he built his life, a life that in other aspects remained unfulfilled. As a young man, he had dreamed of becoming a pilot, but the family obligation to run Inglenook compelled him to spend his career on the ground in Napa. He had an increasingly troubled marriage, with two daughters but no obvious heir for a winemaking estate that earned renown but rarely made a profit. His devotion to quality was a harbinger of things to come, but in the early 1960s he must have felt hopelessly out of step with the rest of American wine. Inglenook's Cask Selection Cabernet simply had nothing in common with the fortifieds and generics that dominated the market. In 1964, Daniel sent shock waves through the insular Napa winemaking community when he sold Inglenook—to Louis Petri and United Vintners. Petri

promised him that United Vintners would respect the Inglenook legacy. Within ten months, however, production was
moved off the estate. A year later, a line of Inglenook generic
wines appeared. Then in 1968, Petri sold 80 percent of United
Vintners to Heublein, the giant Connecticut-based spirits producer, whose leading moneymaker was Smirnoff, America's
best-selling vodka. Two years later, a line of jug wines appeared
under the Inglenook Navalle label, Navalle being the name of a
stream on the old Niebaum property. But the wine in those
bottles did not come from grapes grown there. Instead, most of
the grapes came from the Central Valley. They were shipped
north, to the largest winemaking facility in the United Vint-
ners/Heublein empire—the old Italian Swiss facility at Asti,
where nearly fifty million bottles of generic Inglenook wine
rolled off the assembly line each year.

Italian Swiss Colony itself still existed as a label. In the
early 1970s, it produced some varietal table wines in its Private
Stock line, but many more fortifieds and "pop" wines—lightly
carbonated, fruit-flavored drinks with names such as Annie
Green Springs and Zapple, some of which were not even made
with grapes. So too, Virginia Dare still existed. Paul Garrett's
heirs, who had moved production to California after Repeal,
sold the business in the early 1960s, and Canandaigua Industries purchased the marketing rights to what once had been
America's most popular wine. Still a bulk producer, Canandaigua sold an assortment of generic wines under the Virginia
Dare label, all aimed at the low-end market. Louis Petri, a millionaire many times over, retired to Hawaii in 1971. John
Daniel had died the year before, reportedly of a heart attack but
actually from an overdose of barbiturates. In only six years, his

cherished Inglenook had turned into just another purveyor of cheap plonk, no better than the new Virginia Dare or Italian Swiss.

Inglenook's fall, though more rapid than most, mirrored that of American wine at large. Yet by 1970, the rise already had begun. More and more Americans were beginning to discover table wines, first as an alternative to fortifieds and cocktails, then as a part of meals and daily life. Soon the quality of those wines would improve dramatically—so much so that, in the final quarter of the century, American wine would earn a place among the world's best, becoming an object of admiration and indeed imitation. The iconoclasts' shared vision then would come true, as would the still older dreams of men like Hilgard, Husmann, and Longworth. "Nature has designed this to be [a] great Vineland," wrote Husmann in 1888. A hundred years later, in the last decades of the American Century, he would be proved right.

4

First
Families

P EOPLE WATCHED AND GAPED. Not only did this strange
ranch-style building mark the first significant new winery construction in the Napa Valley since before Prohibition, and not
only did it look unlike anything anyone had seen before, but in
late September 1966, wine was being made in it literally before
the roof was on. Along with the heady scent of freshly crushed
grapes, change definitely was in the air. Fifty-four-year-old
Robert Mondavi, the eldest son of the late Cesare Mondavi, an
Italian immigrant who twenty years earlier had revitalized the
Charles Krug operation, had struck out on his own. First he
had purchased a piece of the venerable To Kalon estate in
Oakville. Now he was building his own winery and beginning
to make wines under his own label. The people watching were
not surprised that someone might try to start a new business.
Even in the insular world of Napa, property changed hands
fairly frequently. Hanns Kornell had bought the Larkmead estate eight years earlier; Joe Heitz had started a new company in
1961 on the site of the small Only One vineyard; and just the

year before, Jack and Jamie Davies had begun to renovate Jacob Schram's old mountainside cellars. No, the surprise came from the scale and scope of Mondavi's ambitions.

This building itself, admittedly stylish, seemed ostentatious and out of place. It was mighty big—with a sweeping arch and a tower, looking vaguely Spanish, nothing like the valley's other large wineries, stately Victorian edifices such as Beringer or Inglenook. Moreover, it sat right out in the open, where anyone driving up and down the road could see it. According to Mondavi, it was designed that way. He planned to operate it as a sort of visitor center, giving tours and pouring samples. What made him think that tourists would come to the sleepy Napa Valley? Why, the wines would draw them, he said—like bees to honey. Robert Mondavi told anyone who would listen that he was not just starting another wine business. Instead, he was starting a new kind of wine business, one dedicated to producing a product whose quality would be on a par with the very best in the world, which in 1966 meant red Bordeaux and white Burgundy. The good wines at Charles Krug, like those at Beaulieu and Inglenook, were fine, but few tasters considered them to be in the same league as the French first growths and grand crus. Even before he crushed a grape, Mondavi was determined to chart a new course. His wines would compete head to head with the world's best. They would change how people thought about American wine because they would change people's tastes. Onlookers gaped, then, not so much at the novelty of the enterprise as at the hubris of the entrepreneur.

Some one hundred miles to the south, Ernest and Julio Gallo watched what was happening in Napa with bemused disdain. Although they did not own any Napa vineyards, the Gallo brothers purchased over 40 percent of the valley's grapes every year. Those grapes got trucked down to a sprawling complex of steel tanks and warehouses in Modesto, where they were crushed and fermented into wines that then were blended with wines made from different grapes grown all over the state. The resulting reds, whites, and rosés were Gallo's finest. Yet no one ever thought of them as being on a par with the best from France. No one ever expected them to be. They simply were sound, reliable, unpretentious products that sold at affordable prices—which according to Ernest and Julio was all that their customers wanted.

By 1966, Ernest Gallo had become renowned in American wine circles for his ability to read sales reports like tea leaves. He had an uncanny talent for introducing new products to meet untapped demands, Thunderbird being the best (because best-selling) example. He would spend countless hours on consumer research, studying both his and his competitors' sales figures, commissioning sophisticated market analyses, interviewing thousands of store managers and retail salesmen. Whether selling fortified or table wines, his goal was always the same: to understand the market by understanding his customers' desires. He knew that table wine sales were rising, but he also knew that most of the table wines that Americans bought came in half-gallon or gallon jugs, with screw tops, generic labels, and bargain-basement price tags. Sales of cork-finished, vintage-dated wines constituted only a tiny proportion of sales. Most of these were imports, and Ernest insisted that people bought them primarily to show off. He had little patience with people who talked about making American wine more sophisticated or changing American tastes.

Robert Mondavi could aim for the stars, but Ernest Gallo knew that his sales figures didn't lie. To his mind, talk of raising American wine to the level of great Bordeaux was nothing but pretentious claptrap. His company was about to become the country's, indeed the world's, largest wine producer, all because he and his brother knew better than anyone else what Americans wanted.

But in 1966 American tastes and attitudes toward wine were beginning to change. With sales of table wines poised to overtake those of fortifieds, new consumers were starting to approach it as something chic and sophisticated rather than as a skid row drink. In line with wide-ranging shifts in cultural tastes, all sorts of people who never thought about wine before were beginning to drink it. Being new to wine, they often were unsure exactly what they wanted. So even though sales were rising and consumer demand was growing, the demand itself proved unpredictable.

In terms of sheer sales, the Gallo brothers certainly met it successfully. Ernest and Julio released their first varietals in 1974, their first vintage-dated bottles in 1983. They then proclaimed in advertisements that "today's Gallo" was "all the best a wine could be." Gallo continued to produce huge amounts of both fortified and generic jug wines, but the company's focus gradually shifted to premium wines. Then in 1993, the brothers released their first estate bottlings, a Cabernet Sauvignon priced at $60 and a Chardonnay selling for $30. The very idea caused quite a stir in Modesto. Senior executives argued that the company's reputation would make it difficult to sell anything labeled Gallo at such prices, as the family name worked against the wines' being taken seriously by consumers and critics alike. The Gallos had never had to worry about wine critics before, but they knew that many of the new consumers who purchased expensive wines looked to reviews and ratings to help them decide what to buy. The company often had used other names on its bottles — Thunderbird, Boone's Farm, Carlo Rossi, and more. The sales team now urged doing the same at the high end. But this time Ernest and Julio resisted. These estate wines were the very best they had ever made, and theirs was a family company. For once, Ernest went against the market research. Not only did he and Julio call the wines Gallo, they also put their signatures on the front labels.

A similar sort of discussion had taken place back in 1966, this time around a kitchen table rather than in a boardroom, when Robert Mondavi left Charles Krug and made the decision to start his own company. He had contemplated using a fancy French-sounding name, but finally opted for his own. As he explained years later, "Wine to me was family." Beginnings often are difficult to date, but the construction of the Robert Mondavi Winery marks the effective beginning of American wine's rise in both quality and prestige. What happened there helped ignite the revolution in American tastes. It also helped change broad public attitudes toward wine in general and American wine in particular. This facility, so open, so different, so new, suggested that Prohibition's long legacy had run its course.

Down in Modesto, Ernest and Julio Gallo still operated with a Prohibition-era mindset. With their company poised to become the industry leader, they too were building in 1966 — a new "contemporary-classical" headquarters, modeled loosely on the North Carolina state capitol in Raleigh, a building that Ernest admired. But the Gallos had no intention of opening it to visitors, or of taking American wine in new directions. Mondavi, frequently accused of being elitist, wanted to use everything at his disposal to popularize American wine by demonstrating that it was more than booze. By contrast, the Gallos, who produced what they thought of as the people's wines, operated in legendary secrecy behind tightly closed doors. Nonetheless, like Mondavi, they took pride in what they built. The labels on Mondavi's wines featured a picture of his winery, with its familiar arch and tower. Soon the Gallos followed suit, a drawing of their headquarters finding its way onto their labels as well.

Over the next thirty years, the Gallos would follow in many other ways. Whether the issue involved using corks rather than screw caps, bottling by vintage instead of making blends, or identifying wines by grape variety and geographic origin rather than employing generic names, they repeatedly took paths that Robert Mondavi cleared ahead of them. But Mondavi was by no means the only trailblazer. In the 1970s and 1980s, scores of viticultural pioneers altered the world of American wine, taking it in directions that went far beyond what its most ardent nineteenth-century advocates could have imagined. First in California, then in the Pacific Northwest, and finally back east, they raised American wine to unprecedented heights. By the 1990s, American wines no longer were considered inferior. Instead, connoisseurs and consumers regarded them as the equal if not the better of wines made anywhere. Robert Mondavi was not the first to turn heads or change palates. Nonetheless, he was the leader, American wine's self-proclaimed but also widely acknowledged "ambassador." Unlike the Gallos, who followed the often dizzying marketplace, he predicted, inspired, and compelled change. "Maybe there was no market yet for fine wine in America," he recalled later, reminiscing about his decision to build his winery. "So what? I was determined to create the market we needed."

Only one thing connected Mondavi and the Gallos in 1966: their remarkably similar family histories. Unlike the vast majority of people who would play prominent roles in the American wine industry during the next decades, they had blood ties to Prohibition and its legacy, their Italian immigrant families having sold grapes for home winemaking during the dry years. What so starkly separated them was their relationship with those histories. Although Ernest and Julio rarely talked publicly about their past, their work was linked inexorably to it. They had succeeded where their father failed, and the memory of that failure served as their constant inspiration. All their work was an attempt to make right what they had inherited. Robert Mondavi, on the other hand, quite consciously rejected his inheritance. Wine may always have been family to him, but his notion of family had little to do with where he came from and everything to do with where he was going.

In 1966, Mondavi and the Gallos had fundamentally different philosophies, radically different visions of wine's place in American culture. Gradually, over three decades, the differences lessened. As they did, the Mondavis and the Gallos became American wine's first families — multigenerational households with ties to both American wine's great fall and its even greater rise. Ernest and Julio, professing disdain for alleged elitism, had watched bemusedly when Robert Mondavi first declared that he wanted American wines to "stand shoulder to shoulder with the great wines in the world." By 1993, they were saying much the same thing. When the expensive estate wines were released with their names and signatures on the labels, Ernest looked back over their careers and concluded that, despite having accomplished so much, one goal remained unrealized: "to create wines that will be recognized as among the world's best." A few months later, *Wine Spectator* reviewed the Chardonnay. "This wine," the magazine told its readers, "will change the way you think about Gallo."

The Gallo and Mondavi stories begin with the two fathers—Giuseppe and Cesare, men who, like so many young Italians of their generation, came to America because life back home promised only toil and struggle. Giuseppe Gallo emigrated from Piedmont in 1905, Cesare Mondavi from the Marche in 1906. Born only six months apart, each was twenty-three years old when he landed at Ellis Island. Both came from large families, both had followed brothers across the Atlantic, and both first found employment as miners, Giuseppe digging coal in Pennsylvania, Cesare iron in Minnesota. Neither much liked working in the mines, and both soon decided to try something else. After a trip back to the Marche to marry his childhood sweetheart, Cesare Mondavi opened a small grocery store in Virginia, Minnesota, where he catered primarily to Italian miners, selling them pasta and salami, bread and wine. And Giuseppe Gallo moved west to California, where he too got married, and along with his brother, Michelo, began to buy young wine in bulk to sell to fellow immigrants. Wine at first for both men was simply what it had been for their families in Italy—a staple.

They soon learned that things were different in America. Here many people, influenced by the loud and strident rhetoric of the temperance movement, associated wine with liquor. Cesare and Giuseppe may not have accepted that association, but they certainly used it to their advantage. As soon as they made enough money, they each bought saloons, with rooms to rent upstairs, and more profitably, bars to tend below. Giuseppe, who now called himself Joe, operated his Oakland saloon for nearly a decade, while Cesare ran his in Minnesota for five years. Both kept a jug or two of red table wine behind the bar along with the stronger stuff—brandy and grappa, whiskey, rum, and the obligatory fortifieds. They did well as saloon keepers, and the two families prospered. Joe and Susie Gallo had three sons—Ernest born in 1909, Julio the year after, and Joe Jr., born in 1919. Cesare and Rosa Mondavi had two daughters, Mary and Helen, and then two boys—Robert, who appeared in 1913, followed by Peter a year later. These children grew up at least dimly aware of a tension that has marked American wine from the very beginning. On the one hand, it was liquid food, at home in the kitchen and on the supper table, where it became as much a part of everyday family life as bread. On the other hand, it belonged in the masculine, hot-tempered world of the saloon, where like whiskey it served the family by providing income but not fellowship. Four of the seven children (Ernest and Julio, Robert and Peter) would end up in the wine business. How they responded to that tension would help shape their careers.

Prohibition brought dramatic changes to the Gallos and the Mondavis. With the saloons shut down, both families soon found themselves on the move. The Gallos moved first, heading north to Antioch in Contra Costa County, where Joe bought a farm. Although he made some money there, the work was hard, and he increasingly felt lost in the heavy shadow cast by his brother, Michelo, now called Mike, who was fast on his way to becoming one of the Bay Area's most successful bootleggers. Mike ran wine, brandy, whiskey, anything that he could sell. He drove fancy cars, wore gold jewelry, and had cash to spare. When he offered Joe a job, Joe jumped at it. For about a year, the brothers took midnight rides from still to still, picking up booze and delivering it to speakeasies in Oakland and San Francisco. Then the police raided them. Mike got the charges dropped, but the experience frightened Joe enough to persuade him to try something else—grape growing. This time he moved to the San Joaquin Valley, eventually settling in Modesto, where, if only briefly, his luck turned. The California grape market was booming, and in the fall of 1925, Joe shipped eighteen freight cars full of grapes to Chicago. He sold them one by one to dealers and pocketed a healthy profit. Because he didn't much like the frenzied, somewhat sinister world of the railyard, he sent his oldest son the next year. Ernest took to sales right away, returning with $17,000 and a reputation for driving a hard bargain. The business took off. According to one Chicago dealer, the Gallos "had a good reputation" and their "grapes were in big demand." Buyers soon recognized the name. Much the same was true of grapes sold by other conscientious Italians from California—both old-timers like the Rossis from Asti and newcomers such as the Mondavis, freshly arrived from Minnesota.

Cesare Mondavi had first gone to California in 1919 on behalf of the local Italian Club to see about buying grapes and shipping them back to Minnesota for families to use when making home wine. California was a far cry from the cold north. It seemed something like the country of his childhood, and he loved it. So in 1922 he moved his family west, to Lodi in San Joaquin County, and became a full-time grape buyer. His business prospered, and Robert and Peter recall a rather idyllic adolescence, filled with what Robert calls "the values of the old country: love, discipline, and hard work."

Cesare was a frugal man. Because he saved his money, he lost little when the stock market crashed in October 1929. By contrast, Joe Gallo lost his proverbial shirt. He had invested some of his money with his brother, but then saw it all evaporate when Mike finally was sent to jail for bootlegging. He also had speculated in the stock market, and the crash left him deep in debt. To make matters worse, a grape surplus had led to depressed prices. Unable to sell all his crop, Joe crushed some of it illicitly and stored the wine in underground tanks, hoping for better days to come. He then tried growing grapes for a legal product, raisins, but the next couple of years only brought heavier losses. No one wanted his wine, and the market was awash in a sea of grapes and raisins. When Ernest went to Chicago in 1932, he found no buyers, and so ended up with nearly seventy cars of unsold fruit as well as a bill for $70,000 from the railroad. With debt piling ever higher and Mike nowhere in sight to bail him out, Joe was in serious trouble. He must have felt completely overwhelmed. In a tragic moment that would haunt his sons throughout their lives, he shot his wife and then himself in June 1933. Repeal was only six months away.

"None of us talked much then or later about what happened," Julio recalled years later. "What was there to say?" There was, however, plenty to do. Ernest in particular was determined not to lose the family business. Yes, there was a mountain of debt, but the vines hung heavy with fruit every year, and Prohibition was just about over. He persuaded Julio to join him—not as grape growers but as winemakers, and more important, wine sellers. No middlemen, he said. We can make the wine and sell it too. Ernest didn't have a cent to his name, but Julio had managed to save $900. That was about a sixth of what they needed to start a winery. After everyone else turned them down, Ernest's mother-in-law loaned them $5,000, and in September 1933, the E. & J. Gallo Winery was bonded. The brothers immediately began crushing grapes. Their bond had been for a facility with a 50,000-gallon capacity, but they quickly saw that they had room for more. So after petitioning the Bureau of Alcohol to raise the limit, they bought grapes from their neighbors and crushed nearly 180,000 gallons. Julio made the wine, using a pre-Prohibition University of California handbook for guidance. Then in December, Ernest boarded his first airplane and flew to Chicago, where he got a jump on his competitors who traveled by rail, and began to sell it. He did not come home until he had found a buyer for every last drop.

In later years, Ernest and Julio would try to conceal the connections between the company they started at Repeal and their father's failed Prohibition-era business. Their obfuscation came in part from their sense of shame concerning their parents' deaths and in part from their desire to protect what they considered rightfully theirs. Both of these came into full public view in 1988 when their younger brother sued (unsuccessfully) for a third of the business, alleging that the three brothers had inherited equal shares of the Gallo company back in 1933. Yet the legitimate legal distinction between the E. & J. Gallo Winery and Joe Gallo's grape-growing business could not obscure the deep psychological ties binding Ernest and Julio to their family history. The new company was a way—the only way—to fix what had gone so terribly wrong. According to Julio, "staying together in Modesto was a must." And in *Our Story*, the two brothers' autobiography, Ernest writes: "I never considered for a moment the thought of giving up. I was determined to make good on the pile of debts our parents had left behind." He and Julio made good on more than debt. They took what their father and their uncle had started, and they set it right—meaning both that they made money at it, and that they made it legitimate. Their wine, unlike their father's and uncle's contraband, was perfectly legal.

At first, the Gallo brothers sold all of their wine in bulk, primarily to dealers in Chicago, New York, and other eastern cities, who then bottled it under different labels. These dealers wanted only red wine—"dago red," which they sold to Italians and other immigrants. But as the business grew—and it grew each year, to 350,000 gallons in 1935, then more than 2 million by 1938—people began to demand variety. Some wanted white wines, but many more wanted fortifieds. So in 1937, Ernest added a distillery to the operation. Gallo sold 310,000 gallons of high-alcohol wine that year, compared with about 1.2 million gallons of table wine, but the gap soon narrowed. By the early 1940s, fortifieds had become the big sellers. By then, the company was making a full line of wines: burgundy, claret, rhine, barbarone, tokay, muscatel, sauterne, sherry, port, angelica, white port, and more. The business expanded every year, with fortifieds providing the biggest growth. Those were the

wines the market demanded, and Ernest and Julio were determined to meet the demand. Wine for them was tied to liquor
just as it had been for their father back in his Oakland saloon or
for their uncle during Prohibition. Like Joe behind the bar or
Mike in the speakeasy, they gave their customers what their
customers wanted, which for many people simply meant alcohol. In the process, they became what Joe had always dreamed
of but had never come close to—they became rich.

Cesare Mondavi didn't become rich, but he did well—
well enough to send his two sons to Stanford. He had resisted
the impulse to make commercial wine, and instead had stayed
put in Lodi, selling grapes and banking his profits. Nonetheless, he envisioned a bright future for post-Prohibition commercial wine, going so far as to become a financial partner in at
least one winery, Sunnyhill in Napa. And he advised his eldest
son, who clearly was not cut out to be a farmer, to think seriously about wine as a career. Robert listened, and after graduation went to work at Sunnyhill (the name soon was changed to
Sunny St. Helena). While there, he did, as he puts it, "everything from A to Z," and "really began to learn the wine business." In 1940, Cesare's partner at Sunny St. Helena died, and
Robert took over the day-to-day operation of the winery.
Meanwhile, his brother, Peter, started working at Acampo, a
large winery Cesare recently had invested in near Lodi. Wine
indeed was becoming family for the Mondavis. Peter left home
the next year to serve in the Chemical Corps, while Robert, ex-
empt from World War II military service, continued running
Sunny St. Helena. Then the big distillers began to look for
wineries to buy, and all sorts of property came up for sale. Cesare made a tidy profit after Acampo changed hands, so he had

some cash to spare in March 1943, when Robert drove down to Lodi with a business proposition. The Charles Krug facility was up for sale, and Robert wanted his father to buy it. Cesare resisted at first. He still had no desire to become a winemaker, and no interest in setting up the kind of sales network needed to sell bottled wine. He also did not want to leave Lodi. Robert, with his mother's help, eventually persuaded him to take the plunge. They outlined a plan in which the Mondavis would purchase all of Sunny St. Helena's wine in bulk, bottle it down the road at Krug, and then sell it to distributors. Robert would take charge of sales and marketing, and Peter would become the winemaker. Cesare could stay in Lodi if he wished. His sons would run the company, a family dream come true.

It stayed true for almost two decades. Profits came quickly during the remaining war years, enabling Cesare to buy Sunny St. Helena outright in 1946. Then when Peter returned from the service, production grew dramatically. The Mondavi brothers wanted Charles Krug to become a leading Napa producer, on a par with the valley's so-called big four—at that point, Beringer, Beaulieu, Inglenook, and Larkmead. But what exactly this entailed remained unclear. Was it a matter of quantity, as at Beringer and Larkmead? Or was quality more important, as at Inglenook and Beaulieu?

The Mondavis aimed for both. They made two separate lines of wine. The majority of the production, sold in big jugs under the C. K. Mondavi label, continued what had worked well at Sunny St. Helena. It was bulk wine, mostly red, and made mostly from grapes grown in the Central Valley. A smaller percentage of the production, coming from Napa grapes, was bottled under the Charles Krug label. This historic name was reserved for varietals and high-end generics, the best wines Peter made. They did well, not so much in terms of sales —the market for premium American table wines being very small—as in terms of image and prestige. Charles Krug won more medals at the California state fair in the late 1940s and 1950s than any other winery. The Mondavis won for whites as well as reds, with the winning wines often small-production gems—for example, a Traminer (gold medal in 1949) of which they made only eighty-five cases, and their Vintage Select Cabernet, a wine first released in 1956 to compete with Beaulieu's Georges de Latour Private Reserve and Inglenook's Special Cask. At the same time, their overall volume grew to the point that they became the valley's biggest producer.

Some revisionist commentators have pictured Peter as the advocate of quantity and Robert as the spokesman for quality at Charles Krug, but in truth both brothers shared both goals. Peter's work played a leading role in improving Napa wines generally, especially the whites. He experimented with new techniques such as cold fermentation, acid correction, and sterile filtration, and along with André Tchelistcheff enjoyed a reputation as one of the valley's most conscientious winemakers. And Robert, who certainly took great pride in the award-winning Krug wines, always pushed hard in family meetings to increase the growth of the C. K. line, arguing that it generated the greatest profits and thus had to serve as the company's financial foundation. The division of labor matched the two Mondavi brothers' temperaments—Peter careful and disciplined, a technician, Robert gregarious and outspoken, a born salesman. Down in Modesto, popular legend had it that when the Gallo winery first opened, Julio had promised to make all the wine that Ernest could sell, while Ernest pledged to sell all the wine Julio made. In actuality, however, Ernest invariably made the important decisions, with Julio deferring to his dominant, sometimes dictatorial will. But at Charles Krug, Cesare always ran the show. The "patriarch," he regularly went up to St. Helena or called the boys down to Lodi to review company policy. Although he gave his sons plenty of latitude, his word became law whenever disputes arose. This arrangement, "a good combination" according to Peter, worked well. It did so because, as Robert remembers, we "held an even keel." By the late 1950s, the big four had become the big five, with Charles Krug the biggest of all. No privately owned Napa winery, however, was anywhere near as big as the Napa Co-op, which in 1960 counted some 230 member growers and operated two separate plants, with a total capacity of about 2.5 million gallons—every last drop of which was bought by Gallo.

Gallo had started making truly big profits in the 1940s. During the war, some came from the winery, but more came from the distillery, where the company manufactured industrial-strength alcohol from molasses. "[We] had a government contract for 10 percent plus costs," recalls a company manager. "The more you said it cost to produce the alcohol—torpedo juice, we called it—the more the government paid. You can't imagine the costs we put in for!" Then in 1947, the brothers made a killing by correctly anticipating a crash in grape prices. They saw that the big distillers were paying inflated prices for California wine. So six months after selling their bulk wine for an outlandish $1.50 a gallon, they watched the market hit bottom, bought all their wine back for less than 50 cents, then made a further profit by selling it under their own name. They also began to bottle their wine themselves, cutting out yet another middleman. Then they started to sign growers to long-term contracts. In the process, they learned an important lesson —as Ernest put it, to "control the grapes." That lesson is what led them to Sonoma and then Napa, where they made deals with growers and co-ops that guaranteed them a steady supply of top-line fruit. Julio's production team blended Napa and Sonoma juice with that from Central Valley grapes. Improvements in winemaking techniques made the Gallo red table wines softer and less tannic. Paisano, a smooth, slightly sweet jug wine, became one of America's best-selling reds, and in the seven years from 1948 to 1955, the company's total sales soared from four to sixteen million gallons, a 400 percent increase.

Julio came up with the recipe for Paisano after Ernest brought him a wine called Vino da Tavola, made by Guild Wineries. A new label, it tasted smoother and sweeter than most Central Valley red wines, and had found an unexpected niche in the California market. Ernest thought Gallo should offer a competitive product. In effect, he wanted Julio to figure out what Guild was doing, and then to do the same thing on a larger scale in Modesto. "This would happen a lot," Julio recalled later. "The sales and marketing departments would ask production to try and develop a particular product that had commercial potential." In a nutshell, here was the Gallo philosophy: find out what consumers want, then give it to them.

Ernest studied his sales figures to determine which wines Julio should make. He asked for new wines whenever he saw or predicted a new demand. He went on the road constantly, visiting even the smallest retail accounts, and he kept a close eye on both his competitors and his customers. So, for example, he asked Julio for Grenache Rosé, which copied Italian Swiss Colony's popular Vin Rosé of the mid-1950s. And of course Thunderbird, modeled on the lemon juice and white port mixture that customers in Los Angeles were concocting during the same period. At the end of the decade, Ernest noticed how rapidly sales of colas and other soft drinks had risen, and proposed the idea of a carbonated, low-alcohol wine. The result was Ripple, which at the height of its popularity enjoyed sales of more than seven million gallons annually. Ernest insisted on control—of his brother's production, in that he alone decided what Gallo should make, as well as of sales, marketing, advertising, even distribution. State and federal laws prohibited manufacturers of alcoholic beverages from owning distributorships. Ernest worked around these laws by creating separate corporations in which Gallo executives and family members served as shareholders. Yet all the important financial decisions were made in his office in Modesto. By the early 1960s, the company trailed only Louis Petri and United Vintners in total sales. Growers, locked into long-term contracts, grew the grapes that Ernest wanted, just as Julio made the wines he demanded. The company even manufactured its own bottles at the Gallo glass plant. Ernest oversaw the business all the way from the grape on the vine to the bottle on the store shelf.

Back in Lodi, Rosa Mondavi assumed control of Charles Krug after Cesare died unexpectedly in 1959. Rosa soon moved to Napa, settling in a house behind the winery. Robert lived on the property too, and his sister Helen soon built a house there for herself and her children. Peter's home was only a few miles down the road, so for a time Krug became, in Robert's words, "a large, idyllic, happy family compound." Problems, however, surfaced before long. Rosa had no experience in business, and without Cesare's steady hand, the company floundered. Peter and Robert began to disagree, first about profits, then about quality and direction, then about almost everything. Krug had grown at an annual rate of between 5 and 10 percent for a decade, but the growth had been financed by reinvesting almost all the profits in capital expenditures—new tanks, a building addition, new vineyards, and the like. Peter thought it time to slow down and enjoy some of what they had earned. Robert argued for greater growth and, what was more of a problem, new directions. Peter didn't agree. He took pride in Charles Krug wines, which consistently won awards and sold out. Robert, though, only became more strident. He began to talk about competing not with Beaulieu or Inglenook but with Bordeaux and Burgundy. So too, he started to talk about wine as a mark of culture, a form of art, and about helping to change how Americans thought about it. Peter still conceived of wine much as his father had during Prohibition—a staple that provided a good income. He had little patience for his brother's seemingly arrogant attitude.

In November 1965, everything came to a head. During a family gathering at the winery, the brothers began to argue. Robert accused Peter of being lazy, while Peter accused Robert of spending too much money and putting on airs. Fists flew. When the dust cleared, Peter had a black eye and Rosa decided that one person, not two, had to be in charge. She chose Peter. Robert, who had been managing wineries for twenty-five years, was out of a job.

He might well have swallowed his pride, apologized, and stayed at Charles Krug were it not for the fact that Rosa's decision to give Peter control meant that Peter's sons would be the next generation to run the company. Robert had pushed so hard for increased growth in large measure because he wanted to leave a solid foundation for his own children, especially his eldest son, Michael, who he had assumed would take over when he retired. Now Rosa and the rest of the family, along with lawyers and advisers, decreed that Michael, who was about to graduate from college, could not even work at Charles Krug. In an effort to cool tempers, they gave Robert a six-month leave of absence. It didn't work. Rosa's decisions became an even hotter item of gossip than the brothers' fistfight, and Robert's ego was bruised more deeply than Peter's face. In early 1966, Robert decided to make a fresh start. He would leave the family business, abandon the path trod by his father, and go out on his own. He no longer would play the role of dutiful son. Now he would lead. He would himself become the patriarch, not just of his family but of the new world of American wine.

Wounded pride, fraternal resentment, sheer ambition—these were important factors in Robert Mondavi's decision to build the winery that carries his name. But his decision to use that facility to make wines to compete with high-class wines from France came from something (or someplace) else. In the summer of 1962, he had traveled for the first time to Europe. The experience, he remembers, was nothing less than "a revelation." The trip took him to many of the continent's great wine-producing regions. He toured vineyards and cellars, talked with winemakers, visited famous estates, and rubbed shoulders with aristocratic proprietors. He also drank the wines. The best of them tasted different from those Peter and the other top California winemakers were producing. They seemed more subtle and complex, and Robert began to identify some of the reasons — the widespread use of small oak barrels, for instance, and the practice of making wines in small rather than large lots. Yet the wines themselves were only part of the story. "The differences ran much deeper than method and equipment," he recalls. The more crucial distinction had to do with style and spirit, with approach and attitude — with how the wines were perceived even more than with what went into the bottle. The best American wines, and Charles Krug's ranked among them, still were widely viewed as forms of liquor. They competed with spirits and fortifieds for public attention, and the people who made and sold them treated them as such. For in America, any beverage with alcohol in it was still suspect. Wine, like whiskey, was tainted with a suspicion born of the country's hard-drinking past and reinforced by a mentality that the post-Prohibition wine industry had done remarkably little to combat.

But in Europe, or at least in the Europe that Robert Mondavi was visiting, fine wine, like fine food, was part of refined culture — a civilized, because a civilizing, thing. "To my mind," he says, "the contrast was stark: we were treating wine as a business; the great European chateaux were treating wine as high art." Robert may not have known all that much about art, but he felt its pull. During lunch at La Pyramide in Vienne, then France's most legendary "country" restaurant, he marveled at the power of food and wine to "transport us into a world of gentleness and balance, of grace and harmony." The experience, he said later, "epitomized the artistry and aesthetics I had been discovering all across Europe." It inspired "both a vision and a vow." The vow was to make wines with "grace and style" like the ones he tasted that day. The even more audacious vision was of Americans actually drinking them.

As an immigrant's son, Robert had inherited certain Old World sensibilities, including his father's original notion of wine as an important part of family fellowship. But Cesare Mondavi's Italy had been a place of rural poverty, while the Europe that so impressed Robert in 1962 was an aristocratic, not a peasant (or even a bourgeois) world. As such, it seemed starkly different from the small-town America in which he had lived his entire life. Although definitely rich, it kept its money discreetly behind the scenes, employing wealth as a means in service of a greater end. That end, in a word, was taste. Whether in art or architecture, food or fashion, this Europe prized taste —good taste, which meant the ability to make subtle distinctions, to know what to value and why. Its very existence was the great revelation. In one sense, Robert simply was in tune with the times. During the early 1960s, the era of John Kennedy's Camelot, millions of Americans discovered, at least vicariously, European style and taste. Part of the Kennedy mystique was this political first family's ability to convey a continental, especially a French, savoir-faire while remaining unmistakably American. The Kennedy image, with Jackie dressed in Parisian high fashion, charming the socks off Charles de Gaulle, and Jack in white tie and tails, hosting writers and artists at elegant White House dinners, seemed to signal a new direction in American politics. Robert came back from Europe wanting to move, and to take American wine with him, in a similar direction. But in another sense, he was ahead of his time. He did not want to produce European-style wines as a final end. Instead, he wanted to use those wines as a means by which to begin changing how Americans thought about wine. That is, he wanted to bring good taste home.

The Bordeaux and Burgundies that proved so enthralling during lunch at La Pyramide represented only a minuscule percentage of France's total production. The French consumed far more wine per capita than did Americans, and the vast majority of it was coarse, crude plonk. Julio Gallo had discovered as much when he had traveled to Europe three years before Robert Mondavi. He too enjoyed drinking what he called "the exceptional wines," but he came away far more impressed—shocked, really—by the low quality of the everyday table wines. Not only did he perceive a huge gap between the wines served at the finest restaurants and those consumed daily in middle-class homes, but he also saw that the quality of this *vin ordinaire* was actually below that of much American jug wine. When he returned to Modesto, he told Ernest that Europe was "stuck in the past, with old-fashioned equipment and methods," and that their company did a much better job. The whole European attitude toward wine, he said, was backward. At the highest levels, wine was treated with a befuddling sort of reverence. People fawned over it, memorizing vintages, growths, and crus, treating it as an intellectual subject rather than what it really was, a simple beverage. But no one cared about the rest of it. The average Frenchman, Italian, or Spaniard drank whatever was in his glass, no matter the quality. This situation, Julio said later, was exactly "the reverse of what we were trying to do in this country." He and Ernest, in their drive to become number one, always were trying to expand their market. Thus "we were concentrating on producing quality wines at affordable prices. In much of Europe, where the consumption rate was up to ten times greater than in the United States, [the producers] already had their customers."

Julio was in fine historical company. Thomas Jefferson, Nicholas Longworth, and George Husmann all had argued that sound inexpensive wines were the key to changing public perceptions and increasing wine consumption in the United States. Yet a crucial thing separated the Gallo brothers from these early advocates of American wine: their own twentieth-century inheritance, Prohibition's legacy of wine as cheap booze. In the early 1960s, plenty of American table wine already was affordable. And its overall quality was certainly acceptable. What it lacked was prestige. Men and women of good taste just didn't want it. Robert Mondavi intuitively grasped this. He saw that American wine's rise would have to start at the top. Attitudes would change only when the best American wines could hold their own with the best from Europe. Then, and only then, could wine begin to become a respectable part of American life and culture. To an extent, Robert was motivated by pride and ambition. He clearly wanted to become one of the people he so admired in Europe, a man of taste and sophistication. At the same time, he was a genuine visionary. In the summer of 1966, he may not have known how to get there, but he knew exactly where he wanted to go. "I want to belong in the company of the fine wine people of the world," he declared, "and I'll stop at nothing to do it."

From the beginning, even before the ground was broken for his winery, Robert found people who listened and believed — friends in Napa who loaned him start-up money, his children who followed him in the new business, and men and women from all over who came to work for him as winemakers. Many of those who helped to make the early Robert Mondavi wines —people like Rick Forman, Mike Grgich, Zelma Long, and Warren Winiarski—went on either to start their own operations or to become head winemakers elsewhere. Their wines, even more than Mondavi's, won the competitions and earned the plaudits that fueled American wine's great rise in quality, style, and prestige. Robert, though, was the leader—not because he necessarily made the best wines, but because he was American wine's most ardent advocate. If, as Hugh Johnson has written, he "fit the definition of a genius," his genius came in public relations more than winemaking. He promoted his own wines, of course, but he also promoted a revolutionary new vision of wine for America. He insisted that fine wine should not be viewed as something effete and pretentious that only snobs enjoy, just as it should not be thought of as a cheap way to get drunk. Instead, it should be considered an integral part of high culture, an object of pleasure and a subject of fascination. American wines, he declared, had the potential to be just as good as the great European wines. They too could be liquid art.

This was what both Peter and Rosa Mondavi did not understand. They knew wine as either a kitchen staple or a form of booze, the first reflecting their rural Italian heritage, the second the reality of their post-Prohibition business. The concept of wine as a sensory and an aesthetic object with value in its own right seemed foreign—as indeed it was in the mid-1960s, when only a small proportion of the world's wine drinkers valued only a handful of wines, almost all of them French, in this way. Although a new generation would change all that, families like the Mondavis, who knew wine and winemaking from Prohibition, found it hard to go along. But in 1966, there were not many old-guard families left. John Daniel already had sold Inglenook, and the Marquise de Pins, Georges de Latour's granddaughter, was about to do the same with Beaulieu. Louis Petri would soon retire, and back east the Paul Garrett wine empire was just a memory. Here and there grape growers could trace a family legacy in wine, but the only other American wineries with significant production and more than a generation of family history were the Taylor Wine Company in Hammondsport, New York, Sebastiani Vineyards just outside Sonoma, and Louis M. Martini's operation down the road in Napa. And of course Gallo.

Having made a fortune with cheap generic wines and "misery market" fortifieds, the Gallos would shift their focus over the next two decades to premium varietals and what they later called their company's "search for excellence." Neither Ernest nor Julio, however, would ever completely accept the revolution in American attitudes and tastes. They just could not forget all that had happened—their father's suicide and mother's murder, their uncle's bootlegging, the mess they inherited and all the work it took to set things right. Much the same was true for those few other family winemakers who remembered Prohibition. Almost all of them distrusted talk of wine as art or high culture. The Taylors in New York took pride in producing their "uncomplicated wines" from native and hybrid grapes, as did August Sebastiani from *vinifera*. Even Louis M. Martini, himself an Italian immigrant, whose special selections and reserve bottlings were widely regarded as being among America's best, had little patience with people who viewed wine as anything more than something good to drink

with supper. Along with his son, Louis P. Martini, he produced
user-friendly wines at affordable prices. "We make wine for
people to drink," Louis P. once said, "not to sip and spit out."

At Robert Mondavi's winery, people sipped and spat discreetly into earthenware jugs in the tasting room. They also
took guided tours of the winery, where they were shown in detail each step involved in the craft of winemaking. Robert had
initiated a modest program of tastings and tours at Charles
Krug in the 1950s, but he was determined that nothing would
happen on a modest scale here. One whole wing of his winery
was devoted to hospitality, and it often seemed that the real action took place there. He had designed the facility to serve as
"a magnet for tourists," a place where people would come to
learn not only about wine and food but, more broadly, about
taste. So within the first year of operation, he began hosting art
exhibitions and concerts, events that he thought "placed the art
of fine wine in exactly the right context and cultural setting."
In the mid-1970s, he started a culinary instruction program, a
series of weekend seminars and tastings featuring Michelin-
starred chefs from the finest restaurants in France. Then in the
early 1980s, Robert and his second wife, the Swiss-born
Margrit Biever, helped initiate the Napa Valley Wine Auction,
a showcase for American wine, modeled on the annual Les
Trois Glorieuses in Burgundy. That was the not-so-hidden
key. All the publicity and promotion, the hype and hospitality,
served one end—to place American wine in the same class
as the great wines of Europe, especially the celebrated
first growths and grand crus from France. In this regard,
Robert's greatest accomplishment came in 1978, when he
formed a partnership with Baron Philippe de Rothschild, of

Château Mouton-Rothschild in Bordeaux, to produce a Napa Valley wine, Opus One. The first vintage would not be released for six years, but signing the partnership agreement constituted a moment of glory. "Imagine how proud this all made me feel," he says. "The names Rothschild and Mondavi . . . side by side."

The wines that made Robert Mondavi famous, his reserve line of Cabernet, Chardonnay, and Fumé Blanc, were made on French models. The Chardonnay aped white Burgundy, the Cabernet red Bordeaux. Herbaceous whites from the Loire Valley and softer, oak-aged ones from Bordeaux served as dual models for the Fumé Blanc. Robert invented this faux French name in 1967 as a way of glamorizing an unglamorous grape, Sauvignon Blanc, because to his ear, glamour required a chic Gallic accent. Good California wines certainly had been made from these grape varieties before. Both Chardonnay and Sauvignon Blanc had produced award-winning wines in the Livermore Valley before Prohibition, and Cabernet was considered by those in the know (André Tchelistcheff, for one) to be the Napa Valley's finest grape. During the post-Prohibition years, Beaulieu, Inglenook, Louis M. Martini, and Charles Krug all had produced fine Napa wines from Cabernet. These came in different styles, the winemakers having employed different methods and techniques. Peter Mondavi, for instance, aged unblended Cabernet in neutral vats, while Tchelistcheff used young American oak to dramatic effect. Both the Martinis and Inglenook's winemaker, George Deuer, advocated blending other grapes with Cabernet, but while Deuer stored his blends in well-aged wooden casks, Louis M. Martini used redwood cooperage. The resulting wines all tasted quite different.

These winemakers, like the other iconoclasts toiling in the darkness cast by Prohibition's fall, made wines in what Hugh Johnson calls "the vernacular style." Some were "more tannic, some less, some easy to drink young, some husky and demanding a decade in the bottle, but none [came] in any sort of borrowed finery."

Robert Mondavi changed that. His wines, like those from the smaller, so-called boutique wineries that began to spring up in the late 1960s and 1970s, did not look to California's past for inspiration. Instead, they were designed—and "designed" is precisely the right word, the winemaker being viewed as an artistic craftsman—to taste French. Robert regularly set up blind tastings featuring his and other top California wines along with their French counterparts—Chardonnays alongside Puligny-Montrachets and Meursaults, Cabernets alongside the first growths from Pauillac. The object of the exercise was less to crown a champion than to demonstrate how similar the wines tasted, the ultimate accolade being when an expert declared that a certain wine "must" be French, only to have its identity revealed as Californian. "My bit of showmanship opened a lot of eyes," he recalls. "I was preaching the gospel . . . introducing [people] to a new product and a new way of thinking."

All the Robert Mondavi showmanship required a great deal of money. Although Robert had promised his original investors that the winery would make a profit within a few years, his books were awash in so much red ink that he had been forced early on to go into partnership with a heavyweight backer, the Rainier Brewing Company in Seattle. For some eight years, Rainier effectively owned his business. Then in

1976, Robert sued Peter and the Charles Krug board of directors, alleging that he had been excluded from his fair share of profits in the Mondavi family corporation. In line with Cesare's will, each member of the family owned 20 percent of Charles Krug. At issue, then, was how much Krug was worth. Peter claimed a few million dollars, but during the long, 103-day trial, it came out that he recently had rejected an offer to sell the winery for $32 million. The judge then found for Robert on virtually every count. He put a value on Charles Krug of $47 million, ruling that Peter had siphoned off profits in order to depress corporate earnings and make money for himself and his sons. For a time it looked as though Charles Krug would have to be sold, but eventually the brothers (or their lawyers) worked out a deal in which Robert received the money owed him, while Peter, in massive debt, kept control of the family business. With his bank account bulging, Robert could buy out Rainier, so at last was firmly in control of his own destiny.

The Mondavi family wounds began to heal in 1985 when a wealthy collector organized a forty-year retrospective tasting of Charles Krug and Robert Mondavi Cabernets to benefit the University of California enology scholarship program. People paid $1,000 per seat to taste every vintage from 1944 to 1984, with the promise that both Peter and Robert would be in attendance. As the brothers tasted the wines, they tasted their shared histories—the good times even more than the bad. At the close of the evening they shook hands and then, after a moment of silence, embraced to cheers and applause. Although the Charles Krug wines suffered a nearly twenty-year period of decline, resulting in large measure from the burden of Peter's debt, by the mid-1990s they began to regain some of their former luster and renown. With Peter in retirement, his sons took control of the winery and brought it back into the black. They made their best wines, including a line labeled Generations, like most every winemaker in the Napa Valley—according to the model that their uncle had popularized nearly a generation earlier when he first advanced the then radical notion that American wines can taste as good as great French ones.

More than anything else, oak is what made this possible. During his 1962 trip to Europe, Robert had noticed that the finest Burgundies and Bordeaux were aged in brand-new, small oak barrels. The wood imparted a distinct flavor to the wines— a buttery, smoky character to the white Burgundies and a spicy, vanilla note to the red Bordeaux. He persuaded Peter to experiment with imported French barrels at Charles Krug, and when he started his own winery four years later, he bought so many barrels that he ended up selling some to competitors. Here again, he was the popularizer and promoter rather than the innovator. A decade earlier, James Zellerbach at Hanzell Vineyards in Sonoma had pioneered the use of small French oak barrels in California. His production, however, was very small, and while his wines drew acclaim, they did not change many minds or alter much winemaking. Robert's did. His production, although small at first, grew rapidly. The people watching him saw that his goal was to make artisanal wines on a large scale, and anyone who sampled his wines could identify the stylistic thread running through them—the aroma and flavor of French oak. That flavor quickly came to be perceived as the mark of quality, and soon just about everyone wanted it. Many wines ended up tasting more of wood than of grapes, but the crucial discovery was that the seemingly magical flavors of the great French wines could be reproduced elsewhere. The magic apparently came from the hands, and the palate, of the wine-maker.

The romantic conceit of the artist-winemaker that emerged in California in the late 1960s celebrated individual genius, but its greater significance lay in the confidence it inspired. Wine could be considered an art because it had an aesthetic function (one that good taste recognized), but more to the point because it came from human hands—"art" in its first dictionary definition, the "human effort to imitate, supplement, alter, or counteract the work of nature." Since human efforts in Europe were not inherently superior to human efforts in the United States, the focus of American winemaking during the initial years of American wine's great rise shifted from nature to art. Those aspects of winemaking that cannot be controlled by human hands—soil and climate—began to be viewed as less important than those that can be controlled —the choice of grape, the decision of when to harvest and then how to ferment, the question of how long to age and when to bottle.

In America during the 1970s, the winery more than the vineyard came to be thought of as the place where great wine originated. Fine wine came to be identified varietally, precisely because vineyard location, the basis of virtually all European wine classifications, seemed relatively unimportant. In turn, this focus on art rather than nature led people to speculate that the qualities that distinguished the best wines could be echoed if not replicated in other, less prestigious bottlings. Although grapes from the Central Valley obviously would not produce as fine a wine as grapes from Napa, the differences might be lessened if the winemaker used similar methods and techniques— particularly similar oak barrels. This possibility led in the 1980s to the emergence of the "fighting varietals," Cabernets and Chardonnays priced for everyday consumption but modeled on high-end wines. Generic blends fell even more out of favor as consumers came to regard European place names on American wine labels as a sign of something cheap. Varietal labeling, on the other hand, signaled prestige. Many new American wine drinkers did not know that Chardonnay was the name of a grape. They simply recognized it as a wine—a classy wine at that, especially when compared with something called "chablis" that came in a screw-capped jug.

Of course, perception and reality are not always one and the same. Julio Gallo had been right back in 1959 when he returned from Europe and told his brother that many American jug wines were better than French *vin ordinaire*. And he probably was still right fifteen years later when he defended the quality of his generic blends against Ernest's push to follow the market toward varietal labeling and vintage dating. Julio's goal as a winemaker always had been consistency. He blended different grapes from different vineyards and different harvests in order to produce a product that tasted the same no matter where or when the customer purchased it. The results could prove impressive. As part of a 1972 cover story on the emerging American wine boom, *Time* magazine asked a panel of experts (including Frank Schoonmaker, James Beard, and Alexis Lichine) to evaluate a number of California and French wines in a blind tasting. Gallo's nonvintage Chablis Blanc bested both a 1968 Puligny-Montrachet and Beaulieu's 1967 Pinot Chardonnay, while its Hearty Burgundy emerged as the second-highest-scoring red wine, outperforming Château Lafon-Rochet 1969 and even Robert Mondavi's 1969 Cabernet. Every other wine in the competition cost at least twice (and in some cases three or four times) as much as the Gallo wines.

Because good quality at a fair price remained his objective, Julio was understandably skeptical when Ernest and the marketing team began to push for new directions. But he could not ignore the fact that the market itself was changing rapidly. As *Forbes* asked in its 1975 cover story on American wine: "Can Gallo Move Up?" Both Ernest and Julio were determined that the answer be yes. They reduced production of pop wines like Boone's Farm, began marketing cheaper generics under other names (Carlo Rossi became the most successful), and inaugurated what turned into a twenty-year campaign to upgrade the company's image. The initial advance in that campaign came with the release of Gallo's first vintage-dated varietal—a 1978 Cabernet, made exclusively from Sonoma County grapes and aged in oak for thirty-five months.

Throughout the 1980s, the Gallos tried, with varying degrees of success, to earn their company prestige as well as profit. As the *Forbes* story had perceptively noted, their determination "to win respect for their wine and their family name" was itself "the bedrock on which they had built their E. & J. Gallo Winery." Until the mid-1960s, respect in the American wine industry had come almost solely from raw sales. Now, with premium table wine becoming part of the cultural mainstream, it came as much from what a winery produced as from how many gallons it sold. This shift often involved style more than substance. The "fighting varietals" did not really mark an improvement in quality over the generic blends produced a decade earlier by Gallo or the other large-volume producers such as Almadén or Italian Swiss Colony. They did, however, mark a change in style. Everyday, mass-market American wines now were modeled on premium wines, just as ten or fifteen years earlier those premium wines had been modeled on fine French imports. When the Gallo brothers made their fortune, they succeeded where their father failed. But so long as they operated their company with a Prohibition-era mindset, they inevitably were tarred with the same brush as Joe and Mike had been back in the 1920s. To earn respect in the new world of American wine, the world that Robert Mondavi promoted and inspired, they had to do more than sell wine as booze. They had to sell it as art. So in television commercials for their "wine cellars" line that ran in the mid-1980s, scenes of lush vineyards alternated with shots of coopers and winemakers at work, while classical music played in the background, and an announcer intoned: "There are no better ways to make wines. No better land to grow wine. No better wines than Gallo wines—today." The implication was clear: today's Gallo was not the same as yesterday's.

Changing the Gallo image proved to be quite a challenge. Many consumers persisted in identifying the company with Ripple, Thunderbird, and cheap generics. Moreover, the company sometimes seemed almost too big for its own good. Many people associated premium wine with small-volume production, and Gallo was anything but small. By the early 1990s, its various facilities produced about seventy million cases of wine a year, with sales totaling approximately $1 billion. One out of every four bottles purchased in the United States was a Gallo product. Fine varietal wines constituted only a small percentage of this massive production, but they were the wines the company advertised, promoted, and spent millions of dollars developing. They also were the wines that Ernest and Julio cared about most.

When the brothers decided to make the move into premium wine, they began buying land—not in the Central Valley, but in Sonoma, where they soon became the county's largest landowner. They sometimes purchased established vineyards, but just as often they bought orchards and farmland, creating new vineyards by bulldozing the terrain into the hillsides and valleys they wanted. By 1990, they owned about 4,000 acres in Sonoma, the largest single block being in Asti, once home to Italian Swiss Colony. They then constructed a 350,000-square-foot underground aging cellar, capable of holding 60,000 small oak barrels, the largest such facility in the world, as well as a new $1.5 billion state-of-the-art winery in the Dry Creek Valley. The wines made there, an entirely new line called Gallo Sonoma, "will dispel the idea that fine wines can't be made by companies that put out volume," said Julio in 1993. Gallo Sonoma quickly won the critics' favor, earning high scores and winning awards in international competitions. Public acceptance came a bit more slowly, but Ernest, studying the market as carefully as ever, saw that premium varietals constituted the future for Gallo and for American wine at large. Since they were what the public wanted, they became a profitable ticket to respectability. So when asked why the company had shifted its focus so dramatically, he said simply, "It's a matter of personal satisfaction."

When the Asti project began, Julio had noted that "these new premium vineyards [will] benefit our descendants more than Ernest and me." He died in a jeep accident in 1993. The responsibility of managing those vineyards then passed to his grandson Matt, while his granddaughter Gina took over the winemaking. Advertisements for the Gallo Sonoma line featured pictures of Matt and Gina, with the tag line "Taste the wines of our generation." Although Gallo still was very much a family company, the family had changed. No longer were Prohibition-era memories of suicide and bootlegging the primary inspiration for business success. Now, much as at Robert Mondavi, the goal was to make wines that could be considered among the best in the world.

A new generation was at the helm at Mondavi as well—Robert's sons, Michael, the company CEO, and Tim, the managing director and winemaker. The winery that had occasioned such a stir during its construction back in 1966 had become Napa's top tourist attraction. Now people gaped only at the crowds. Production had expanded tremendously over the years, impelled in part by the public's embrace of the Mondavi label and in part by Robert's decision to diversify—not away from wine, but away from Napa. In 1979, he purchased a six-million-gallon facility in the town of Woodbridge, near Lodi, where he began producing mass-market wines. Much as he had done years before with the C. K. line at Charles Krug, and much as the Gallos did with their other labels when they made the move into premium wine, he used Woodbridge to support growth elsewhere. The wines at first were generic blends, Bob White, Red, and Rosé, but they soon became varietal. Sales of Woodbridge Cabernet, Chardonnay, and other varieties, almost all oak-aged, provided the cash flow that enabled the company to grow ever larger, expanding in California and abroad. By the mid-1990s, the Woodbridge plant produced nearly five million cases of wine annually, with the other Mondavi ventures (including partnerships in Chile and Italy) producing another two million. The hubris of thirty years earlier had paid off, in spades.

With his sons in control of the company, Robert next turned his attention to a new project, raising money for the construction of a not-for-profit institution true to his vision, the American Center for Wine, Food, and the Arts, in the town of Napa itself. Scheduled to open in 2001, this educational facility will offer public exhibits and programs. In Robert's words, it will be "a place where American music is played, artists-in-residence work, vineyards grow, wonderful meals are created, and visitors and scholars alike explore the richness of America's cultural heritage . . . a very special place to explore and celebrate the American passion for living well."

Yet insofar as that passion includes wine, America's heritage is only a generation old. The rise of American wine, which began in 1966 with the construction of the Robert Mondavi Winery, certainly involved new approaches to winemaking and grape growing. The more profound changes, however, involved attitudes and perceptions—of consumers, but also of vintners and grape growers. No one better embodies those changes than Ernest Gallo, whose family-owned company continues to discard its Prohibition inheritance. Today, prestigious, limited-release American wines, including Gallo's, are considered to be as good as any made anywhere. They set an international standard, as wines at every price level from virtually every wine-producing country are made in their image. No matter whether the bottle costs $50 or $5, American wine has been reborn. In merely thirty years, it has gone from being an object of derision to an object of respect. For the first time in the nation's history, it garners widespread acceptance and admiration—from critics and connoisseurs, and also from consumers, whose pocketbooks prove the point. The proof will be on display when Robert's center opens in Napa. But it already can be found in Modesto, where Chardonnay, not Thunderbird, has become the best seller. After nearly seventy years, Ernest Gallo's sales figures still don't lie.

5

Machines
in the Garden

ALTHOUGH Robert Mondavi inspired a generation of American winemakers to raise their ambitions, no one person caused American wine's great rise. Consumers first had to believe that domestic wine was worth buying. And winemakers had to be convinced that it was actually possible to make wine in America that resembled what came from fabled European estates. After all, the United States in the mid-1960s had virtually no tradition of either fine winemaking or fine wine appreciation. Mondavi's success helped show the way, but equally crucial was the work of the teachers and researchers who insisted on the systematic application of scientific principles to grape growing and winemaking. Mondavi himself certainly was a believer. "Back then," he says, "we thought anything was possible because we thought our technology gave us control." Controlling the grapes in the vineyard and then the wine in the winery became the key to success for people trying to raise both the quality and the image of American wine. An emphasis on science and technology was important not only because it led to better wines, but also because it enabled American grape growers and winemakers to focus on what they had available to them rather than on what they did not have—current research instead of time-honored traditions. It gave them the confidence —some would say the arrogance—to believe that their ultramodern wines could compete favorably with venerable European imports.

Wine is as old as the Caucasian hills of Georgia and Armenia, where people first cultivated *Vitis vinifera* grapes some seven thousand years ago. But wine made to a consistent, uniform standard, often in dizzyingly large volume, is quite new. Less than a hundred years ago, the vagaries of a frequently fickle nature—what was and was not in season, what spoiled and what stayed fresh—dictated which foods people could consume and which beverages they could drink. But by the mid-twentieth century, food and drink had become standardized commodities, products of nature tamed and mastered by science and technology. Wine's modernization was neither exclusively nor originally an American phenomenon. Nonetheless, twentieth-century Yankee ingenuity led the way, so much so that today, wines the world over bear an American imprint. This is not because they are made with American grapes, but because they emulate American styles and reflect an American vision. That vision sees good wine as the product of good science, and bad wine as the product not just of bad vintages, but of science misapplied and technology misused. In the 1970s, when American wines began to outperform European ones in tastings and competitions, wine growers around the globe took note. Large-volume producers making wines to be drunk on an everyday basis were especially intrigued. Most such wines back then were at best mediocre—often spoiled, usually unbalanced, shrill or dull. Scientific winemaking and grape growing was what would turn them into today's clean, sound, consistent products. Moreover, an increasing number of everyday table wines began to be fashioned in the image of the historically finest wines, so the stylistic gap between expensive, exclusive bottles and *vin ordinaire* narrowed with every vintage. Modern wine was no longer simply the fruit of nature. Instead, it was the fruit of science—particularly science as it was practiced and, more important, valued in the United States.

The University of California was the most respected center of American wine-related research. After Eugene Hilgard's retirement in 1904, Frederic Bioletti took over the program. Because his research involved more than grapes, he kept going during Prohibition, even though the university regents banned wine study beginning in 1916. Following Repeal, wine work shifted from the Berkeley campus to the College of Agriculture at Davis, near Sacramento. Over the next fifty years, the professors there, led by Alfred Winkler and Maynard Amerine, made Davis the leading institution of its kind in the world. This was not because Winkler and Amerine conducted more impressive research than their colleagues elsewhere. Rather, it was because American grape growers and winemakers so readily adopted their mindset, especially the fundamental notion of using science and technology to control an otherwise capricious nature.

Significant research took place in Europe too. Indeed, the single most important person in the creation of modern wine was the French scientist Louis Pasteur, who in the 1860s first identified the basic principles of fermentation. Pasteur was the world's leading authority in the then emerging field of microbiology, pioneering investigation into what he called "the large role played by the infinitely small in nature." He worked on wine for only a few years, but in that time he almost single-handedly created the discipline of enology—the rigorous analytical study of wine, as opposed to the merely sensory appreciation of it. People long had regarded the transformation of juice into wine as a magical or spontaneous act, a gift of nature's God. Earlier French scientists, Lavoisier and Chaptal, had demonstrated that the process involves a chemical reaction, but they had been unable to discover its cause. Pasteur, working in a makeshift laboratory in his father's house amid the Jura vineyards, demonstrated that yeasts, single-celled organisms living on grape skins, initiate the "vital act." They feed on grape sugar, transforming it into alcohol and carbon dioxide. For thousands of years people had made wine using techniques and practices that they never really understood. Pasteur provided them with new knowledge, which in turn led to new practices and techniques. For example, he discovered that wine, being uncooked, contains bacteria that multiply when exposed to air. "Yeasts make wine," he famously said, "[and] bacteria destroy it." When winemakers learned that, they began to treat their wine differently—to handle it more carefully in the barrel (always adding new wine to top off or replace what had evaporated) and to bottle it earlier. In conducting his research, Pasteur looked at the ancient art of winemaking through the lens (literally the microscope) of modern science. His discoveries slowly but inevitably changed how winemakers approached their craft. Traditionally they had wanted only to assist nature. Now they began to try to control it.

This desire to control nature revolutionized all forms of

agriculture. Farmers used science and technology to help them realize larger yields, reduce damage from pests, and produce more consistent results. When the academic discipline of agricultural science began to be studied in universities in the late nineteenth century, research was applied even more systematically—not so much on the small family farm of the old agrarian dream, but on the emerging agribusiness farm of modern capitalism. Although wine grapes did not lend themselves to systemized agriculture as readily as crops such as corn, wheat, and soybeans, wine growing was very much part of the general movement. In the United States, Eugene Hilgard at Berkeley and Ulysses Hedrick at the research station in Geneva, New York, played prominent early roles. Prohibition and its tortured legacy slowed everything down, but once American wine began its mid-twentieth-century rise, wine growers pursued scientific solutions with a passion verging on frenzy. This was in part because their post-Prohibition problems were so acute. But it also was because, at the time, science seemed to promise a bright future in nearly every area of American life. From the miracles of medicine to the delights of technology, from nuclear power to NASA exploration, science defined progress in the American imagination.

In European vineyards, the claims of science always had to compete with those of tradition. Especially in the most famous appellations, home to the most prestigious wines, the techniques of grape growing and winemaking continued to be passed down from generation to generation. Because a famed Bordeaux or Rhine wine owed much of its renown to history, vintners valued knowledge *how* far more than knowledge *why*. Scientific research proved helpful when unexplained problems like phylloxera surfaced, but it seemed of little use at other times. Even when a new generation became exposed to science through some sort of formal training, sons and daughters frequently continued to do things as their fathers did. In addition, for much of the twentieth century, European wine production was mired in a prolonged economic depression brought about by the two world wars. Amid financial uncertainty, the cost of change often seemed too high. Many vineyards did not lend themselves to mechanization, just as many cellars, being small, did not have room for experimental equipment. Growers frequently were tenants, not owners, so they had no desire to take risks on their own. Moreover, the only estates that consistently made money in hard times were those that resisted change the most—the exclusive, premium producers for whom tradition was an essential element in their vintage blends. For a long time, then, most European wine growers knew the controlling power of science only indirectly.

The situation was exactly the reverse in post-Prohibition America. For one thing, the dry years left the United States with virtually no winemaking history. No matter whether a producer aimed to make bulk or premium wine, he rarely could employ past experience to show him what to do. Perhaps more important, though, reliance on tradition was fundamentally foreign to brash American sensibilities. "In most of the operations of the mind each American appeals only to the individual effort of his own understanding," wrote Alexis de Tocqueville in his nineteenth-century classic, *Democracy in America*. "Americans," Tocqueville continued, "evade the bondage of system and habit" because they "accept tradition only as a means of information, and existing facts only as a lesson to be used in doing otherwise and doing better." The almost wholly self-sufficient and present-minded rise of American wine certainly supports his claim. Especially during its first decades, science often determined quality, for laboratory analysis instead of the memory of past vintages had to dictate how a wine should taste. The enologist arrived at a formula for a particular type or variety of wine having to do with the respective levels of sugar, tannin, acid, and the like—all things that could be measured and tested in a laboratory. The winemaker then made the wine to fit the formula, trying as much as possible to minimize the influence of location, climate, or vineyard. Consistency above all else was the goal. "It was the era," recalls Bill Bonetti, winemaker at Charles Krug and then at Sonoma-Cutrer, "[of] the manipulation of wine."

The desire to manipulate both grapes and wine in order to achieve predictable, reliable results reflects the influence of what the critic Matt Kramer calls "the machine in the mind." Kramer argues persuasively that the scientific methodology employed by the researchers at the University of California at Davis came to serve as the basis for this distinctly American vision of wine growing, a vision that went on to influence and often transform production around the globe. The principles of systemized agriculture, promoted by university-trained scientists, turned what largely had been a trial-and-error enterprise into something "quantitative, methodical, [and] verifiable." So too, the microscopic examination of the composition and characteristics of wine turned subjective impression into objective analysis. More than economics was involved. As Kramer notes, "Equally powerful [was] a determined interventionism." To many American vintners, "the offense of European wine growing was its passivity. The machine in the mind offered a more muscular approach."

Within the broader sweep of history, that muscular approach can be thought of as an extension of a persistent American phenomenon—the intrusion of science and technology on the agrarian ideal, a machine not only in the mind but also in the garden. The cultural historian Leo Marx has used the image of the machine in the garden to portray what he calls America's "root conflict," the reality of an industrialized nation-state in tension with a homeland idealized as a pastoral refuge. It makes little difference that the ideal has rarely been realized, he argues. What matters is that it has exerted powerful sway for generations over how Americans understand themselves and their country. American wine's ardent early advocates—Thomas Jefferson, Nicholas Longworth, and George Husmann—all promoted wine as part of America's pastoral ideal. They urged Americans to make and drink it in order to sustain the country's agrarian promise. Yet the late-twentieth-century rise of American wine has been impelled by the machine far more than by the garden. Wine may belong to the pastoral revelry of the classical bacchanal, but it has never played a significant role in the life of rural America. In the New World, the image of wine as part of a simple, "back to nature" way of life is nostalgia for a past that never was.

The machines in the wine garden can be literal—mechanical harvesters, drip irrigation systems, rotary fermenters, and the like. They also can be metaphoric—Matt Kramer's notion of a mindset that values nature tamed over nature unbound. The story of the rise of American wine involves both. Over the past fifty years, technology has enabled producers to make better and better wines that vary less and less from year to year. At the same time, without an analytical, scientific approach to begin with, such consistency never would have been deemed a worthwhile goal. The fact that wine became standardized in terms of both quality and style helped make it a mainstream consumer product. Then, as it became an acceptable part of American life, new energy, often in the form of big corporate money, helped to revitalize it even further—yet another form of the machine in the garden. Without enological science, and a vision that values it, none of this would have happened. Americans were not the first to bring machines into the vineyard in either the literal or the metaphorical sense. Louis Pasteur and his followers did that. Yet because American producers accepted tradition only as a means of information, and existing facts only as a lesson in doing better, they more than their French, German, or Italian counterparts took Pasteur's work to a new level of accomplishment. In effect, they created modern, commercial wine as we know it today.

When Professor Maynard Amerine was asked, near the end of his career, if anything in his background had prepared him for a life with wine, he answered succinctly, "No, nothing at all." Amerine thought of himself first and foremost as a scientist. Wine just happened to be the field in which he worked. In the beginning, he had no interest in it. His family were California prune and peach growers, but he never wanted to work the farm. From the time he was a young boy, he dreamed of going to college and doing scientific research—even though, as he admitted later, "it wasn't quite clear to me what research was at that age." So he earned a B.S. and then a Ph.D., writing his dissertation on how plants of different colors respond to light and temperature. Then in the spring of 1936, he went looking for a job. It was the Depression. A couple of junior colleges had openings for teachers, but Amerine wanted to "do" science, not just teach it. The only offer he got was to work as a researcher under Professor Alfred Winkler, chair of the new Department of Viticulture at Davis. He accepted, even though he knew little about wine. Had there been "a suitable opportunity" elsewhere, he would have pursued it, especially since the university paid so little—supposedly $2,000 a year, but abruptly reduced to $1,800, a situation that "left a bad taste in my mouth for several years." But with jobs so scarce, Amerine kept his mouth shut. Soon he got a raise—then a few years later a full-time professorial position, then a research assistant and a laboratory—and the taste turned sweet. It was, in fact, the taste of wine, which he came to like very much. More to the point, he came to understand it. For he spent nearly a half century analyzing it, until he understood better than just about anyone else what it was made of—wine's biochemical composition. In the process, Maynard Amerine became America's most esteemed enologist, the preeminent member of the generation of scientists who revitalized American wine.

Amerine shared his understanding of wine's chemistry with his students, with the wine industry, and with scientists and wine growers the world over. By the time he retired from Davis in 1974, he had written well over two hundred books and articles, all designed to promote a scientific appreciation of wine. Reticent about his private life, he was adamant in public when discussing what was needed to improve California wine

—better grapes in better vineyards, better winemaking in better facilities. He and his colleagues spent their careers defining
exactly what constituted "better" wine. Through a series of bulletins and other publications, they advised California growers
on what to plant where (and why), and California winemakers
on which techniques to use when (and why). Their books and
public lectures also assisted other growers and winemakers, in
other states as well as in other countries. In the process, they
made the Department of Viticulture and Enology one of the
world's leading centers of wine-related research.

As part of the College of Agriculture, the Davis department initially was supposed to study only viticulture. It started
doing so in 1935, when Frederic Bioletti retired. What little
enological work was being done in those early post-Prohibition
days remained in Berkeley's fruit products department, chaired
by William Cruess. Professor Cruess had studied wine before
Prohibition, but then shifted his research to the technology of
food preservation. At Repeal, his work on frozen foods as well
as fruit and vegetable dehydration took most of his time (he invented, incidentally, the now ubiquitous canned fruit cocktail),
so by default more and more wine research moved to Davis.
For a few years the two campuses engaged in a friendly rivalry,
but before long the department at Davis officially expanded to
include enology. It was small—three professors in viticulture
and, at first, only Amerine in enology—but it grew as the significance of its work became apparent to both the wine industry
and the university administration. By the time of Amerine's retirement, the department had a staff of nearly fifty.

Amerine's first task in his new job was to investigate which
grape varieties grew best in which areas of California. His boss,

the Texas-born and Berkeley-trained Winkler, had inherited Eugene Hilgard's old conviction that better wine could only come from better grapes. "You can't make a silk purse out of a sow's ear," he kept telling his young assistant. Winkler directed Amerine to make experimental lots of wine from grapes grown in different parts of the state. Amerine knew little about wine-making, but with advice from Cruess in Berkeley, he mastered the basics. First in a basement laboratory and then in a winery on the edge of the campus, he made small, five-gallon batches of wine—over five years, some three thousand different ones from 140 grape varieties. He used fruit from all over the state, often harvesting the grapes himself, always keeping the lots separate. "We made an attempt in this research," Amerine re-called later, "to cover California as best we could, from Escondido in the south to Ukiah in the north." He kept meticulous records detailing the growing conditions in each vineyard site —when the vines bloomed and the grapes ripened, how hot the weather got, the average number of hours of sunlight, and more. Each lot of wine was analyzed chemically, subjected to a statistical sensory analysis, and rated as to general quality. Amerine and Winkler then tried to correlate the different data. Was there a causal connection between where the grapes grew, the chemical composition of the wine made from those grapes, and the overall quality of that wine? Gradually, two things be-came clear to them. First, different grape varieties performed differently in different places. Second, the root cause of these differences was the climate, specifically the heat.

Amerine and Winkler's data convinced them that temper-ature was the single most important factor in grape growing, and thus the single most important factor in determining wine quality. For one thing, they found a precise and predictable correlation between heat in the vineyard and the resulting wine's chemical composition. Not only did it take longer for grapes to ripen in cool areas, but the skins had a deeper color and the acidity of the fermenting juice was higher—on average, 50 percent higher than in regions where the growing season was 50 percent warmer. For another, their sensory analysis statistics indicated that some grapes, especially the more delicate white varieties, just did not make good wine in hot areas. The fruit ripened, but the heat robbed the juice of acid and left the resulting wines unbalanced. The data varied with the grape variety, but the overall lesson seemed clear: to improve quality, growers needed to be more selective with the vines they planted. As Winkler told a group of Napa grape growers in 1938, "The only way for you to convince the buying public of the superiority of the wines of your region is to grow the right varieties, pick them at the proper maturity, and convert them, without dilution of their quality, into really fine wines."

In order to teach this lesson, or as Amerine wryly put it, to do their "missionary work," the two researchers needed an easily understandable formula or system with which to summarize the data they had accumulated. Borrowing from the work of French scientists, they advanced the notion of heat summation and degree-days as a way to measure the effect of temperature on vineyards. These measurements calculate the temperature over the course of the growing season. Vines effectively shut down when the thermometer drops below 50 degrees Fahrenheit, so a degree-day is one day's average temperature measured in terms of everything above that point. The total of the degree-days in the growing season then becomes the heat summation figure. Winkler already had done some research on temperature in European countries. Now he and Amerine tabulated the numbers for California. They classified the state's vineyards according to a scale of five climatic zones, ranging from Region I (the coolest, with fewer than 2,500 Fahrenheit degree-days) to Region V (the warmest, with more than 4,000). They then summarized all they had learned by drawing a map of California and painting the grape-growing areas with different colors denoting where they fell on the heat summation scale. With a glance at the map, a grower could determine if it made sense to plant a certain grape variety in a certain area. In 1944, Amerine and Winkler published all their findings. Dryly titled *Composition and Quality of Musts and Wines of California*, their book systematically reviewed the grapes they had tested, giving the results of their analyses as well as notes on the varieties' various problems (susceptibility to disease, for example). It was a truly groundbreaking work.

Amerine and the enologists who worked with him went on to experiment with and report on a host of new winemaking technologies and techniques. These included fermenting wine at low temperatures in stainless steel tanks, using pure yeast cultures in a compressed form, and cultivating strains of bacteria to induce malolactic fermentation, a process just then being understood. The university and the California wine industry worked hand in hand, becoming, as Amerine put it, "mutually dependent on each other." Davis scientists offered extension courses, conducted conferences, and published scores of articles, while wineries put the academic research to practical test. When problems arose, vintners frequently came calling. Amerine and his staff tried not to play favorites. Still, because applied research often was financed by the state's wineries, they inevitably provided more assistance to large, bulk producers than to small independents. In 1956, for instance, when some of the big wineries asked for help getting cheap fortifieds onto the market quickly, the Davis department initiated a study on aging wines rapidly, going so far as to hire an enologist (Vernon Singleton) to direct it. Amerine, who would have preferred to see more premium table wines produced, defended both department policy and industry practice by drawing an analogy between wine and automobiles: "General Motors doesn't produce just Chevrolets but produces Buicks and Cadillacs . . . So the wine industry must cover an entire consumer market." Not surprisingly, during the 1940s and 1950s, the era of cheap fortified wine's supremacy, the majority of the Davis research was directed at bulk wine production.

Winkler's viticultural work also focused on large-scale production. Because many California vineyards were infected with viral diseases, Winkler and his staff developed high-yielding, healthy clones of the more prolific grape varieties. Harold Olmo, the university's grape breeder, went a step further, creating a slew of new disease-resistant *vinifera* hybrids. Even though many of the varieties that the Davis scientists promoted never became popular, the virus-free vines they propagated produced much of the fruit that ended up yielding the award-winning wines of later decades. Olmo and Winkler also studied pruning and vine-training techniques, as did Vincent Petrucci, who, with a grant from the Roma Wine Company in 1947, started a viticultural science program at Fresno State College (now Fresno State University and an important research center in its own right). In addition, Winkler spent considerable time researching vineyard spacing. He concluded that a standard system, with eight feet between each vine and twelve feet between each row, ripened the grapes evenly, increased yields, and allowed for mechanization, twelve feet being wide enough for a tractor to pass through. By 1962, the year of Winkler's retirement, virtually all new or replanted vineyards followed this model. Soon they would be planted on a new rootstock, AXR-1, which the Davis scientists recommended growers use instead of the old St. George. University studies showed that AXR-1 consistently produced higher yields, and just about all of the new plantings in the boom years to follow used vines grafted onto it.

Not all of the important American research took place in California. The largest machines in the country's vineyards came from New York, where Cornell scientists under the direction of Professor Nelson Shaulis introduced mechanical harvesters in the late 1950s and early 1960s. New York was the country's second most prolific wine-growing state. Most of the grapes there were native or hybrid varieties, and most of the wine was cheap. Unlike in California, where low-paid migrant Mexicans picked the crop, eastern labor costs proved high. Harvesting by machine rather than by hand provided a way to save money. The challenge was to train the vines appropriately, trellising the fruit high above the ground so that the grapes could fall onto the harvester's conveyor. Shaulis devised a system in which a divided canopy of leaves and fruit was trained downward from high cordons. Called the Geneva double curtain, this system worked especially well with hardy native varieties, but over the next decades, as mechanical harvesting found its way into *vinifera* vineyards (in Australia and Europe even more than California), the Geneva double curtain came to be used with classic wine grapes as well. Even more important than this trellising system were the various experiments Shaulis conducted to improve yield and fruit quality. Working primarily with Concord grapes, he discovered that he could grow better fruit if he increased the amount of sunlight on the grapes. Manipulating the position and exposure of grape clusters so the vine grows the way man (rather than Mother Nature) wants was a radical idea at the time. Shaulis's techniques have since been refined and popularized, notably by Alain Carbonneau in Bordeaux and Richard Smart in Australia, and today his research informs new vineyard plantings throughout the world.

Yet despite all these advancements, American wine in the early 1960s had not changed all that much since Repeal. Quality had definitely improved, as nearly all of the wines being marketed commercially were clean, but the overwhelming majority of them remained either skid-row fortifieds or undistinguished table blends. The big problem still was in the vineyards. In New York, most growers grew only foxy native grapes. No matter how well made, the wines from them remained unremarkable. In California, even growers in the cool Regions I and II, the areas that Davis proclaimed best for premium grapes, were reluctant to replant with better grape varieties. Their biggest concern was yield. Ordinary varieties such as Carignane and French Colombard produced four, five, or six tons of grapes to an acre, while more noble grapes produced only a third as much. Unless a grower could sell better grapes for three times more than standard grapes, he was bound to lose money. But with the limited market for premium American wine, producers buying grapes could not afford to pay that much. In retrospect, one can identify harbingers of changes—Konstantin Frank's Finger Lakes vineyard and John Daniel's wines at Inglenook, for example—but at the time only a handful of growers cared about better grapes and varietal wines. The Davis scientists knew that their most important work involved matching grape variety with location, and they shuddered every time they heard about a new planting of inferior grapes in a prime area. Amerine in particular felt discouraged. He had chosen, or rather fallen into, a scientific field that had distinct practical applications. While virtually everyone agreed that his research made theoretical sense, hardly anyone followed it in practice. "As late as 1965," he recalled later, "I couldn't see very much influence of that work. If I had found the right biochemical job, I would have left the university . . . I felt that I'd wasted all those years as far as application of our results was concerned."

Then came the sea change. It began in Napa and the other North Coast counties, soon swept over the rest of the wine-growing regions of California, and then gradually spread east. In New York, Virginia, and Missouri, French-American hybrids replaced native varieties in vineyards whose owners aimed to make better-quality wine. New growers began to experiment with *vinifera*, and before long a small but growing number of high-quality wines emerged from eastern wineries. Meanwhile, the composition of California's vineyards changed radically. For one, there simply were more of them. For another, the grapes being planted were no longer the old standbys. Growers in Regions I and II began to demand only premium varieties, especially Cabernet Sauvignon and Chardonnay. Growers in the warmer regions still grew Alicante Bouschet and Carignane, but they now also planted Chenin Blanc, Ruby Cabernet (one of Harold Olmo's hybrids), and Zinfandel. In 1965, out of a total of nearly 113,000 acres of wine grapes in California, fewer than 4,000 were devoted to Cabernet and Chardonnay. (By way of comparison, nearly 6,000 still were planted to Mission grapes.) By 1985, the total acreage under vine had increased to 343,000, with nearly 23,000 devoted to Cabernet and 27,000 to Chardonnay. Maynard Amerine was sure he knew the cause of the escalating demand for high-quality grapes: "This is a reflection of the university's insistence . . . that you have to have better varieties if you are going to make better wines, and they have to be grown generally in good regions."

But the scientists at Davis did not change American wine by themselves. California growers began to plant better grape varieties only when consumers developed a taste for better wines, and as important, when those consumers showed a willingness to pay for them. Again, the changes began in the mid-1960s, when a number of factors—increased foreign travel, the Francophile tone of the Kennedy years, greater middle-class affluence, and more—led millions of Americans to sample table wine. In 1967, sales of table wines passed those of fortified wines for the first time since Prohibition. This shift in taste was in part a reaction against the staid conformity of the preceding decades, in part an embrace of things natural, in part a response to the lure of the exotic and new. Whatever the reasons, wine in the late 1960s began to enter the American mainstream, where it remains today, long after other fads and fancies of the era have disappeared.

At first, Americans bought mostly white wines, which they

drank both with meals and as an alternative to spirit-based cocktails. Soon many turned to rosés or blush wines, initially Portuguese imports in cute bottles, then California white Zinfandels. The white and rosé booms in turn were followed by a huge increase in red wine sales, fueled in large measure by medical studies that linked moderate wine consumption with a reduced risk of heart disease. Sales of fortifieds fell, as did sales of cheap jug and generic wines, while sales of premium table wines skyrocketed. Over three decades, the American palate gradually moved from sweet to dry, and varietal wines became the norm rather than the exception. During the same period, American tastes in food also changed, becoming more global and more adventurous. A "new American" cuisine emerged, a melting pot of culinary styles from Asia, Mexico, and the Caribbean, as well as Europe. Originating in northern California, this cuisine emphasized the importance of fresh ingredients and healthful eating, and featured dishes that proved to be not only wine-friendly but also wine-inspired.

Ever so slowly, fine wine became disassociated in people's minds from other forms of alcohol. Not everyone saw it that way, as prohibitionist sentiment enjoyed a resurgence in the 1980s, but more and more Americans came to connect wine with a healthy, civilized lifestyle rather than with inebriation or debauchery. For a small but economically important segment of the population, fine wine became a weekly if not daily part of life. So although per capita wine consumption remained relatively stable (roughly two gallons per year, as opposed to forty gallons of cola and other soft drinks), the kind of wine people drank and the kind of people who drank it changed radically. Put simply, American wine finally left skid row.

Growing consumer demand for better wine led wineries to increase production, which spurred both replanting and new vineyard development. By the end of the 1960s, consumption of cork-finished wines retailing above $3 a bottle was increasing approximately 25 percent annually. Growers suddenly could make money with fine varietals, even though these vines had lower yields than standard ones. Maynard Amerine had been preaching the gospel of premium varietals in premium locations for three decades. At long last, the industry was putting his words into widespread practice. In 1971, California produced five million gallons of varietally labeled wine. Ten years later, production had reached more than twenty-five million gallons. And during those initial boom years, everyone who planted or replanted knew by heart the degree-day and heat summation figures for the area in question. Winkler and Amerine's color-coded map, along with their list of recommended varietals for each of the state's five regions, had become the California wine grower's irreplaceable guide.

The only problem was that the map was never very precise. A multitude of microclimates exist within any one of the five regions, so a grape variety that performs wonderfully in one vineyard might not do well in another, even though both sites have a comparable number of day-degrees over the growing season. Moreover, the scale measures only heat. It does not take into account other climatic variables—for example, wind, sunlight exposure, humidity, or nighttime cold. This is the primary charge that revisionist commentators have leveled against the Davis scale. But Amerine, for one, readily acknowledged that degree-days are a crude measurement. "Neither Winkler nor I have ever said that the law of the Medes and Persians lay in the Region I to V concept," he replied somewhat testily when asked about it. "We just say that it's the best picture we have at the present of the most important factor influencing the composition and the quality of California grapes." More to the point, in the late 1960s and early 1970s, when vineyard development first accelerated, the Davis map was the only guide available. Although it seems clear in hindsight that some vineyards were planted with inappropriate varietals, at the time most growers, like most consumers, knew little about fine wine. They thought of it as something foreign, and a crude guide proved better than no guide at all.

It may seem surprising that California winemakers and grape growers during the initial boom years almost always turned to the university for guidance rather than to their compatriots abroad, the European producers whose wines they wanted to emulate. The explanation is twofold. First, the boom came amazingly fast. The California industry needed help right away, and it trusted the university from years of working together. Second, although American winemakers admired European wines, they did not necessarily admire European winemaking. To a Davis graduate, answers grounded in scientific fact invariably proved more attractive than those based merely on traditional practice. Not until the 1990s, when the best American wines had repeatedly proven themselves to be on a par with the best from Europe, did extensive collaboration between European and American wine growers begin. At the start of that decade, a new wave of replanting got under way in California, necessitated this time not by changing consumer tastes but by the return of an old foe—phylloxera. This time, the approach was less monolithic. Yet while growers frequently employed European models, they first made sure that those models had been refined and endorsed by a new generation of scientists, who tested them in controlled experiments and then offered extensive explanations as to why they might prove advantageous. A lot had changed over the years of American wine's rise, but one element stayed constant: tradition was worth heeding only if it made good scientific sense.

The phylloxera plague of the late 1980s and 1990s erupted because the pest had mutated, with a new biotype attacking the AXR-1 rootstock used in most post-1960 plantings. Although replanting cost millions of dollars, it had definite benefits, as it allowed growers to upgrade their vineyards by taking advantage of new knowledge. Some of that knowledge had deep historical roots. Many high-quality varietal vineyards, for example, began to be replanted with much tighter and denser spacing systems than Winkler or Amerine had ever promoted, systems based on traditional European practices. The old European way, however, now had a sound scientific explanation: each vine would produce less but more concentrated fruit, and with more vines planted per acre, the total yield would stay the same. Most important, no longer did university scientists advise all California growers to follow a single model in any one region. Viticultural practices increasingly became less uniform—not just with spacing, but also with the choice of varietal, the trellising system, the selection of clones and rootstocks. Amerine was not surprised. "There are undoubtedly more regions and more factors than the ones we used," he acknowledged in a 1985 interview. "A whole series of things could be added to influence the ripening and the composition of the grapes . . . Good research always reveals more problems than you can solve."

In the same interview, Amerine defined what he called "the gospel according to the University of California":

> [We] always started in with the basis that winemaking is a branch of biochemistry, and grape growing is a branch of genetics and plant physiology. And if you don't know anything about plant physiology, you don't know anything about grapes. If you don't know biochemistry, you don't know anything about wine. Therefore, you have to study wines from the biochemical point of view, and you have to study grapes from the genetic and plant physiological point of view in order to develop new techniques of doing things. The applied research comes out of or is based on the basic research.

This scientific vision, Amerine said when asked about its influence beyond California, "[has] spread everywhere now." As evidence, he cited the large foreign enrollments at Davis, the number of graduates working abroad, the consulting work done by Davis scientists around the globe, and the changing mentality of grape growers and winemakers in traditional wine-growing countries. Even in Bordeaux, he noted, "they preach the gospel in that way." In fact, "It's pretty hard to find someplace in the world where somebody from Davis hasn't had some impact." No one, he could have added, more so than Maynard Amerine himself. If, by the time of his death in 1998, his specific recommendations to some degree had become outdated, that was only because his "good research" had been followed by that of others—at Davis, Fresno State, Cornell, and other centers of American enological and viticultural research.

Some of today's most valuable research comes from

abroad, especially from Australia, where Roseworthy Agricultural College has played a similar role as Davis in the development of that country's wine industry. Australian viticulturists, led by Richard Smart, certainly share the machine-in-the-garden mindset. Building on the work of Nelson Shaulis at Cornell, they have pioneered all sorts of new techniques, the most significant being a sophisticated canopy management system designed to control the vine's vigor. Their research demonstrates that growers can manipulate a vine so as to moderate the influence of other factors, including local climate, thus making it possible to grow better-quality fruit in areas that previously had been deemed unsuitable. Aussie viticulturists now travel throughout the world, lecturing and advising grape growers. So too, "flying winemakers" from down under consult extensively abroad, taking advantage of Northern Hemisphere harvests that come six months after their own. At least where science and technology are concerned, the Americans and the Australians together have led the New World to challenge and often convert much of the Old.

Such globalization does have a potential downside. Today, a number of grape varieties, notably Cabernet, Chardonnay, and Merlot, are being planted virtually anywhere they will grow, and more and more of the wines made from them taste alike. But there is a far greater upside, for more and more of these wines also taste good—much better, in fact, than most wines made a generation ago. As Hugh Johnson writes in *Vintage: The Story of Wine*, wine has entered a global golden age: "It has become a subject of intense worldwide interest, competition and comparison, an industry comparable in some ways with fashion, with the great difference that for all the style and glamour of its market image, its roots are in the earth." There can be little doubt what raised it to these new heights. Without the controlling power of science, consumer demand for high-quality table wine never could have been satisfied, and fine wine would have had to remain an esoteric luxury enjoyed by only a privileged few. Although the research of today's Australian and European scientists is as significant as that of their American counterparts, it was the American faith in the power of science to comprehend and thus master nature that first set the stage. That faith now has spread across the globe, as agricultural science has made the world of wine a much smaller place. Contemporary research, whether conducted in Davis or Dijon, Adelaide or Asti, Cornell or Conegliano, has a common core. Enologists and viticulturists share their findings with one another; multinational conferences and symposiums appear regularly on the calendar; and scientists from all over the world publish in the same journals. Maynard Amerine, America's great proponent of scientific winemaking, would be pleased. Tradition held no appeal for him. When critics said that Davis and other schools should provide students with more practical experience and less laboratory training, he had a simple retort: practical experience can teach only the status quo, and the status quo cannot improve anything. Given the depths to which American wine had fallen when he began his career at Davis, his logic was unassailable.

The biggest impact made by the advance of the machines in the garden, first in California and then elsewhere in the United States as well as the rest of the wine-growing world, involves the improved quality and the changing style of wines made to be drunk every day. A generation ago, these were mired in an economic and qualitative depression. The elite growths may have tasted ethereal, but most of the world's wines, the sort that the vast majority of people actually consumed, were just plonk, their primary virtue being their heady effect. Today, consumers can choose from a bevy of delicious, affordable everyday wines. Some come from the New World—America of course, but also Argentina, Australia, Chile, New Zealand, and South Africa, countries that have emerged in the past two decades as important players. Some also come from previously neglected Old World regions (for example, southern Italy, the French Languedoc, and Navarra in Spain) as well as from tradition-laden areas (Bordeaux and Burgundy, Piedmont and Tuscany, the German Pfalz). In all of these places, the old distinctions between elite and everyday wines have become blurred. The machines in the garden—in terms of actual equipment and in terms of attitude—have impelled a tremendous rise in the overall quality of the world's wine.

Producers the world over used to be divided between what Robert Skalli, owner of the popular Fortant de France line of French varietal wines, calls "mystery or misery." Elite wines, "cloaked in mystery and mystique," were appreciated only by connoisseurs. They had little in common with the coarse, heady (and in America, usually fortified) "misery" that millions of people consumed on a daily basis. Today, such distinctions no longer hold true. This is in part because far less plonk, including far less cheap fortified wine, is being produced. People everywhere are drinking less but better, and the rise in premium production has corresponded with a decline in cheap, generic, or *ordinaire* production. But it also is because inexpensive table wine increasingly has become modeled on premium wine, sometimes to striking effect.

Nothing illustrates these changes better than the rise of the varietal wine that has become the world's favorite—Chardonnay. Back in the days of the polarity between mystery and misery, elite white Burgundy was just about the only table wine made from Chardonnay. It had little besides alcohol in common with generic French wines from the Midi or Languedoc. So too, when American boutique producers began to make Chardonnay in a Burgundian style, their wines had nothing much to do with American generics, including so-called "chablis." Today, however, the premier cru Burgundy and the American boutique bottling share a stylistic profile with a slew of mass-produced wines, no matter the country or appellation of origin. This is in large measure due to viticultural and enological advances, including Harold Olmo's clonal research at Davis, that have brought widely available, inexpensive wines closer to exclusive ones in terms of both style and quality. As indicated by the example of Robert Skalli's varietal wines made from grapes grown in the Languedoc, including Chardonnay, the gap between the two categories has narrowed even in France. But the narrowing began in California, where large-volume producers first demonstrated to the world that inexpensive table wines successfully could emulate the most elite premium bottlings. That approach was soon adopted nearly everywhere else—in Australia, Chile, and other New World countries, but also in Italy, France, and much of the Old World. Skalli's Fortant de France Chardonnay, for instance, resembles white Burgundy, but its true inspiration is American—specifically, Kendall-Jackson Vintner's Reserve Chardonnay, the world's leading example of a mass-produced, blended varietal, a type of wine that simply did not exist before the machines entered the garden.

"There was a hole in the market I could drive a truck through," recalls Jess Jackson, a white-haired lawyer turned wine magnate and Chardonnay's chief American popularizer. Back in the early 1970s, Jackson purchased an eighty-two-acre pear and walnut orchard in Lake County, north of Napa, as a tax shelter. He at first just wanted a place to relax with his family on the weekends. But Jackson was a shrewd businessman. He took note of the rising price of wine grapes, converted the property to vineyards, and began selling grapes to North Coast wineries, especially Fetzer Vineyards. Then in 1981 prices fell, and Jackson found himself with a vineyard but no buyer for his grapes. He took the logical step and began making wine. At first he thought he would sell it in bulk, but after researching the market, he decided to start his own brand, which he named after himself and his then wife, Jane Kendall. Jackson wanted to feature what he calls "high-profile" wines, but he did not have the financial resources to follow the state's highest-profile Chardonnay producers and make vineyard-designated estate wines. So he did the next best thing and blended high-quality grapes from different regions—Lake and Sonoma Counties, also Monterey and Santa Barbara—and sold the wine under a general California appellation. But he did not put it in a screw-capped jug and charge $2.49, the going price for most California-designated white wines. Nor did he charge $10.99 as the boutique producers did. Instead, he sold his wine for $5 a bottle. The first Kendall-Jackson Chardonnay, some fifteen thousand cases, came on the market in 1983. Tasting totally ripe, slightly sweet, and full of fruit flavor, it had been made from only premium grapes (primarily from Regions I and II on the Davis scale) and fermented and aged in French oak barrels. While it cost twice as much as generic jug wines, it tasted like the higher-priced super-premiums. The inaugural vintage was named "Best American Chardonnay" by the American Wine Competition, and it sold out in six months. "I saw that hole in the market," says Jackson, "and I created a new category — really good wines that the average person could afford." These were the wines that soon became known as the "fighting varietals."

Jackson and his winemaker, Davis-trained Jed Steele, defined a flavor profile of really good varietal wines that they believed consumers would enjoy. They then made their wines to match the model. Kendall-Jackson's Chardonnay retained a trace of sugar (due to Steele's including a small percentage of off-dry Gewurztraminer in the blend), so it tasted sweeter and riper than most Burgundies. It helped define an American style, one marked by honeyed softness and expressive fruit. That style proved enormously popular at home and abroad. It came to be imitated by winemakers in the Old as well as the New World — first in an effort to appeal to American consumers, then, before long, to meet the demand of wine lovers everywhere. In little more than a decade, Chardonnay made in this slightly sweet, barrel-aged, fruit-driven style became the world's most popular wine. For many consumers, it defined what white wine, any white wine, should taste like.

As important as the specifics of the Kendall-Jackson style was the fact that the wine was a blend of grapes from different vineyards and different regions. Jackson and Steele never tried to express a taste of place. Instead, they made wines to fit the stylistic profile they had defined. Blended wines traditionally had been low-end generics, but this one clearly was something more. Jackson had a simple philosophy, "to blend the best with the best," and as production grew rapidly, Steele proved to be a master at staying true to the model or recipe. By 1990, he was producing more than 600,000 cases of Vintner's Reserve Chardonnay, made from fruit from thirty vineyards in five counties.

The very notion of using a recipe for anything other than jug wine marked a new stage in American wine's rise. Scientific winemaking enabled Steele and his staff to analyze precisely the composition of each lot, and thus to blend to the model they wanted. While they could not completely avoid vintage variation, they could minimize stylistic variables, and so were able to create consistently accessible, large-volume wines with the qualities usually associated only with boutique or estate wines — complexity, richness, harmony, and balance. Evidence of just how important the recipe was showed up in 1992. After Steele left the company, Jackson sued him, alleging that he had stolen "trade secrets." It was a messy trial, since Steele countersued for back pay and bonuses, but on this issue, Jackson won. The judge barred Steele from revealing Kendall-Jackson's winemaking techniques to potential competitors, as the enological formula was deemed the defining factor in the wine's character.

Other "fighting varietal" Chardonnays joined Kendall-Jackson's in the 1980s to help transform a largely unfamiliar grape into the trendy choice of wine drinkers everywhere. Former lumberman Barney Fetzer quickly followed Jackson's lead with Sundial, a blend made from coastal grapes. Sundial made Fetzer and his family (who had been selling wine under their own name since 1968) a small fortune, since the public clamor for Chardonnay grew louder with every vintage. Meanwhile, Bruno Benzinger, formerly half owner of a New York liquor-distributing business, started selling huge amounts of blended wine under the Glen Ellen label. "These three brands," says Jess Jackson, "Fetzer, Glen Ellen, and Kendall-Jackson, made Chardonnay in America." They attracted a host of imitators, particularly since all three enterprises proved highly profitable. By 1995, more California acres, nearly seventy-three thousand, were planted to Chardonnay than to any other variety. Blended varietal wines had become America's favorites.

Most inexpensive varietals were (and are) fashioned in the stylistic image of elite premium wines—those made by boutique American producers and by prestigious European, particularly French, estates. The one exception was Zinfandel, a *vinifera* variety of uncertain origin with no European model to either imitate or rebel against. Back in the 1880s, Zinfandel had been one of California's most widely planted grapes. During Prohibition, it enjoyed popularity with home winemakers, and after Repeal it served primarily as a blending grape for inexpensive generic red wines. In the 1950s and 1960s, some producers did make varietal Zinfandels. Because the grape often ferments to a high degree of alcohol, these wines proved popular among drinkers who liked their wines heady and strong. Connoisseurs liked to call them America's own, and by the early 1970s Zins from producers such as Ridge Vineyards, Joseph Swan, and Sutter Home had acquired a small but loyal following. The Sutter Home Winery in the Napa Valley, abandoned during

Prohibition, had lain silent until the Trinchero family, Italian immigrants from New York, purchased it in 1947. Although Mario Trinchero made mostly bulk wine to ship east, he also developed a wide array of small-production wines, including red and white ports, sherries, vermouths, a number of different "burgundies," and a Zinfandel, which customers could buy by the gallon at the winery. Then in the late 1960s, after Mario's son Bob had taken over the winemaking responsibilities, Sutter Home began to concentrate more and more on Zinfandel. It was Bob Trinchero's favorite variety, and he made award-winning wines from old vine grapes grown in Amador County, in the Sierra foothills gold country. Almost black in color, with intense, robust flavors, these wines satisfied the tastes of the day. Brash and forward, they were America's own because they were anything but subtle.

In an attempt to make his 1972 Zinfandel even bigger and more powerful, "to out-zin the competition" as he put it, Bob Trinchero drew off some of the free-run juice after crushing the grapes, thus intensifying the red wine by reducing the amount of liquid in contact with the skins during fermentation. It worked, but it left him with 550 gallons of pale juice. He fermented these to dryness, and on the advice of the Sacramento wine merchant Darrell Corti, bottled the wine as Oeil de Perdrix (Eye of the Partridge), a French term for white wines made from dark grapes. The federal Bureau of Alcohol, Tobacco, and Firearms, which approves all commercial wine labels, required him to include an English-language description, so he added the phrase "a white Zinfandel wine." Trinchero sold Oeil de Perdrix only in the winery's tasting room. A winemaking byproduct, it was very much a commercial afterthought, and consumer response proved unenthusiastic. Then in 1975 the fermentation unaccountably stopped before all the grape sugar could be converted into alcohol. The resulting wine had a pale pink color and about 2 percent residual sugar. Labeled simply White Zinfandel, it proved extremely popular, and to everyone's surprise was the first wine Sutter Home sold out that year. The same thing happened the next year, and the next. "We were sitting around, sort of scratching our heads, wondering what was going on," recalls Bob's younger brother, Roger. "We weren't the brightest guys in the world, but eventually it dawned on us that maybe we should make more white Zinfandel."

They did, purchasing grapes from the Central Valley and blending them into a consistent product that they began to market nationwide. In 1979, Sutter Home produced nearly 20,000 cases of White Zinfandel, a number that already strained capacity at the small, family-run winery. Ten years later, production had grown to 3.7 million cases. A massive new plant on Zinfandel Lane processed the grapes coming to Napa in a steady stream of trucks from far afield. What Bob Trinchero liked to call his "fortuitous accident" had become the best-selling wine in America. Its success spawned a host of imitators, and by the late 1980s more than 125 White Zinfandels were on the market. (Beringer Vineyards produced the second most popular one, a wine whose commercial success provided the capital to revitalize that venerable winery.) White Zinfandel's popularity had nothing to do with Old World models. "It was really quite revolutionary," says Bob Trinchero. "Normally, we try to replicate something that was created in Europe — usually in France. You know, 'my Cabernet tastes just like Bordeaux,' or 'my Pinot Noir tastes just like Burgundy.' White Zinfandel doesn't taste like anything in Europe. It's totally American." It also is the ultimate blended wine, for it owes nothing to vineyard location. Made from high-yielding vines in often otherwise marginal, because warm, regions, it can be rushed onto the market only a few months after harvest. In the 1980s, when national wine consumption increased just about every year, White Zinfandel was what many new wine drinkers purchased.

In New York and Chicago, Minneapolis and Atlanta, Tokyo, London, and Zurich, corporate accountants took note of wine's new place in American culture. The machines in the garden had made moderately priced table wine a better and, as important, a more consistent consumer product. Sales were booming. Back in 1965, Americans had consumed 190 million gallons of wine (a per capita average of 0.98 gallons), over 60 percent of which was fortified. By 1985, consumption had increased to 580 million gallons (2.43 per capita), with over 80 percent being table wine. Market forecasters confidently predicted growth in all segments of the table wine industry. Banks foresaw a bright future ("the brightest of any agricultural enterprise in California," read one Wells Fargo study), so were more than willing to make loans. Plenty of people took them up on it. At the same time, big corporations such as Coca-Cola, Nestlé, Pillsbury, R. J. French, and Schlitz Brewing, lured by the prospect of big profits, entered the industry. Some prospered. Swiss-based Nestlé, for instance, revitalized Beringer, turning a sleepy relic into an industry leader. Others floundered, Coca-Cola being the most spectacular example. In the late 1970s, top executives at the Atlanta-based company decided to invest heavily in American wine. They purchased the Taylor Wine Company of New York, and then started a high-volume West Coast counterpart from scratch—Taylor California Cellars. Coke's strategy with wine was much as it had been in the cola wars with Pepsi—no-holds-barred competitive marketing. It launched a dramatic advertising campaign, including blind tastings in which Taylor California wines were pitted against those from their chief competitors, with names named and results broadcast. As a form of wine demystification, it worked—to a point. Taylor California Cellars wines sold well, but not well enough to cover the cost of the company's investments. So with the bottom line in red, Coke sold its wine properties in 1983 and swallowed its losses.

Then in the late 1980s, to the surprise of most everyone in the wine business, American per capita wine consumption fell, going from the 1985 high of 2.43 gallons to a low of 1.74 gallons in 1993. (It has since gone back up, to roughly 2 gallons today.) Certainly the recession of the early 1990s hurt sales, as did the revival of an anti-alcohol movement that associated any sort of alcoholic beverage with illegal drugs. Much as had happened eighty years earlier, these neo-prohibitionists lumped wine together with spirits, blurring the distinction between moderation and abuse. They campaigned for warning labels, limitations on advertising, and higher taxes on all alcoholic beverages, but they increasingly were out of touch with people's tastes. For ironically enough, the biggest factor in the drop in consumption was the change in how Americans treated wine. Hardly anyone drank it as booze anymore. Instead, people increasingly used it as a mealtime beverage. As a consequence, Americans were drinking less but enjoying better-quality wines, so that while the volume they consumed went down, the amount of money they spent on wine went up. And the wines they bought were varietals. The forecasters, then, had missed the proverbial boat when they predicted growth in all segments of the wine industry. Really only one segment continued to grow, and grow rapidly—varietal wine.

Moderately priced varietal wines made like more expensive ones first emerged in the early 1980s to fill the gap in the consumer market that Jess Jackson had so presciently seen. Today that gap is just about gone. Some companies still produce generic "chablis" and "burgundy," just as some companies still make cheap fortifieds, but more and more inexpensive wines, even those bottled in screw-capped jugs, come from premium varietal grapes. Chardonnay and Zinfandel remain the most popular varieties, but Cabernet and Merlot do not lag far behind. For many consumers, even those who do not recognize them as the names of grapes, varietal designations on the label stand for quality. This means that premium grapes are being planted in areas that viticulturists a generation ago would have judged marginal if not inappropriate, especially California's huge, hot San Joaquin Valley. But the twenty-five years since Maynard Amerine's retirement have seen significant advances in both viticulture and enology. Machine harvesting at night, more precise temperature-controlled fermentation, the widespread use of stainless steel tanks, improved clonal selection as well as canopy management, and judicious blending have enabled bulk wineries to produce palatable varietal wines made primarily from grapes grown in Regions IV and V. Obviously there is a large gap in quality between an estate-bottled Carneros Chardonnay and a bag-in-a-box version, but in a basic sense both wines aim for a similar stylistic profile. For in America today, cheap wine increasingly is blended so as to resemble elite wine. The machines in the garden have made that possible.

The big companies now recognize as much, for they too are making premium wine. Gallo is a leading example, as is its biggest volume competitor, Canandaigua Brands, based in New York. Long a producer of fortified wines made from eastern *labrusca* grapes, Canandaigua first ventured into the California table wine business in the 1970s. With fortified wine sales falling fast, management thought it saw a rosy future in inexpensive, primarily generic table wines. For nearly twenty years, Canandaigua purchased wineries big and small. Presidents Marvin and Richard Sands oversaw the production of a variety of products, including wine coolers, flavored pop wines, and a bevy of jug generics. The company grew to become the second-largest supplier of wine (as well as the second-largest importer of beer and the fourth-largest supplier of distilled spirits) in the United States. Yet so long as it concentrated on low-end, generic wines, its market kept shrinking. So in the spring of 1999, Canandaigua entered the quality wine business with a rush. In March, it purchased the venerable Simi Winery in Sonoma for $35 million. A month later, it acquired Napa Valley–based Franciscan Estates (producers of the Franciscan, Mount Veeder, and Estancia labels) for $240 million. All of a sudden, a company that had never evidenced any fine wine ambition became an important player. The reality of the bottom line explains why. "These acquisitions give us a major stake in the rapidly growing premium wine market," says Richard Sands. "We believe that this category will continue to grow at impressive rates in the years to come."

Beginning in the 1960s, Americans in significant numbers began to drink table wine. Not everyone kept drinking it, but many did—so many that it became an accepted and acceptable part of life for millions of people. Then in the following decades, American wine's quality improved dramatically, thanks primarily to the achievements of the viticulturists and enologists who helped transform American *vin ordinaire* into something quite special. As the infusion of corporate capital in the 1970s and 1980s demonstrates, it was not difficult to see that American tastes were changing. Yet as both the Coke and Canandaigua stories also demonstrate, it was sometimes difficult to predict the direction they would go—white or red, generic or varietal, French inspired or New World style. Americans had developed an interest in wine, but exactly where that interest would take them was anyone's guess.

One person who kept guessing right was Jess Jackson. By the late 1990s, Kendall-Jackson's production had grown to nearly three million cases a year. Blended Chardonnay remained the biggest seller, but it now sold for close to $15 a bottle. Jackson raised the price in response to the escalating cost of premium Chardonnay grapes. He was determined not to use Central Valley fruit in the blend and not to tinker with the original recipe. The future of American wine, he insisted, was quality. Over the years Jackson had purchased vineyards up and down California, from Mendocino to Santa Maria. In the process, his portfolio expanded to include a number of small, essentially boutique wineries, specializing in estate-grown wines. (So too the Trinchero family had expanded their portfolio to include small-production premium wines, including a $40 Cabernet and $30 Chardonnay under the M. Trinchero label.) Yet Jackson never abandoned his commitment to blending. He bought vineyards in order to better control the farming as well as the winemaking, and so set aside the majority of grapes grown on the various estates for use in the Kendall-Jackson blends. "Control," he said, "is what matters most. I want to control the wine on the vine because I want to make the best."

The very notion of controlling a wine, from vine to bottle, underlies the scientific and technological advances that have led to the creation of modern wine as we know it. Critics sometimes argue that excessive control can lead to excessive uniformity—cookie-cutter winemaking and homogenous production. But the stylistic uniformity of wine today is less a reflection of standardized winemaking than of consumer demand. The market has changed, becoming ever more global and sophisticated. Fine wine has gone from being something traditional and mysterious purchased by an elite clientele to a readily enjoyable beverage consumed by people of all social backgrounds. At the same time, cheap generic plonk, the historic staple of millions of wine drinkers, is fast disappearing. In its place are varietal wines made on a Kendall-Jackson or Sutter Home model, if not according to their exact formulas. The real result of wine's scientific revolution is better quality. Whether in the New or the Old World, modern viticulture and enology have given wine growers more choices than ever before, enabling them to better control the fruit of their labors in both the vineyard and the winery. Proof is in the glass.

6

Small
Is Beautiful

W ARREN WINIARSKI was restless. A lecturer in political philosophy at the University of Chicago, thirty-five years old and working on his Ph.D. dissertation, he felt strangely unful-filled. It was 1963. While he enjoyed teaching, he found his ur-ban routine sterile and impersonal, and in tune with the chang-ing times, dreamed about a new kind of life, close to nature and away from the city. Winiarski loved wine. He had begun to drink it regularly when studying in Italy a few years earlier, and back home in Chicago he tried to taste everything he could, vis-iting local shops and talking with anyone who could teach him about it. His wife came from Maryland, where he had met Philip Wagner, the iconoclast at Boordy Vineyard who helped revitalize eastern wine growing. Wagner's example at Boordy served as an inspiration. Winiarski, though, felt the lure of the West. He was a voracious reader, and the books and newsletters he devoured suggested that California's vineyards had the po-tential for excellence, no matter that the wines he tasted rarely demonstrated it. "It was sort of crazy," he recalls, "to think that

I could have anything to do with that. But I knew or had a very strong sense that there must be people out there who were at the brink of achieving this excellence." So he decided to see if he could apprentice himself to one of those people—to learn by doing rather than reading or talking.

But who? Philip Wagner volunteered to ask his friend Maynard Amerine at Davis. Amerine's response was that "it's practically impossible to get started these days the way you want to do it, with no formal training." But enrolling in school was the last thing Winiarski wanted to do. So he wrote to a handful of smalltime wine growers who he had heard were doing something special. When a couple replied encouragingly, he took a trip to California to check things out. In northern Napa, one thousand feet up Howell Mountain, he got a job offer—from J. Leland Stewart at a tiny winery called Souverain Cellars. The job was to work as Stewart's assistant in what otherwise was a one-man operation. So the next summer, the Winiarski family piled into an old station wagon pulling a trailer full of books and headed west. Their car broke down on the first day out of Chicago. But a week later, with a rebuilt engine, they arrived in the Napa Valley, ready to begin their life with wine.

Warren Winiarski was in the vanguard of a new approach to American wine—men and women drawn to it because of the lifestyle and values it represented rather than the profits it could bring. Some were beatniks and hippies, others refugees from corporate life, still others just restless spirits looking for change, but their shared passion for wine involved more than just liquid in a glass. Like Nicholas Longworth 150 years earlier, they saw it as an agent of social change, a vehicle for improvement. While Longworth used wine to battle frontier drunkenness, they used it to counteract something equally uncivilized — a modern urban or suburban way of life in which food and drink had become mere sustenance and taste had little or no value. Wine for them was always more than a business. They came to it in large measure as a reaction against cultural conformity and the status quo, specifically the self-satisfied conformity of 1950s America, in which wine was categorized by both producers and consumers as booze. Their wineries were small, their boutique wines limited, and their share of the industry's economic pie minuscule. But by the close of the 1960s, itself a decade of cultural change, they began to exert an influence that far outweighed their financial import. As Winiarski notes, because their "tastes and aspirations were formed elsewhere," they brought to a sleepy industry new energy and vision — the desire to "pursue excellence." That vision helped American wine as a whole change course.

These boutique wineries were the antithesis of virtually everything that had happened since Prohibition — the antithesis of companies like Gallo and United Vintners, of the distillers like Schenley and Heublein, and of the big corporations like Pillsbury, Nestlé, and Coca-Cola, all of which would buy wineries but viewed wine as only one in a stable of consumer products. They also were different from the large California premium producers like Beaulieu or even Robert Mondavi, where the production of fine wines always was supported by the larger output of generic wines. Although the proprietors and winemakers at these boutique wineries shared Mondavi's revolutionary vision of American wine as art, theirs was a more narrow focus. Happy to work on a small scale, they tended to produce a single line, sometimes even a single bottling or varietal, always at the highest level. They wanted to make money, of course, but their volume was so small that they had little need to promote or proselytize. Nonetheless, because they insisted on hands-on, nonindustrial production, they brought a new spirit and energy to American wine. Theirs became the domestic wines that collectors and connoisseurs sought out, in much the same way that people traditionally had prized small-production Burgundies. Small then became chic—so chic that by the 1980s many consumers considered a winery's size a mark of its supposed quality. Robert Mondavi, for one, noted the irony. "People consider [my winery] a volume producer," he complained in a 1987 interview. "We have been hurt by that. They look only at boutique producers."

Back in 1964, when Warren Winiarski moved his family west, the term "boutique winery" had not yet been coined. (It would enter the vernacular about a decade later.) There was nothing chic or glamorous about his new job. Souverain Cellars was a winery, but also a farm, and farm labor proved long and hard. Lee Stewart, his new boss, had come to Napa twenty years before, an early defector from the gray flannel corporate world. For a time he raised chickens. Then, with direction from André Tchelistcheff at Beaulieu, he began to make wine. Stewart's wines regularly won medals at the state fair, but because production was so small and demand for premium California wines so limited, hardly anyone outside Napa knew about them. Frequently strapped for cash, he was willing to hire Winiarski in large part because this neophyte came so cheap. In turn, for Winiarski, being Stewart's assistant meant watching, learning, and doing a bit of everything. "That was a very good experience," he recalls. "Every step was available, every single step was open to observation, and [I] had to do every step, from the most inconsequential to the most important." Stewart was both a skinflint and a perfectionist, obsessively concerned with minutiae. So the difficult work taught invaluable lessons. Winiarski apprenticed at Souverain for two years, long enough to learn what he calls "the essentials of the winemaking process" from an "enormously beneficial master." Then in 1966 he came down Howell Mountain and took a job at the new winery that had everyone in Napa all abuzz—Robert Mondavi's. Already, though, he was planning for the time when he would grow grapes and make wine on his own.

Winiarski was not Lee Stewart's first assistant. One notable precursor was Miljenko (Mike) Grgich, a Croatian émigré who had studied enology and viticulture at the University of Zagreb. Like Winiarski, Grgich's first taste of American winemaking came at Souverain Cellars. And like Winiarski, Grgich found Stewart a hard taskmaster. "He asked for perfection— perfection in cleanliness and performance. Everything had to be done in a particular way—not a second way, only one way, the best way." Winemaking with Lee Stewart was a labor of love, but it was labor nonetheless—a way of life more than just a job. Grgich left after less than a year, not because the work was too hard but because his winemaking experience got him a better-paying job. Still, in even that short time he learned an important lesson: "to watch over a wine as I would watch over a baby."

Mike Grgich's new job was at Beaulieu, where he worked as André Tchelistcheff's second-in-command for nine years. Then in 1968 he received an even better offer, to head the winemaking team at Mondavi. He remembers why he made the change: "I was very much charmed by his new building . . . He had stainless steel tanks, French barrels, and very interesting new things." One of the first wines Grgich made at Mondavi was the 1969 Cabernet Sauvignon, which three years later was crowned California's best at a well-publicized tasting. He worked on all of Mondavi's wines during his four years there, years in which the production grew tenfold. For Grgich, himself a perfectionist, it became too much. With production increasing so rapidly, he no longer could control every aspect of the winemaking, and he worried about quality across the board. In addition, Robert's sons were being groomed to succeed their father, and he knew that his future possibilities at Mondavi were limited. So he was ready to listen when in early 1972 Ernest Hahn, a southern California developer, and James Barrett, Hahn's friend and attorney, offered him a job as the viticulturist and winemaker at an old winery near Calistoga they were restoring. It was called Chateau Montelena, and Grgich would be a limited partner. He accepted, and started drawing up plans for the future. Hahn and Barrett were red wine lovers. They wanted Chateau Montelena to produce only Cabernet Sauvignon, but Grgich told them that this was unrealistic. It would take five years before the first bottle of red wine would be ready to sell, years in which the winery would spend money but generate no income. "Start with white wines," he advised them, "wines which you can make and sell and have cash flow until your Cabernet comes into the market." They did, and the second Chardonnay that Mike Grgich made at Chateau Montelena (from the 1973 vintage) was the wine that triumphed over the premier cru and grand cru white Burgundies in July

1976 at Stephen Spurrier's Paris tasting. The red wine that won the laurels that day also came from a new winery—Stag's Leap Wine Cellars in southern Napa, owned by Warren Winiarski.

Winiarski, along with a number of investors, had purchased the property for his winery in 1970. The Cabernet that turned all those heads in Paris came from only his second crop of grapes. Like Grgich, he wanted to control every aspect of his winemaking. This involved more than mastering the technology. He was convinced that the best wines combined science and poetry. They came from the heart as well as the head, reflecting artistic desire as much as professional discipline. Winiarski had come to California because he felt the stirrings of just such desire, and his triumph in Paris served as a sort of validation or confirmation—not just of his individual talent, but more crucially of California's, and by extension America's, potential. "It was a kind of consummation for my notion that the California grapes had potential which was not being expressed or was not being exploited; we were not doing the best we could."

Just as surprising as the fact that the expert judges in Paris could not distinguish French from California wines was the discovery that the two top-scoring wines came from producers whose names virtually no one outside the Napa Valley recognized. Production at Chateau Montelena and Stag's Leap in 1976 was extremely small. Even devoted connoisseurs of California wine (and there were beginning to be a few of these by then) were likely to know little if anything about them, let alone ever to have tasted the wines. Both wineries have expanded in the quarter century since their Parisian triumphs, but in the early 1970s they each made minuscule amounts of wine. All of it was of very high quality. Other, larger producers also made fine premium wines, but only as a part, and usually a small part, of their total production. When the Gallo brothers, for instance, decided to make the move to better varietals, they made sure to use their already established line of mass-produced generics as a financial foundation. So too, Robert Mondavi's production of premium wine always was supported by his larger output of everyday table wine, Bob's Red and White. By contrast, wineries like Montelena and Stag's Leap aimed to make only expensive, elite bottlings. Hence their wines appealed to only a small percentage of the wine-drinking public. Yet as their success in Paris signaled, they and other boutique wineries would lead American wine to new heights. Before long, even the big-volume producers would join them.

Warren Winiarski and Mike Grgich followed in Robert Mondavi's footsteps. Not only did they both work for Mondavi, but like him they were determined to make world-class wines on a French model—Chardonnay that tasted like grand cru white Burgundy, Cabernet that tasted like classified-growth Bordeaux. The plaudits in Paris proved they could do just that. But they also followed another model, one that they knew from their days on Howell Mountain at Souverain Cellars, where Lee Stewart treated each tank and barrel as a newborn child, and winemaking was considered more a way of life than a business. In 1977, helped immeasurably by the publicity generated by the Paris tasting, Grgich (along with a financial partner) started a winery of his own—Grgich Hills. Like Winiarski, he wanted personal control. Over the years, Stag's Leap and Grgich Hills both would grow, and Winiarski's and Grgich's ambitions would change aplenty. Yet when they started making their own wines, they were committed to the ideal of winemaking as an art form and fine wine as an individualistic expression. As Mike Grgich put it: "That's why I came to America . . . I felt a little artistic blood in my veins . . . I wanted to do it my own way."

The pulse of artistic blood sent many hearts racing during the initial years of the American wine renaissance. Small premium wineries, often financed by entrepreneurs who had made their fortunes elsewhere, began to pop up all over the place—in Napa and Sonoma certainly, but also in Mendocino, Monterey, and Santa Barbara, and soon outside California, in Oregon and Washington State, Virginia and New York. The number of small, bonded wineries in the country more than doubled during the ten years between 1965 and 1975. Not all of these made premium wines, but more and more tried to do so, particularly since small was fast becoming beautiful in the eyes of consumers. Leon Adams, who remembered the bad old days, marveled that some small wineries could "sell all they can make, at prices considerably above those of the nationally known premium brands, by merely sending announcements to customers on their mailing lists." Although the big national brands were experimenting with new wines and starting to move from generics to varietals, small producers more often played the pioneering roles. As André Tchelistcheff perceptively observed, "The apostolic mission of the future belongs to the small wine grower."

The boutique phenomenon was not entirely new. Here and there, artisanal winemakers had been crafting small-pro-

duction gems for years, sometimes as an outgrowth of Prohibition-era home winemaking, sometimes in a self-conscious effort to create something truly memorable. For the most part,
their efforts had little if any influence on others. In a few cases,
however, they made a difference, opening the eyes of larger
producers to new possibilities. These possibilities might involve a specific grape variety (as with Chardonnay at Fred and
Eleanor McCrea's Stony Hill), a winemaking technique (aging
in French oak at James Zellerbach's Hanzell), or a more general
approach (Lee Stewart's meticulous craft at Souverain). One
winemaking pioneer embodied all these and more. The most
influential of the post-Prohibition era's small, elite producers,
he also was the most controversial, because of his hubris as well
as his missionary zeal. Martin Ray made wine, first under the
Paul Masson label and then under his own name, for forty
years. He died in 1976, so only saw the beginning of the revolution in American taste. Yet he was the father of the boutique
movement, for he more than anyone before or since had a genuinely apostolic vision for American wine.

Martin "Rusty" Ray was born in 1904 in the northern California lumber town of Etna Mills. The son of a teetotaling
Methodist minister, he grew up in Saratoga, a small community
in the foothills of the Santa Cruz Mountains, west of San Jose.
Ray's father died in 1910, but the boy found a surrogate a few
years later when he sneaked into Paul Masson's La Cresta estate
on Table Mountain and was befriended by Masson himself.
Paul Masson then was in his mid-fifties. He had emigrated
from Burgundy as a young man in order to work for Charles
Lefranc, the Santa Clara Valley's pioneering wine grower. After
purchasing vineyard land high in the mountains, he started the

Paul Masson Champagne Company, where he made table as well as sparkling wines, many of which received considerable acclaim in the years before Prohibition. The company was especially renowned for a rosé sparkler widely considered one of California's finest. Masson cut a dashing figure and had a commanding presence. Strong and imposing, he was a cultured man of the world who at the same time never shrank from physical labor. Whether working in the vineyard or hosting an elegant dinner party, he conveyed an infectious *joie de vivre*. One of the few things missing from his life was a son, and he quickly came to look on young Martin Ray with paternal affection. In turn, Martin revered Paul Masson, trying all his life in ways large and small to emulate him.

As a teenager, Ray worked in Masson's vineyard and winery, concealing the specifics from his mother, who honored her husband's memory by condemning all alcohol. The winemaker's art fascinated him, as did the way of life that went with it—a combination of hard, disciplined work and rich, sensuous enjoyment, an integration of honest, rural toil and cultured charm. Ray visited Masson often. Once when the old man asked him what he planned to do with his future, he supposedly replied: "Find some way to make money. And then buy a mountain like this one." Yet with Prohibition in full swing, wine promised only a dismal future for anyone with ambition and drive. Consequently Ray became a stockbroker after college, eventually starting his own firm in San Francisco, Ray & Company. Meanwhile, Masson struggled to keep La Cresta going, in part by shipping grapes east and in part by making sparkling wine, his being the only winery in the United States licensed for the production of "medicinal champagne." The fourteen years of struggle exhausted him. Early on the morning of December 5, 1933, the day of Repeal, Martin Ray drove up Table Mountain to ring in the good news with a giant bronze schoolhouse bell he had surreptitiously carted up there the day before. Afterward the two men shared a bottle of sparkling rosé and stood together, gazing out at the vineyards. One saw the past, while the other looked to the future.

Drained by his battles with bootleggers and lacking the energy to face the new challenge of Repeal, Paul Masson decided to sell his winery and retire. Martin Ray used all his savings to buy it. In 1936, he and his wife moved into La Cresta, the old man having retained a plot of land for a small home of his own. For the next four years, until Masson's death, the two men shared a life centered around wine—walks in the vineyards, trips to the cellar, long dinners filled with bottle after bottle and story after story. These, Ray would say later, were the best years of all. Around that time a rumor started to the effect that he was Masson's illegitimate son. It wasn't true, but the two did have a great deal in common. Both were stubborn and principled. Both loved what Ray called the good life, and were willing to work long and hard to attain it. Most important, both viewed the havoc wrought by Prohibition and its legacy with disdain. They considered fine wine an essential part of that good life, and they thought the sweet, fortified swill beginning to flood the market an abomination.

At La Cresta, Ray kept the Paul Masson brand alive. He bottled the wines with the old labels, adding in small print, "Martin Ray, proprietor." His goal quite simply was to make world-class wines. That there was no American market for them hardly bothered him, for even then he had an arrogance that some people attributed to genius and others to near insanity. In 1941, a fire destroyed La Cresta. Ray rebuilt the winery, but with its founder now dead, he felt free to sell the estate—to Joseph Seagram, the Canadian spirits conglomerate, which like all the big distillers during the Second World War was willing to pay top dollar. With the profits, Ray and his wife purchased property on the other side of Table Mountain, up a road named Mount Eden. They cleared the land, planted Cabernet, Chardonnay, and Pinot Noir, and settled down to make what Ray loudly proclaimed were America's best, and indeed America's only great, wines. For the next thirty years, his Martin Ray Vineyards produced tiny quantities of those three varietals, along with blanc de blancs and blanc de noir sparkling wines, all of which developed a fiercely loyal following. "He [makes] the best wines that have ever been made in the United States," declared the revered connoisseur and Francophile Julian Street. "They prove what California can do if it ever gets around to following the best practices of the best vineyards."

Since few people actually tasted them, Martin Ray's significance in the larger history of American wine comes less from the wines themselves than from his at times visionary and at other times paranoid attitudes toward them. He was one of the most important winemakers of his day because he adamantly refused to grow grapes and make or sell wine in anything but his own way. Virtually alone in his generation, he understood that premium wines would have to be the ones to lead American wine out of its post-Prohibition depression. "The market for fine wines is limited," he wrote presciently in 1955. "Yet the market for all other wines is supported by it."

Ray was convinced that American wines could be the equal

of the best from France, and he complained angrily that the industry itself conspired against improved quality. Nothing infuriated him more than the then standard practice of blending inferior grapes with premium varietals. Regulations required that a wine contain a minimum of 51 percent of any one variety in order to be labeled as such. Since inspectors hardly ever checked, many blends contained far less. Ray railed against both practice and rule, insisting that authentic varietals needed to be made completely from a single grape variety. (The requirement was raised to 75 percent in 1983; he would not have been satisfied.) He also objected to the use of generic names, arguing that they made good American wines appear to be mere copies of foreign originals. So too, he argued strenuously for an American appellation system, a quality-control program that would regulate which grape varieties could be grown in which locations. In an era when over 90 percent of California vineyard land was planted to poor wine grapes (Alicante Bouschet, French Colombard, and such), he pioneered using only the most noble varieties. "*Prestige* is the key," he declared. "Look at the French. Because their fine wines are truly elegant, their prestige permits France to market not only those finest wines at fabulous prices, but a vast volume of shippers' mediocre wines at prices far higher than our volume wines . . . California can never compete with French wines until we protect truly fine varietals as they do."

In making this argument, Martin Ray was ahead of his time. During the 1950s, the California wine industry made its profits by selling vast amounts of cheap wine, and even those few producers who aimed to make something better financed their premium lines with the sale of inexpensive blends and fortifieds. Ray regarded them with contempt. "California wine-growing from the first has unfortunately drawn to it unprincipled profit-seekers," he wrote, adding that it will take "many years to overcome their influence."

Although he issued diatribe after diatribe in both print and conversation, Martin Ray's more characteristic response to the sad state of American wine was retreat—up his isolated mountain to what he called his "vineyard in the sky." He never joined the Wine Institute, refused to enter his wines in fairs or competitions, and had nothing to do with the regular business of selling wine—mass-market distribution, restaurant sales, competitive tastings. His production was so small that he never had to do any of these things. Instead, he made and sold his wines by hand, bottling them in thick, heavy glass replete with wire cages atop the corks, and shipping them in polished wood cases. He charged astronomical prices—$6 for a bottle of 1948 Cabernet and $12 for the 1952, $24 for the 1962 Chardonnay (which he proclaimed "the world's greatest white wine"), and $50 for the 1970. He defended such prices by noting that the top growths from France cost much the same, and argued that he made wines to "be favorably drunk against the best." He felt no need to go down Table Mountain and proselytize as a salesman. People with taste, he always insisted, would find their way to his door.

One who did just that was Warren Winiarski, who had read about Martin Ray in Chicago. Although Winiarski had not tasted the wines, he wrote what he remembers as "sort of a fan letter," asking "Mr. Ray" about the possibility of going to Saratoga and apprenticing there. Ray, surely flattered, invited him for a week's trial, during which the young would-be vintner did a bit of everything—pruning, driving a tractor in a newly cleared vineyard, bottling wine in the winery. Recalling the experience years later, Winiarski described life up Table Mountain with wonder:

> It was a fantastic experience . . . Everything had its special magic . . . Martin had accumulated a number of bells from schoolhouses that were no longer being used as schoolhouses. On occasions, when visitors came, they rang those bells. It was like a cathedral with all its bells ringing. It was ceremonial; it was formal; it was very special. It called for your taking strong notice, that this was not without its "breath of divinity," for it invited comparison with its churchlike original. The quality of life there—there was nothing ordinary; not a thing was left to its ordinary disposition. It tried to be heightened, enhanced, increased in meaning. After a while you had to sort of rub your eyes, because you couldn't believe all this was happening.

The heightened experience of life on the mountain extended to the wines themselves, which Winiarski remembers as "extraordinary, stunning, [with] a degree of artistic excellence that I had not experienced in California wines before." The week's trial never led to anything more, Ray having decided that his academic visitor seemed too headstrong and independent. But after returning to Chicago, Winiarski knew where his future lay —in a vineyard and a cellar, not just with wine but with really fine wine, someplace where he could make art out of nature's bounty and take "strong notice" of life itself. Less than a year later, he moved to Napa and started work at Lee Stewart's Souverain Cellars.

Not everyone found time with Martin Ray magical. Opinionated to the point of obstinacy and proud to the point of petulance, he took affront at even the hint of any disagreement, and regularly would expel guests from his property for having the gall to express their own opinions. It made little difference that he sometimes was wrong. He insisted, for instance, that all great wines were made from single grape varieties. When people who had been there told him that winemakers in Bordeaux blend Merlot and other varieties with Cabernet, he blew up, declaring them liars and infidels. And in truth, not everyone loved his wines. He refused to use sulfur in winemaking and never filtered anything, with the not surprising result that some of his wines became oxidized and spoiled. Rather than admit that a particular lot had gone bad, he would drink the wines, declare them wonderful, and expect everyone else to agree. When someone demurred—a customer, for example, who might complain that an expensive case of white wine was brown and dirty—he would respond with attacks, often refusing to serve or sell the person anything more. Yet since he made so little wine, and since so much of it indeed was special, he never had trouble selling it.

The last decade of Martin Ray's life saw him become even more demanding and difficult. He organized a group of investors to buy stock in an expanded vineyard he called Mount Eden, but his relations with them soon soured and he ended up in court, where he lost almost everything he had. By the time he died in 1976, he owned only five acres at the very top of the mountain. The rest of the property, now a separate entity controlled by the stockholders, had become Mount Eden Vineyards. Merry Edwards, one of California's first important female vintners, was the winemaker there, and she remembers him in his last years, frail but still fiercely proud, coming down to the winery where she helped him make his final vintage. "Crazy," she says with a shake of her head, "just crazy." But she also remembers the wines—"some of them . . . incredible."

Had he lived longer, Martin Ray would have seen much of what he championed come to pass. Accurate varietal labeling, the demise of generics, the emergence of geographic appellations, and the radical shift of focus in the industry at large, with fine wine leading and supporting the broader market—all this is what his example helped inspire. And the next generation of wine growers often found personal inspiration in his story. For Martin Ray created a life in which wine was more than a source of income and more than a simple beverage. To him, wine was rich and exciting, vibrant and vital—deeply, truly *fine.* "I think the lesson was invaluable for me," says Warren Winiarski, recalling his week atop the mountain. "To see something of what I wanted to achieve . . . it took someone of that huge magnitude and capability to show what was possible."

Martin Ray's own inspiration was plain. In all he did, he followed the example of the old Burgundian Paul Masson, who in the days before Prohibition had created a winemaking estate devoted to artisanal production. The boutique producers who followed Ray in the 1970s and 1980s tried to do much the same thing. They wanted their wines to convey something of their own individual styles and personalities, but they shared a common goal—to handcraft elite, exclusive wines that could compete with the finest imports. Those wines were made on a sometimes unconscious but perhaps inevitable French model. Cabernet producers like Warren Winiarski at Stag's Leap paid homage to Bordeaux's classic character. In a similar vein, Jack and Jamie Davies's sparklers at Schramsberg Vineyard emulated Champagne. The Davieses also had been inspired by Martin Ray. "It was quite something," Jack Davies later recalled when describing his and his wife's first afternoon spent atop Table Mountain, a lunch that lasted well into the night and included wine after memorable wine. "It certainly made an impact on us." The impact proved strong enough to entice the couple to invest in Ray's stock scheme, and then a few years later to go into the wine business by themselves. In 1965, they purchased Jacob Schram's historic estate, where they decided to make *méthode champenoise* sparkling wines. "We thought there was a possibility to pick out a niche where somebody else wasn't already paying a lot of attention," Jack recalled. "It really grew out of that experience with Martin Ray . . . [who] made some very interesting champagnes . . . We had a chance to taste them; not many people ever had a chance to taste those wines." In 1972 President Nixon took Schramsberg "champagne" with him on his historic trip to China, where it was served at his state dinner with Premier Zhou Enlai. By then, for Jack and Jamie Davies, as for a growing number of boutique winemakers, the future Martin Ray had envisioned was dawning fast.

Wines from Bordeaux and Champagne clearly gave American winemakers stylistic targets, but for small producers in the 1970s aiming to make exclusively premium wines, Burgundy provided a more enticing model. To some, especially those focusing on Chardonnay, that model might include winemaking styles and techniques. More often, though, it involved broader

matters of philosophy and desire. For the notion of wine providing a way of life rooted in the land, the notion that Martin
Ray inherited from Paul Masson and in turn passed on to a new
generation, was at heart Burgundian. Unlike Bordeaux and
Champagne, where the wine trade traditionally was controlled
by aristocrats (and today by corporate executives), wine in Burgundy remained by and large the province of small, independent growers. It still does. Champagne houses usually operate
on a large scale, their production facilities in Rheims or Éper-
nay lying behind (or beneath) glittering architectural and marketing façades, while producers in Bordeaux invariably think of
their estates, even ones that are actually humble, as *châteaux*. By
contrast, a Burgundian *domaine* is likely to be little more than a
farm or townhouse, the cellar small, the production limited. No
patrician or nobleman, the successful Burgundian wine grower
is still a farmer—probably an haute bourgeois farmer with
plenty of francs in the bank, but a farmer nonetheless. In California in the 1960s and 1970s, the notion of the winemaker as
gentleman farmer became grafted onto the politics and culture
of the day, particularly the "back to nature" environmental
movement and the more general anti-establishment tenor of
the times. This is not to suggest that the boutique producers
were counterculture radicals. Far from it. Starting and running
a winery takes money—lots of money—and most of these
new, small facilities were funded by wealthy businessmen who
espoused fairly conservative political views. However, they
were looking for an opportunity to exchange their suits for
jeans (albeit usually designer jeans) and start a new life in nature
—not the raw, cruel nature of wilderness, but the refined nature of the vineyard. Jack Davies, himself a refugee from the

corporate world, spoke for many of his generation when he said of his and his wife's decision to buy Schramsberg: "We didn't view this as a business venture in totality; we wanted to try to figure out if we couldn't do something that was a life in itself. The place itself was very important."

For some boutique producers, the place was important primarily because of the lifestyle that came with it—or that they brought to it. In Napa, and to a lesser degree Sonoma, that lifestyle often included a democratic, distinctly California version of English country living. A kind of rural chic, it soon became featured in the pages of *Town and Country* and was neatly symbolized by the Napa Wine Auction, an annual fundraising event to benefit local hospitals that quickly became the year's premier, because most visible, social event—*the* place to see and be seen. Being a vintner began to carry a certain cachet, one that, as James Conaway notes in *Napa*, his chronicle of the valley's economic and social changes, "involved the *idea* of wine rather than the reality of producing and selling it."

Elsewhere, especially in wine-growing regions beyond California, the way of life was more down-to-earth. Because of lower vineyard prices, less money was needed to get started in other states. Consequently, the desired lifestyle did not necessarily involve wealth, or at least not conspicuous wealth. The proprietor of a small winery in the East or Pacific Northwest most likely could not afford to hire a winemaker or vineyard manager, so probably did those jobs him- or herself. On the North Fork of Long Island, for example, Louisa and Alex Hargrave opened the region's first commercial winery (named Hargrave Vineyard) in 1974. They aimed to make French-style wines and operate on a Burgundian model, all with a distinctly

American twist. "We wanted the Jeffersonian ideal," says Alex. "To have a small farm, to connect with the land, and to use our minds." The North Fork was home mainly to potato farms then, and land was relatively cheap. "One reason we came here," recalls Louisa, "is that it was a farm community, so we knew we could get tractor parts." The image of the artisanal, agrarian yeoman, working the land and enjoying the rarefied fruit of his labor, inspired a new generation of winemakers across the country who either raised the standard in established regions or brought viticulture to new or abandoned areas. The Hargraves on Long Island, Douglas Moorhead near Lake Erie in Pennsylvania, Gary Figgins and Rick Small in Washington, Dick Erath, David Lett, Dick Ponzi, Susan Sokol and Bill Blosser in Oregon—these were some of the agrarian *artistes* who in the 1970s pioneered premium *vinifera* grape growing and winemaking outside California. For all of them, the land and the life they made on it was very, very important.

Place mattered for yet another reason. Some winemakers had the Burgundian model so fixed in their sights that they searched for land that geologically, even more than culturally, would sustain it. In the summer of 1973, for example, a young academic émigré who had spent a couple of months in the Côte d'Or and fallen in love with the wines and the way of life there went looking for vineyard land to buy in California. He carried around with him a bottle of sulfuric acid to pour on the ground whenever he found an interesting site, in order to determine whether the soil contained limestone, which he had been told was the crucial factor in Burgundy's vineyards. He looked all over northern California, finally finding a place where the acid fizzed and bubbled. So on the eastern side of the Gavilan

Mountains in Monterey County, in rattlesnake-infested back-country that no one before had thought of cultivating, Josh Jensen planted Pinot Noir and set about trying to make American versions of classic red Burgundies. His model was quite specific: the Domaine de la Romanée-Conti, the famed estate where he had picked grapes during the 1970 harvest. Now at his own property, called Calera, he copied as much as possible the estate's methods of pruning and harvesting, as well as its noninterventionist, natural style of winemaking. Jensen's imitative vision was very narrow. If he was the winemaker as artist, his aesthetic was the ancient Greek one of mimesis rather than the more romantic one of originality, for he thought of Calera's vineyard-designated wines as echoes of Burgundy's Platonic forms—Romanée-Conti's La Tâche, Échézeaux, and the rest.

Others were somewhat less narrow in their focus but equally committed to an artisanal imitation of Burgundian ideals. Over the mountains, with the Pinnacles National Monument rearing in the background, a Harvard music graduate and wine lover, Richard Graff, had resuscitated a remote vineyard (with its share of limestone) in the late 1960s. Graff took a year's worth of classes in enology at the University of California at Davis before plunging into winemaking, but a trip to Burgundy convinced him to adopt an old-fashioned attitude in addition to using modern, technology-centered techniques. He did not emulate one particular *domaine*, but rather followed what he considered the French "holistic" approach to wine. "Most Americans, most scientifically trained enologists, look at wine in a very linear, very objective manner," he explained. "But the other way of looking at it is holistically. Wine is perceived as coming from a vineyard and the function of the winemaker is to permit the grapes to achieve their maximum potential." Graff's winery, Chalone, soon gained renown for rich, mineral-scented Chardonnay that resembled Meursault, and earthy, rich Pinot that sometimes echoed Corton or Gevrey-Chambertin. Full of entrepreneurial energy, Graff would go on to expand Chalone, not with new land on the mountainside, but with the acquisition of separate estates that together formed a small, Burgundian empire—Acacia in Carneros, Carmenet in Sonoma, and Edna Valley in San Luis Obispo. In 1984, he and his partner, Philip Woodward, took the company public, but Graff's approach stayed resolutely hands-on. He would commute to each of the four wineries every week, and continued to look to Burgundian practices for guidance.

While Graff and Jensen were motivated by memories of specific wines and specific places, other producers aimed more broadly, their goal being simply to "make the best." So said Brice Jones, a former air force pilot who formed a grape-growing concern in Sonoma County in the early 1970s primarily to try to profit from his country's shifting tastes. Jones liked wine but was no connoisseur. "Back then my wife and I drank Hearty Burgundy and C. K. Mondavi in jugs," he remembers with a laugh. He quickly learned that experts considered grand cru Burgundies to be "the best" white wines. So when he discovered that real money could come from selling premium wines rather than just grapes, he decided to build a winery—Sonoma-Cutrer Vineyards—dedicated solely to the production of Chardonnay. From the start, Jones wanted to produce the finest wines possible, so he spared no expense on equipment and technique. Sonoma-Cutrer quickly became known for a nearly obsessive concern with detail, including the use of specially ventilated picking boxes, a chilling tunnel, an incredibly severe process of grape selection, twice-weekly topping of barrels, and much more. "The finest fruit, handled in the finest way," was Jones's mantra. "We could make wine much cheaper," he acknowledged. "Golly, we don't have to cull every bad grape out. But if you want to make the best Chardonnay in the world, you do." Jones was no eccentric Burgundy wannabe. His goal was to ride, indeed to lead, the white wine boom of the 1970s and 1980s, but like Jensen and Graff, he advocated artisanal imitation. "Remember," he says, "it's the sincerest flattery."

Jensen on his mountain, Graff flying by Cessna between the different Chalone Group estates, Jones in his office (or on the manicured croquet lawn) at Sonoma-Cutrer—these different men represent in different ways the first stage of the boutique movement that helped change the face of American wine. For them, fine American wine was defined exclusively in terms of fine French wine, because fine French wine seemed so obviously different from the mass-produced generics that dominated the American market. None of them produced large numbers of bottles, so none of their wines was ever widely consumed. Their small production enabled them to sell more to restaurants than to retail shops, and their wines, which cost a pretty penny, soon developed a reputation as something exclusive—much, indeed, like the great but rare wines from Burgundy. Their bottom-line success helped inspire the large-volume producers to begin to change, for that success demonstrated that Americans would spend top dollar for American wine.

Some of the changes at the large companies were cosmetic

—bottle shapes, for instance, or corks rather than screw caps. Others were more substantial—huge expanses of vineyard land being replanted with Chardonnay rather than French Colombard, or the new trend of importing small French oak barrels for aging. As consumers shifted from fortifieds and spirits to table wines, the market shifted with them, especially since these new wine drinkers (as opposed to the skid-row drinkers of old) had money to spend. Soon Gallo, United Vintners, and the other large producers began to change the style of their better wines. In doing so, they did not follow French models so much as the American wines that had become successful by imitating French models—Robert Mondavi's most obviously, but also the artisanal bottlings from boutiques like Calera, Chalone, and Sonoma-Cutrer. For these wines, primarily because of their exclusivity, were raising the image and prestige of American wine at large, winning plaudits from critics and winning places on the toniest restaurant lists and in the most exclusive cellars. Soon Sonoma-Cutrer's Les Pierres Chardonnay was competing for space on restaurant lists with the wines of Puligny-Montrachet; Chalone's Reserve Chardonnay was selling out even before it was released; and Calera's vineyard-designated Pinot Noirs were being described by the wine critic Robert Parker as "the Chambertins of California." There could be no greater praise. Like Martin Ray, who toiled in isolation before them, Graff, Jensen, and Jones had a simple goal—to create handcrafted American versions of the greatest French wines. As Richard Graff explained, "I'm simply carrying forward a tradition that has hundreds of years of history before us in France."

But did first-rate American wine necessarily have to taste like first-rate French wine? That was one way to interpret the results of Stephen Spurrier's Paris tasting, where unknown American wines triumphed by seeming indistinguishable from celebrated French ones. Yet a more radical view of the Paris tasting revealed that greatness no longer needed to be defined in a traditional fashion — that is, as a product of historic appellations. Equally fine wines apparently now could come from vineyards that did not have centuries of grape-growing history. The elements constituting great wine thus had to be reconceived. Rather than being thought of extrinsically, in terms of fabled vineyard or property, great wine could be thought of intrinsically, in terms of its present composition. This sort of reformulation appealed to many American vintners. Since they did not have the sort of tradition that distinguished great European wines, they focused instead on inherent quality, defined by terms such as length and depth of flavor, balance, and most important, complexity. These words had been used for generations by connoisseurs, but because the pool of the world's great wines had been so limited, they were linked in people's minds (and taste memories) with specific examples. Balance in white wine, for instance, was not just the interplay of fruit and acid, but more precisely that interplay as realized in premier or grand cru Burgundy. And length was not just the amount of time that sensations lingered on one's palate, but that time as expressed in the intensity of a first- or second-growth Bordeaux. The rise of American wine gradually challenged such associations, as American wine growers slowly discovered that obedience to foreign models did not really produce clones of foreign wines. American growing conditions were not the same as French ones, so no matter how closely they might follow traditional techniques, their wines tasted different—sometimes subtly, sometimes extremely so. Some winemakers viewed that difference as a problem and worked to minimize it. Others, however, began to exploit it. They strived to make wines that would resemble the Old World originals while simultaneously asserting a New World identity all their own.

For the most part, these wines had to come from the classic grape varieties. After all, *vinifera* was itself an import. In this regard, it is helpful to remember how few intrinsically good wines were being produced in the world in the 1950s and 1960s. American jug wine was pretty bad, but so was a great deal of French *vin ordinaire* or Italian *vino da tavola*. As soon as people felt the stirrings of the ambition to make something more than *ordinaire*, they had to look to classic models. The question became what to do with those models—whether to imitate them slavishly or to use them primarily as inspiration. In one sense, the die already had been cast: premium American wines by and large would be made from European grapes. Yet in another sense, the game was just beginning. It gradually became evident that American wines could have the inherent marks of quality—balance, depth, length, and complexity— and not necessarily copy foreign styles. Thus the next stage in the rise of American wine, again led in large measure by boutique wineries, involved the often difficult struggle to define American styles, ones that someday might lead to the establishment of genuinely American winemaking and wine-drinking traditions.

It began with Chardonnay. Although famed for centuries as Burgundy's great white grape, Chardonnay hardly grew anywhere in America before Prohibition. Some acreage had been cultivated here and there, notably twenty or so by Carl and Ernest Wente in the Livermore Valley, east of the San Francisco Bay. (The Wentes almost single-handedly kept the variety alive in the 1920s with the "Wente clone," which later became the source of many of California's most successful plantings.) A few iconoclasts, Martin Ray among them, grew it in the post-Prohibition era, but as late as 1959, fewer than two hundred acres of Chardonnay existed in all of the United States.

It is worth considering why this particular grape variety was not more popular. For centuries, people grew Chardonnay in only three places: Champagne, Chablis, and the Cote d'Or, all in northern France. What unites these three (and separates them from most other European wine-growing regions) is weather—specifically a cool, sometimes bone-chilling climate. All three lie near the northern limit of European viticulture— Champagne, in fact, being so far north that grapes there rarely ripen sufficiently for table wine. Growing Chardonnay in such marginal conditions can be difficult, as spring frosts and autumn rains always threaten to ruin the crop, but the cool climate gives the grapes a relatively high level of acidity, which in turn is what provides the young wines with structure and gives them the ability to age and develop in the bottle. Without sufficient acidity, Chardonnay will produce flabby, innocuous wines, which was precisely the problem in warm, sunny California. (The grape also tends to rot in hot, humid weather, which remains a problem in vineyards east of the Rockies.) So for years, American growers had no incentive to plant Chardonnay. There was virtually no consumer interest in it; most of the wines seemed unexceptional; and the vines had lower yields than many other grape varieties. Generic "chablis," made from French Colombard, Chenin Blanc, and plenty of Thompson Seedless, did just fine—until, that is, the emergence of the fine-wine passion that inspired a new generation of vintners to try to make wines on a par with the world's best.

Why that generation pursued Chardonnay rather than Sauvignon Blanc and Sémillon, the classic white grapes of Bordeaux, or even Riesling, the great German wine grape, remains a minor mystery. The best explanation is probably the most obvious—namely, that because white Burgundies were regarded by connoisseurs as the greatest white wines in the world, a producer with a fine-wine ambition invariably wanted to make Chardonnay. Then in the 1970s, when consumers began to drink more and more white wine, the producers who were shifting from generics to varietals all scrambled to include it in their portfolios. A glass of Chardonnay fast became a popular alternative to the more potent before-dinner cocktail, and for growers, the grape brought big profits. Acidification, the practice of adding acid to a wine in order to bring it into balance, was legal in California, so grapes grown in even hot regions could produce palatable wines. Chardonnay, a grape variety that previously had been considered difficult (because it was both untested and shybearing when compared with the other popular white varieties), actually turned out to be very adaptable. By 1970, more than 3,000 acres were under vine in California, with a few fledgling plantings in the Pacific Northwest. A decade later, the number had grown to 20,000, and by 1990 nearly 60,000 acres in the United States were devoted to Chardonnay—a name that for many Americans had by then become almost synonymous with premium white wine.

Over those twenty years, a recognizably Californian and then American style of Chardonnay emerged. It emphasized ripe, rich, succulent fruit, sometimes going so far as to substitute power and brawn for subtlety and grace. Full of flavor, it was ideal for wines drunk by themselves, without food, as many were in the era's fern bars and discos as well as kitchens and living rooms. During the late 1970s and early 1980s, some producers reacted against this emerging style by making what came to be known as the period's "food wines"—thin, sour, early-picked Chardonnays that claimed sophistication but actually provided only unpleasant tartness. These denied the ripeness that the vineyards naturally wanted to provide, and soon the movement toward rich, lush wines resumed momentum. Chardonnay grown outside California often turned out to be more restrained, but even on Long Island and in Texas and Washington, all places where the grape now grew, the goal usually was ripeness above all else. By the late 1980s, American Chardonnay could assert a full-blown, fruit-driven identity of its own, one inspired but not constrained by the original French model.

This is not to say that all American Chardonnays tasted the same. Different techniques produced different results in different regions, and the variety lent itself readily to winemaking experimentation and exhibitionism. Some wines, like Sonoma-Cutrer's Les Pierres, remained dressed in Burgundian garb—not only in the choice of name, but also in character, being initially austere and mineral-scented, then long and intensely elegant. Others, like Richard Arrowood's vineyard-des-

ignated wines at Sonoma's Chateau St. Jean, were more forward and unabashedly American. Yet despite these differences,
the top American Chardonnays (at first exclusively from California, but then later including wines from Washington, Oregon, Virginia, New York, even Pennsylvania) almost all shared
certain inherent characteristics: a sometimes tenuous balance
that worked against longevity but that provided plenty of near-
term pleasure; a depth of flavor and aroma marked by intensity
rather than nuance; a concentration of fruit instead of mineral
or earthy character; and a rich, almost opulent texture. In
terms of winemaking, the one constant was oak—specifically,
small imported barrels of French oak. Used for aging and
sometimes for fermentation, French oak gave the wines a
nutty, vanillin flavor and a creamy, buttery texture—as
Hanzell's James Zellerbach and then Robert Mondavi had so
presciently discovered years earlier. Oak barrels, however, were
expensive. Small wineries aiming to produce only premium
wines could afford them, but larger wineries had to be more
cautious. At the beginning of the white wine boom, when no
one was sure that the public at large (as opposed to the connoisseur who bought boutique wines) liked the character these
barrels imparted, it made no sense for a volume producer to
spend hundreds of thousands of dollars on them. Oak-aged
Chardonnays thus initially came almost exclusively from small
wineries, and even today some consumers associate this style
primarily with boutique winemaking. Before long, though, it
became clear that the public loved the taste and smell of oak.
Inevitably, the large producers followed suit, buying (sometimes even manufacturing) barrels or, in the case of their inexpensive Chardonnays, using oak chips to flavor the wines. The

taste of oak rapidly became a defining element in American-style Chardonnay.

By the mid-1980s, nearly every California winery included Chardonnay in its portfolio. Many of these wines were quite good, but only a few proved extraordinary. One winemaker whose wines were consistently rated exceptional was Mike Grgich, who had a winemaking style very much his own. Four years after his Parisian triumph, his 1977 Grgich Hills Chardonnay was named "the best in the world" at an international Chardonnay tasting in Chicago, and in 1990 the critic James Laube declared, "If I were forced to choose only one California Chardonnay to drink and cellar each year, it would probably be Grgich Hills." Grgich's techniques were not special. In order to help the wines age, he did eschew malolactic fermentation (the transformation of malic acid into lactic acid, which softens white wines), but he employed all the other methods that had become commonplace at premium wineries —for instance, fermentation and aging in French oak barrels. What, then, made his wines special? "I believe in a small operation with direct contact," he told an interviewer in 1992. "That way [I] have one style." Grgich did not rely primarily on technology, though he did hire Davis graduates as his assistants and never was averse to change. Nor did he emphasize soil, though he was sensitive to how different vineyards produced different fruit. Instead, he remained true to a vision of artisanal creation that had first become clear during his short stint at Souverain Cellars. "The winemaker makes a big difference," he insisted. "People say grapes, grapes, grapes, but anyone can make vinegar out of the best grapes." This Croatian-born winemaker with the accented voice and trademark beret embodied the most American of virtues—self-reliance. "I, as one person, oversee everything," he insisted. "I keep the winery [small] so that I can keep it under control." Grgich did not even bother to taste his wines against the competition's. "I used to do that at Robert Mondavi," he recalled. "Mondavi always compared his wine with somebody else's. [I] have [my own] style, and I'm only going to compare my style with my new wines so that [I] stay not in the style of somebody else but in [my] own style." As much if not more than any other, the Grgich Hills style, which deftly navigated a middle course between opulence and restraint, helped raise the standard for American Chardonnay. It demonstrated that New World wines need not be marked by excess, and at the same time that excellence need not entail slavish imitation of foreign models.

Things proved more complicated with Burgundy's classic red grape, Pinot Noir. The California heat, just the factor that made growing Chardonnay easy (although getting the wine in balance difficult), made most Golden State Pinots taste fat and clumsy. The obvious solution was to pick the grapes earlier, but the resulting wines then tasted thin and weedy, if not downright bizarre. Part of the problem came in the winery, where winemakers tended to treat Pinot as they did Cabernet or other red varieties, handling it without sufficient care and trying to extract too much color from it. Part also came in the vineyard, as Pinot is a notoriously fickle variety, sensitive to minute variables of soil, climate, and drainage. Most California Pinot Noir in the 1960s and 1970s simply was planted in areas that were too warm. Chardonnay in similar sites produced acceptable wines, but Pinot proved more temperamental. Consequently, while a few first-rate wines emerged, many more turned out to be disappointments. Moreover, the good wines seemed idiosyncratic, with little stylistic consistency between vintages and producers. Not until the 1990s would California wineries produce more than the occasional fine bottle of Pinot Noir. By then, site selection had become more specialized, and better clones were being used. A wine's stylistic identity was being conceived in the more precise terms of region, as opposed to state or county—Carneros, for example, or the Russian River or Santa Maria Valleys.

The one place that achieved some success with Pinot Noir in the early years of American wine's rise was Oregon, specifically the Willamette Valley south of Portland. Here too, small producers led the way. The initial pioneers were David Lett and Chuck Coury, refugees from the University of California at Davis, who planted Oregon's first Pinot Noir grapes in 1966. Coury went broke and returned to California, but Lett struggled and survived. The turning point for him came in 1979, when his 1975 Eyrie Reserve finished in third place in the Gault-Millau Wine Olympiad in Paris. Hardly anyone in the French wine trade had even heard of Oregon, so the widespread suspicion held that the wine's strong showing must have been a fluke. The respected Burgundy *négociant* Robert Drouhin organized another tasting the next year, featuring venerable wines from his own cellar. The 1975 Eyrie came in second this time, behind Drouhin's 1959 Chambolle-Musigny but ahead of his 1961 Chambertin Clos de Bèze. Soon a new wave of producers began to buy land and plant vineyards in Oregon, including Robert Drouhin himself. There still was no recognizable Oregon style, since virtually every winemaker with serious aspirations deliberately copied Burgundy—often in terms of technique, always in terms of the desired result. Nonetheless, for a time the Willamette Valley seemed the one place in the country capable of producing world-class Pinot Noir. At least it could do so every once in a while, the vintages there being extremely variable.

There was no such problem with Cabernet Sauvignon, the grape that regularly produced California's and indeed the United States' finest wines. Of all the classic French varieties, Cabernet had the longest and most illustrious American history, having made the reputation of more than one nineteenth-century estate. It is impossible to know what those wines tasted like back then. But in 1960, when André Simon, the undisputed leader of the British wine trade and founder of the International Wine and Food Society, tasted the 1887 Inglenook Cabernet Sauvignon, he pronounced it "every bit as fine as my favorite pre-phylloxera clarets." Cabernet's history gave it a leg up on other varieties when the American wine boom got under way in the 1960s. Because people had grown it sporadically but successfully in northern California all during the long, dark post-Prohibition era, it was universally acknowledged to be the region's finest red wine grape. When the new generation of producers with their new fine-wine ambitions arrived on the scene, it only made sense that they would plant more. The dominant grape in the celebrated first growths of Bordeaux's left bank (Châteaux Haut-Brion, Lafite-Rothschild, Latour, Margaux, and after 1973, Mouton-Rothschild), Cabernet had a special affinity for the North Coast's growing conditions, so it was the obvious choice to lead any American challenge to French supremacy. The legend of pre-Prohibition glory, coupled with the obvious high quality of the fruit in the vineyard and the quite good wines already being produced in small quantities by wineries like Beaulieu and Inglenook, made it inevitable that Cabernet Sauvignon would make a bold statement on the world scene. At first the exciting wines came almost exclusively from Napa. Soon, however, superb Cabernets were coming from Sonoma, especially the Alexander Valley, and then Mendocino, Paso Robles, Santa Cruz, the Sierra foothills, and the Columbia Valley in Washington State.

It did not take long for an American style of Cabernet to emerge. Much as happened with Chardonnay, this style emphasized bold flavor over finesse and fruit over earth. Yet while many of the era's full-blown Chardonnays flirted with excess, the acids and tannins in Cabernet tended to harness the wine's energy and keep the different elements in check. There certainly were variations between and even within regions. In Napa, for instance, grapes grown in the southern end of the valley usually produced more herbaceous wines than those grown near St. Helena or Calistoga. Many of the valley's finest wines, however, were blends of grapes grown in different locales, thus minimizing local distinctions in favor of a more general stylistic goal. That goal, the Napa style of effusive fruitiness and sweet oak spice, soon came to be emulated by winemakers in other California wine-growing areas and then in other states. Robert Mondavi's Cabernets, especially his Reserve, played an important role here, especially after 1972, the year in which his 1969 Cabernet (made by Mike Grgich) triumphed in a tasting held at the Buena Vista Winery that allegedly identified California's best. Small wineries played equally important parts. Joe Heitz, at Heitz Wine Cellars, led the way. He had started his business in 1961, and by the mid-

1970s his two single-vineyard Cabernets, from Bella Oaks and Martha's Vineyard, had become collectors' items, the first Napa wines to achieve cult status. (They soon were followed by others, most prominently Al Brounstein's from Diamond Creek Vineyards, and in the 1990s small-production gems from wineries such as Dalla Valle, Harlan, and Screaming Eagle.) As important in terms of style were the Cabernets from such boutique producers as Chateau Montelena, Freemark Abbey, Mayacamas, Joseph Phelps, and of course Stag's Leap. They tasted as inherently good as classic Bordeaux—meaning complex, balanced, deep, and long—but they managed at the same time to convey a robust, exuberant New World character.

Two notable small producers exploited the California (née Napa) style of Cabernet in the 1970s and early 1980s, raising it to new heights of renown. The first was the father-and-son team of Charles and Chuck Wagner at Caymus Vineyards. Fruit growers in Oakville since 1906, the Wagners decided in 1971 to hold on to some of their grapes and try their hand at small-scale commercial winemaking. They produced their first Cabernet the following year. When it and the following couple of vintages did well, they increased production and hired as their winemaker a young doctoral student (in entomology, not viticulture or enology), Randy Dunn, who previously had helped them out during harvest. Dunn fashioned the Caymus Cabernets until 1985. His wines established Caymus's reputation as one of California's finest Cabernet producers, a reputation that Chuck Wagner's work since then has only enhanced. A Caymus Cabernet, especially one of the elite Special Selection wines, possessed the same elements as a top red Bordeaux, the difference being a matter of proportion and degree. Its complexity encompassed an array of fresh and dried fruit flavors, whereas the Bordeaux more typically included notes reminiscent of leather or earth. Equally deep and long, its lingering sensations seemed slightly sweeter and softer. And it relied less noticeably on harsh tannins to provide structure. Like most top-flight California Cabernets, a Caymus wine seemed rich and ready to enjoy. Although deeply concentrated, with layer upon layer of flavor, it never felt heavy or brooding. In turn, this sort of accessibility became a critical component in the emerging American style.

The other prominent boutique producer who exploited this style was Justin Meyer at Silver Oak Wine Cellars. A former Christian Brother (and winemaker for the order), Meyer and his silent partner, Ray Duncan, founded Silver Oak in 1972. From the beginning, his philosophy was simple — "that wine should taste good when consumed, and that this expectation should be delivered whenever a customer buys a bottle." To this end, Meyer employed unconventional techniques of pressing, fermenting, and aging (using specially coopered new American oak, for instance, rather than imported French barrels) to craft soft, supple, highly perfumed wines that were ready to drink when released. Because he insisted that Silver Oak Cabernets could age, he held on to a portion of each vintage for later sale. At the same time, he insisted that his wines never needed bottle age to be enjoyed. This marked a real break with the classic model, for the greatness of top Bordeaux, especially as it historically had been defined by the British wine trade, was its ability to develop subtlety and nuance during time spent in bottle. Meyer liked young, lush, fruit-driven wines more than old, dusty ones. He wanted Cabernet to taste of plums and blackberries, not raisins or prunes, and he was willing to forgo a level of complexity in order to retain freshness. Apparently the American wine-drinking (and money-spending) public agreed with him. Silver Oak Cabernets, one bottling made from Napa fruit, another made from grapes grown in Sonoma County's Alexander Valley, attracted a fanatical following. No one mistook them for anything but unabashedly American wines.

Silver Oak's seductive wines represented only one side of premium American Cabernet production. On the other side sat plenty of harsh, tough, more tannic and less immediately friendly wines. Some, especially those made from grapes grown in mountain rather than valley vineyards, were intentionally made that way, but more often the grape growers and winemakers tried to tame the tannins, reduce any weedy or vegetal flavors, and soften (but hopefully not lighten) the wines. Such was the case in Washington State, where a reborn wine industry began to make a national mark with its red wines in the 1980s. Washington wine growers planted plenty of Cabernet, but they also emphasized Merlot, the second most important Bordeaux variety, largely because they thought it would help them produce softer, more accessible wines. Something similar happened across the country on Long Island, where Merlot slowly became the red grape of choice. Long Island red wines were not particularly rich and supple, the Atlantic climate being more severe and unforgiving than that out west, but they too were crafted with accessibility in mind. Bottle age may historically have been a mark of class, but the new American wines — no matter whether made in a big, rich California style or a more lean, aromatic one — defined quality somewhat differently. More and more of them provided delicious drinking when young. In terms of aroma and flavor, fresh fruit was what mattered most.

These grape varieties—Chardonnay, Pinot Noir, Cabernet Sauvignon, and to a lesser extent Merlot—were in no sense the exclusive province of boutique producers. As American wine's rise continued, it increasingly became clear that public tastes indeed were changing. The big-volume producers then devoted more attention to these varieties—both with their top-end wines and with their "fighting varietals." In doing so, they quite plainly followed the boutiques, who had paved the way by first emulating and then trying to assert independence from the classic French models.

Independence from those models necessitated a redefinition of the very notion of "classic"—especially as California wines began to command prices equivalent to collectible Burgundies and Bordeaux. Perhaps because of his academic training in philosophy, Warren Winiarski was one of the first people to realize as much (although Mike Grgich, for one, surely was practicing it). To Winiarski, the real lesson to be learned from the Paris tasting had been that great wines embody characteristics that transcend a specific place. Winiarski defined those characteristics as what he called "the three Rs—richness, ripeness, and restraint." He argued that while many wines are good because they represent a region, the best wines qualify as "best" precisely because they embody these more universal characteristics. "They are good any place and every place, any time and every time." If the winemaking challenge in Bordeaux and Burgundy involved attaining sufficient ripeness, the challenge in California was to restrain exuberant varietal character, thus giving the wines complexity. "There are certain wines which are regional, and their excellence is understood as an expression of the region," he argued. "[Those were] the wines that many people in California were trying to make then . . . wines that had very rich, very powerful, very ripe fruit characteristics . . . The Paris tasting showed what California grapes, with all their richness and ripeness, could attain if the wines also were styled to embody a certain restraint. These would not be wines noted for the most massive expression of ripe fruit, but would be wines expressing our regional abundance, *balanced* by moderation and restraint." That is to say, they would taste classic.

When American wine began its rise, producers large and small were dazzled by its potential. Especially in California, carefully tended vineyards produced rich, ripe wines—high in alcohol because full of sugar, with heady aromas and opulent flavors. Consumers, particularly those new to wine, were impressed, and many winemakers pursued this seductive style. Moreover, modern science and technology in both the vineyard and the winery allowed large-volume producers to make wines with a similar ripe, fruit-driven character, so that style became extremely popular. Yet other winemakers, almost always working at boutique wineries, went a step further. Like Warren Winiarski and Mike Grgich, they viewed richness and ripeness as means to a greater end—their goal being to make wines that, in Grgich's words, "are the best in the world or at least equal to the best in the world." Wines such as Grgich Hills Chardonnay and Stag's Leap Cask 23 Cabernet became the touchstones for the finest American wines, which in turn inspired larger producers to aim for greater complexity and at least a modicum of restraint. American tastes were continuing to evolve. Martin Ray had been right—the wine market functioned like an inverted pyramid, with the top end supporting all the rest. Small indeed had become beautiful. As the sales figures at wineries like Grgich Hills and Stag's Leap attested, small also had become very profitable. Demand was on the rise. For producers and consumers alike, American wine had changed. No longer was fine wine exclusively European, and no longer did the desire to make it, or simply to appreciate it, entail isolation. Now fine wine, specifically fine American wine, was becoming part of the country's cultural main current. "After four centuries during which Americans dined without wine," wrote Leon Adams in 1985, "it is finally here to stay."

7

Beyond
California

THEY CAME to wine from far afield. Whether scientists or farmers, corporate executives or urban exiles, the men and women who inspired American wine's rise in states outside California had little experience in vineyards or cellars. Even more than their Golden State counterparts, they worked without benefit of tradition and the reassuring knowledge of past accomplishment. Walter Clore, for instance, the son of teetotaling parents in Oklahoma, had never even tasted wine when he started growing grapes in 1937 as part of a horticulture fellowship at Washington State College. Clore worked at a small research center near the town of Prosser in the Columbia River Valley. Most of the area was tumbleweed desert, but irrigation was beginning to bring commercial agriculture to the region. Clore experimented with apples and other fruits, including pears, all sorts of berries, and some twenty varieties of grapes in a small test plot. "With one million acres of the Columbia Basin to be irrigated," he recalls, "I felt like a pioneer."

Walter Clore's work at Prosser blazed new trails in many

agricultural fields, but none more than viticulture. It took nearly forty years, but by the 1970s his scientific studies had completely transformed Washington wine growing, positioning Washington to become what it is today, America's second most important wine-producing state. He provided conclusive, objective evidence that premium *vinifera* wines could be made from Washington grapes, and soon the best of those wines began to compete successfully with the best from both Europe and California. A similar transformation took place in other parts of the country, as areas with either no history of wine growing or a post-Prohibition history of low-quality production started to experiment with premium table wines. The pioneers included other scientists, men such as George Ray McEachern in Texas and Bruce Zoecklein in Virginia, as well as investors with deep pockets and big ambitions such as John Dyson in New York and Earl Samson in Rhode Island. They also included farmers like Jim and Betty Held in Missouri who were looking for a new crop to grow, urban refugees like Dick Erath, David Lett, and Dick Ponzi in Oregon who wanted to "get back" to nature, and wine-loving individualists like Kip Bedell on Long Island and Dennis Horton in Virginia who dreamed of doing something different, and better, than anyone had done before. Whether motivated by research or reward, and whether to the manor born or to the land returned, they all came to wine with fresh hopes and dreams. Working primarily by trial and error, they made many mistakes, but at the same time, and in an amazingly short period of time, they brought high-quality local wine to parts of the United States that had never known it before.

Today, just as it did thirty years ago, California dominates

American wine, being home to about 90 percent of all commercial production. Nonetheless, the story of American wine's rise extends well beyond California. As of this writing, forty-eight states produce wine. Four of these have only one winery, but a dozen have more than twenty-five—including New York with 136, Washington with 125, Oregon with 116, and Virginia with 54. Indeed, just about half of the country's more than 2,000 licensed wineries are located outside California. They are mostly small, with owners and winemakers who often have upscale, boutique-style ambitions. More than anything else, those ambitions themselves reveal how much American wine has changed. During the first forty years after Prohibition, pretty much all winemaking outside California was dominated by big producers such as Taylor and Canandaigua in New York and American Wine Growers in Washington. Much like Gallo and United Vintners, these large operations focused on cheap table wines and high-alcohol fortifieds. They controlled a significant share of their local markets. Over the last twenty-five years, things have changed drastically. For one, due to shifts in consumer tastes and to advances in agricultural science, more and more *vinifera* vines have been planted in more and more places. For another, with the exception of American Wine Growers (now Chateau Ste. Michelle and part of a large multistate operation named Stimson Lane), the large producers have gone out of business or moved their winemaking operations to California. Canandaigua, for instance, remains headquartered in upstate New York, but the vast majority of its production (under mass-market labels such as Cook's and Cribari, devalued historic ones like Inglenook and Paul Masson, and premium brands like Franciscan and Simi) comes from California. The big eastern bottling plants are mostly empty now, as American jug wine production, itself a dwindling segment of the market, is centered in California's Central Valley. So over the past twenty-five years, while the percentage of American wine produced outside California has fallen slightly, the quality of that wine has risen tremendously. And for the most part, much as in California, small producers have led the way.

In the late 1960s, at the start of American wine's rise, anyone wanting to make fine wine outside California faced challenges unknown to Robert Mondavi, Warren Winiarski, Mike Grgich, and California's other renaissance winemakers. Some of these challenges involved nature—forbidding climates and untested soils. Others, though, involved politics—specifically, a host of state laws and regulations that made wine growing difficult and fine-wine growing nigh impossible. Large portions of many states, especially in the South and West, were dry, local prohibitionist laws having remained in effect long after national Repeal. In addition, in many "wet" states it was illegal to sell wine directly to consumers, as all alcoholic beverages had to be distributed either by liquor wholesalers or by government agencies. Moreover, local protectionist regulations often levied large excise taxes on wines imported not only from other countries but also from other states. These regulations appeared to benefit local winemakers, but they actually discouraged improvement by economically supporting the status quo—American wine as mass-produced plonk. They severely restricted consumer choice, and served as disincentives for anyone even thinking about trying to make different, and better, sorts of wine.

The state of Washington had especially restrictive regulations. Producers there, led by American Wine Growers, made generic "burgundy" and "sauterne" from indiscriminate blends of *vinifera* and native grapes, the prevailing wisdom holding that one type of grape was as good as the next—wine, after all, being just another form of hooch. Wines produced out of state, some of which might aspire to a higher level of quality, were charged a more than 50 percent markup and could be sold only through the state liquor board. The situation so irked California vintners that in 1958 they persuaded their state attorney general to bring suit in the United States Supreme Court, alleging a restraint of trade that violated the constitutional guarantee of freedom of commerce. "Can a state," asked their brief, "which does not prohibit the use and consumption of wine by its citizens, prescribe a wholly different economic system for the distribution, marketing, pricing, and sales promotion of wine produced elsewhere?" But the Supreme Court refused to hear the case. One of Prohibition's most insidious legacies is the tangled thicket of laws and regulations that govern the sale of alcoholic beverages throughout the country. The justices apparently considered any violation of the Constitution's Commerce Clause to be less important than the post-Repeal legislation that gave states control of the liquor trade within their borders. For ten more years, Washington wineries kept churning out cheap swill, leaving Washington consumers who might be interested in fine wine with few legal alternatives. As one well-heeled consumer complained, the law "protects Washington 'wines,' which to my palate are undrinkable."

That consumer was a University of Washington physician and professor of medicine, Belding Scribner, who issued his complaint in *Seattle Magazine* after he was arrested for "possession of illegal alcohol"—not moonshine, but his personal collection of Bordeaux and other fine wines, all of which he had by necessity purchased out of state. Agents of the state Liquor Control Board raided Scribner's house and confiscated his cellar while he was attending a medical conference in New Jersey. After he returned, he was hauled into court, where the judge ordered a six-month (suspended) jail sentence along with a $250 fine and decreed that Scribner could buy back his wine only if he paid the state a "tax" of roughly 75 percent of what he had paid for it originally. Scribner then wrote an angry article titled "A Wine Smuggler Spills All." In it, he criticized not only the law and the judge's ruling, but also the state's myopic wine industry. He called for the repeal of protectionist legislation, declaring that with an open market "Washington might well become as famous for its wines as it is for its apples and its airplanes." This was in 1969, when the change in American attitudes toward wine was just beginning its sweep across the country. Scribner's article caused a small stir, and that same year the Washington legislature did in fact act. House Bill 100, which when passed brought thirty-six years of protectionism to a close, inaugurated a new era in that state's wine history, an era rich in possibility that helped open the eyes of growers, winemakers, and legislators elsewhere.

The heated debate over Washington House Bill 100 represented in microcosm the struggle for the future of American wine. On one side were growers and winery owners with bank accounts full of profits made from selling generic table wines and heady fortifieds in a largely monopolistic environment. On the other were consumers and restaurateurs demanding choice. Both sides were well financed. The Washington Wine and

Grape Growers Council had amassed a war chest to fund lobbying efforts, while the California Wine Institute (which in the short run stood to gain the most from any change in the law) had organized a public relations campaign to drum up support for open trade. The crucial issue concerned what would happen to Washington wine if the market was opened. Ivan Kearns, executive secretary of the Wine and Grape Growers Council, predicted doom. Oregon had passed a similar free trade bill a decade earlier, and Kearns cited statistics showing that California wine had come to account for over 90 percent of Oregon sales, with two companies (Gallo and United Vintners) controlling the majority of the market. "We feel the very same thing would be applicable to us in this state," he declared. The advocates of open trade countered that the Washington industry was more established than Oregon's, and that Washington wine growers could, if they wanted, produce wines every bit as good as the new varietal wines being made in California. The turning point came when they offered proof—in the person of an agricultural scientist from the state's eastern hinterlands, Dr. Walter Clore.

Although Clore had been growing grapes at the Prosser Research Station for more than thirty years, he had only recently begun to experiment seriously with *vinifera*, largely (and ironically) because the Wine and Grape Growers Council had lobbied Washington State University to initiate new research. That research, a ten-year study launched in 1966, came to be known as the Washington Wine Project. It included both grape-growing and winemaking trials, with a total of 149 different varieties tested in various locations throughout the Columbia Valley and some 88 different types of wine produced for evaluation. Clore led the Wine Project, assisted by a team of horticulturists, agricultural economists, and chemists, notably George Carter and Charles Nagel, who assumed responsibility for the winemaking and taste testing. Although the study was only in its third year when Clore was called to testify before the state's joint senate and house Commerce and Agricultural Committee, the evidence was clear. "We have investigated the variety of grapes that are known around the world for their high quality in producing premium wines," he told the legislators, and "we have found thus far that many of these varieties seem to be well adapted here from the standpoint of producing good yields and wine of good to excellent quality."

Despite the fact that these wines came from young vines, Nagel's taste trials showed that they had "considerable promise." Clore noted that because the commercial wineries produced lower-quality wines, few farmers grew these *vinifera* varieties. Nonetheless, there was no agricultural reason for them not to try, and no enological reason for the wineries not to use their fruit. "We feel," he concluded, "that [Washington] can compete very favorably in producing top table and varietal wines with any other region in the United States. We can do it with California, and we can do it with other parts of the world." The legislators paid attention. They pointedly questioned why the state's wine industry had not tried to improve quality and concluded that, more than anything else, their own protectionist laws were to blame. So they voted to open the market and, in the process, to send Washington wine down a new path—toward *vinifera* grapes and premium quality. Ivan Kearns certainly was right: cheap California wine outperformed (and soon outsold) cheap Washington wine. But Walter Clore was right too:

premium Washington wines could hold their own with wines from anywhere. The path of quality led to the future.

Similar changes occurred in other states. In New York, the second-largest grape-growing state, the rise in consumer demand for wine in the 1960s led the big, well-established companies like Taylor and Canandaigua to increase their plantings of *labrusca* and other native grapes. When the market for these "uncomplicated wines" began to shrink, the company managers tried using neutral blending wine from California to lessen the foxy native flavor, but the advent of the California "fighting varietals" dealt them a crushing blow. Canandaigua recovered by moving aggressively into bulk and mass-market California production, while Taylor, purchased first by Coca-Cola and then by Seagram, ultimately went out of business, the only vestige of its long history being the name (which is now in fact owned by Canandaigua).

Meanwhile, a wholly different New York wine industry was born. Small producers, focusing primarily on quality table wines, began planting *vinifera* grapes on Long Island, in the Hudson River Valley, along the shores of the Finger Lakes, and in the largely Concord "grape belt" near Lake Erie. In 1976 Governor Hugh Carey sponsored a bill in the state legislature to encourage the growth of this segment of the industry. His "farm winery" bill allowed producers to sell their wine directly to consumers, thus bypassing the liquor wholesalers, who had no incentive to carry low-production products that were largely unknown to consumers and thus had to be hand sold. Carey also started a program to promote New York wines in retail stores and restaurants. He funded what became the New York Wine and Grape Foundation, which organized well-publicized tastings and an extensive public relations campaign. Using the slogan "Uncork New York," the foundation worked to change how consumers thought of the state's wines and to assist wine growers in their drive for quality. Within a year, twelve wineries opened, and by 1985 more than fifty new ones were in business. Much of their wine was not all that good, but an increasing amount of it clearly was of high quality, especially in regions where specific *vinifera* varieties performed well. In particular, Rieslings from the Finger Lakes and Merlots from Long Island demonstrated how rapidly and radically the face of New York viticulture was changing.

Similar farm winery laws revitalized wine growing in many other parts of the country. Pennsylvania passed the first such legislation in 1967. Before then, any wine made in the state could be sold only by the Liquor Control Board, which had little interest in promoting local wines. Pennsylvania was an important source of grapes, mostly Concords grown near Lake Erie, where the Welch Company operated a huge facility, but when farmers grew wine grapes, most of their crop ended up being sold out of state, usually to New York wineries. Douglas Moorhead was one such farmer. The third generation of a Concord-growing family, he returned home in 1958 from military service in Germany, his eyes (and palate) opened to how good wine could be, determined to try to grow *vinifera* grapes and make wines like those he had enjoyed when visiting the Rhine. He obtained Riesling and other grape varieties from Dr. Konstantin Frank in the Finger Lakes, and for a number of years contented himself with homemade, noncommercial wine.

As Moorhead's vines matured, though, he became convinced that the Lake Erie region could produce quality com-

mercial wines. Encouraged by the evidence in his own vineyard, he organized a number of local farmers to lobby the legislature to allow wineries to sell their wines directly to the public.
The liquor board opposed the bill, but for one of the few times
in post-Prohibition Pennsylvania history, the board did not get
its way. Within a year after passage of the state's landmark farm
winery bill, Moorhead opened Presque Isle Winery in North
East, Pennsylvania, where for more than thirty years he has
produced small lots of *vinifera* wines. Others soon followed
him, not only in the Lake Erie region but also in the southeast
corner of the state and the Lehigh Valley. Equally important,
other states began to follow Pennsylvania's legislative lead.
Some of these, like Indiana (where a farm winery act was passed
in 1971), Connecticut (1978), and Virginia (1980), had a pre-
Prohibition history of wine growing. Others, like New Hamp-
shire (1971) or Mississippi (1976), were new to wine. In some,
wine growing would go on to become a sizable industry in
terms of employment, tax revenue, and tourism. In others, it
would remain on a largely mom-and-pop scale. But no matter
the size of the operation, local wine began its rise to respectability in state after state only after it was separated from liquor
distribution and government control.

In any state where wine production became a significant
commercial enterprise, agricultural scientists, usually working
through the public university system, played a leading role.
Most of the viticultural work done at state agricultural stations
involved table and juice grapes, but the emphasis shifted when
wine production began to become commercially viable. Although the scientists rarely had much experience with wine
growing, their academic positions brought them the trust and

confidence of local farmers, many of whom were at first skeptical about grapes and wine. George Ray McEachern, for example, an extension horticulturist at Texas A&M, had advised farmers about orchard management before he began working with grapes. In 1973, he received a university grant, financed by businessmen, to conduct a trial of different grape varieties to determine whether commercial wine growing could be a realistic enterprise in Texas. He planted test vineyards throughout the state, from Texarkana to Abilene. At first "we did not know which way we wanted to go," he recalls. Texans, led by the viticulturist and grape breeder T. V. Munson, had grown wine grapes before Prohibition, but no one had made a commercial bottle of wine in the state for over fifty years. McEachern experimented with the native Munson grape varieties and with French-American hybrids, as well as with *vinifera*. About half of his vineyards died within only two years, but a few prospered, including a six-acre plot of Cabernet Sauvignon near Lubbock.

Inspired by McEachern's research, two Texas Tech professors, Clint McPherson and Robert Reed, soon planted a vineyard and started a winery. They called the vineyard Sagmore, because their trellis wires sagged so much, and the winery Llano Estacado, the Spanish name for the "staked plains" of west Texas. This was in 1976. Today, Llano Estacado is Texas's most esteemed winery, its wines having won a plethora of awards over the years. Meanwhile, the University of Texas planted another experimental vineyard. In 1983, when that experiment had been deemed successful, a French-Texan consortium called Gill-Richter-Cordier began building a 1.5-million-gallon winery in Fort Stockton. Today Cordier Estates, its wines sold under the Ste. Genevieve label, is the largest producer in the state. Looking back, George Ray McEachern notes that vineyard expansion proceeded carefully in the initial wine boom years of the 1970s and early 1980s. "[We] went about it slowly, deliberately, methodically, and in an exacting way," he says. But "when people from outside tasted the early Texas *vinifera* and said, 'Hey, this is good, I'm surprised!' it was wonderful."

It was wonderful too in Michigan, where Professor Gordon Howell of Michigan State University's Department of Horticulture conducted research to assist that state's fruit growers. Most growers planted native grape varieties, especially in the 1960s and 1970s for use in producing Cold Duck. Made mostly from Concord and other *labrusca* grapes, Cold Duck was an American version of a German drink — *kalte ente*, a mixture of leftover wine, fresh sparkling wine, lemon juice, and sugar. The American rendition originated in a Detroit restaurant in the 1930s, but it only began to be bottled and sold commercially in the 1960s. Cold Duck briefly took the country by storm, with vintners in most every wine-producing state offering their versions, including blueberry, strawberry, even cranberry "ducks." But the sweet fizz fell out of fashion just as quickly, and Michigan growers started to experiment with French-American hybrid and *vinifera* grapes. Edward O'Keefe, scion of a prominent Canadian brewing family, planted forty acres of *vinifera* near Traverse City in 1975. "People must have thought I had more money than brains," he quips. "But I wanted to grow European *vinifera* grapes and the research indicated it could be done." The quality of the wines from O'Keefe's Château Grand Traverse turned more than a few heads, and before long a number of other boutique wineries opened for business. Northern Michigan may seem an unlikely place for fine wine growing, but the Leelanau Peninsula, with Lake Michigan to the west and Traverse Bay to the east, offers protection from winter cold, giving it a microclimate similar to that found in many northern European appellations. Not surprisingly, varieties such as Riesling and Chardonnay do particularly well there.

Similarly in Ohio, wine growing began to enjoy a renaissance along the shores of Lake Erie. Most of the wineries there emphasized *labrusca* wines, but a few adventurous growers experimented with *vinifera*. Arnulf Esterer, for one, a former navy officer and industrial engineer, began planting Riesling at his Maarko Vineyard in 1968. His wines tasted crisp and refreshing —amazingly so, according to Leon Adams, who, when he first tasted them, asked, "Is it an accident? Can [you] duplicate this?" Subsequent vintages proved that the answer was yes, and before long other wine growers joined Esterer in trying to root Ohio's renaissance in *vinifera*. Their efforts gained momentum when the state legislature adopted a tax-supported plan to assist viticulture, including a long-range program of research through Ohio State University. Wes Gerlosky, who started Harpersfield Vineyard in 1985 with the ambition to "make something as good as anywhere in the world," was one of the leaders. The state's large-scale Concord and Catawba growers considered his ambition odd, but Gerlosky insisted that premium *vinifera* wines represented the future. "You've *got* to have a vision beyond the end of your nose," he told an interviewer. "If we do this right, we can make a mark."

Vinifera, however, couldn't be done right everywhere. In many states, particularly in the Midwest, the combination of frigid winters and hot, humid summers wreaked havoc in the vineyards. University scientists like Justin Morris in Arkansas and Larry Lockshin in Missouri kept conducting research, but the short-term future lay more with hybrid and native grape varieties. That future turned bright quickly in Missouri, where a research program under the direction of enologist Bruce Zoecklin was launched in 1980. Before long Missouri wines were not only selling well to local customers but also winning international awards. Zoecklin advised wine growers to concentrate on grape varieties that, though not always fashionable, could produce wines of high quality. A good hybrid wine, he was fond of saying, is always better than a poor *vinifera* one. He was especially partial to Seyval Blanc and Vignoles, two white French-American hybrids. Proof that his advice was sound came in 1992, when a Missouri Vignoles from the Hermann-hof Winery stunned the wine world by being named Best of Show at the New World International Wine Competition in California.

By then Bruce Zoecklin had moved on—to Virginia, where in 1985 he began work as the state enologist through Virginia Tech University, and where he concentrated more on *vinifera* than on hybrids. That state's climate is more temperate than Missouri's, and new spraying materials could combat black rot and other fungal diseases. Zoecklin's appointment was part of an enlightened state government program that, in addition to funding scientific research, included tax advantages for wineries, a marketing plan, and a campaign to promote winery destination travel as part of Virginia's tourist trade. "The state realized that if the industry is going to be competitive, it needs to have help," he recalls. "We got more support commensurate

to our size than our California counterparts with UC Davis."
State support, or at least state noninterference, was connected
with university research in many parts of the country. Not surprisingly, in states without it—states like Tennessee, Oklahoma, and Utah—the combination of heavy taxes and prohibitionist regulation discouraged wine appreciation, and serious
wine production had a difficult time getting started.

The pioneers who revitalized wine growing across the
continent, whether farmers or scientists, winemakers or financiers, almost all had little experience with it. Nonetheless,
they shared a passion and commitment for it. Regardless of
which grapes they worked with or where they did that work,
they had a common desire—to bring an appreciation for wine
home by producing it at home. That appreciation gradually began to develop nationwide. In 1974, for instance, Dorothea
Checkley, inspired by a meeting with Walter Clore in Prosser,
founded the Enological Society of the Pacific Northwest. "We
tasted nine different wines [that day]," she remembers. "Dr.
Clore was almost seeing visions of what was going to happen."
Checkley's Enological Society, which grew to become one of
the largest consumer wine groups in the world, did not focus
exclusively on Washington wines. Instead, it promoted wine
appreciation by introducing people to wines and wine regions
from around the globe. Washington wines, though, always received special attention, and Checkley made sure to organize
regular excursions to the vineyards in the Yakima and
Columbia Valleys, as well as regular tastings of the local wines.
"It was almost as if it was magic," she says, recalling the time
when people first discovered that world-class wine could be
made in Washington State. Slowly, then, two things happened

to encourage American wine appreciation beyond California. First, as American wines got better, they attracted an audience —locally, then regionally, nationally, and eventually internationally. Second, as the wines got better, more people became interested—not just in them, but in wine generally as part of a civilized, cultured way of life. California certainly continued to dominate national production, but the rise beyond the Golden State of an interest in wine went hand in hand with the rise of local wines.

"The best way to make a small fortune in the wine business," runs an oft-repeated adage, "is to start with a large one." Premium wine growing anywhere requires money—lots of money. The money buys and maintains land, labor, and equipment. It also finances the pursuit of quality, for without deep pockets a wine grower will not be able to take the steps necessary to produce truly fine wine—eliminating substandard lots in order to preserve character, for example, or lowering yields in order to produce less but better volume. In northern California during the heady boom years of the 1970s, money poured into the wine business. Investors were attracted by the lure of an emerging wine-country lifestyle as much as by anything else, and before long Highway 29 in Napa became a thoroughfare of glitz and glamour. Things were different elsewhere, particularly in places where fine wine growing was wholly unknown. Fewer people invested in those places, and those who did concentrated on the wines themselves. They knew that what was in the bottle had to speak for itself, especially since many consumers were understandably skeptical about whether high-quality wines really could come from vineyards in the East, Midwest, or even the Pacific Northwest. At the same time, the wine growers needed money just as their California counterparts did —not to finance a *Town and Country* lifestyle, but to make premium wine where no one had made it before. In virtually every region where fine wine gained a foothold, moneyed investors played a significant role. Their financial commitments helped raise standards and turn heads, as their wines changed people's perceptions and enlarged people's sense of possibilities. And in virtually every case, this money originally had nothing to do with grapes and wine. It too came from far afield.

Susan and Earl Samson had backgrounds far removed from agriculture when they purchased Sakonnet Vineyards in Little Compton, Rhode Island, in 1986. He came from the world of Wall Street investments and capital ventures, she from Broadway. Their past success in those fields is what gave them the financial resources to pursue their quixotic dream—to make premium *vinifera* wines in Rhode Island. The Samsons had caught the wine bug a decade earlier, with Earl going so far as to become a principal investor in a California boutique winery. They had no desire, though, to move west. "We had summered for years in Rhode Island," Susan says, "and even though we had decided to make a change in our careers, we wanted to stay here." Sakonnet Vineyards had been founded back in 1975 by Jim and Lolly Mitchell, who with relatively meager resources produced decent wines—mostly French-American hybrid varietals, but some experimental *vinifera*. By 1986, the Mitchells were ready to sell. As Susan Samson recalls, "It had come to a point where the choice was clear—either put more money into the enterprise and move ahead or go backwards."

After researching the local climate and soil conditions, the Samsons decided to take the plunge. They concluded that the only reason no one in coastal New England had produced quality wine before was that no one had really tried. It seemed clear that there wasn't any scientific reason why it couldn't be done. So the Samsons invested heavily, replanting vineyards and starting new ones, purchasing new winery equipment and upgrading facilities. "We had to learn about cool-climate grape growing and winemaking," says Earl. "And we had to instill professionalism." The Samsons threw themselves into their work with a passion. By the mid-1990s, Sakonnet had established itself as New England's leading premium winery, with production nearing fifty thousand cases annually and many of its wines winning awards in international competitions. Earl oversaw the wine growing, while Susan took charge of the marketing. "That was the biggest challenge," she observes, "getting people to take our wines seriously." To many consumers, quality American wine by definition came from California. "People had to taste our wine," she says "in order to believe."

Some of the people who tasted and believed went on to grow grapes and make wine themselves, as the Samsons' success helped inspire a number of other New Englanders to invest in wine growing. These included William Chaney, the CEO of Tiffany & Company, at Chamard Vineyards, and Steven and Catherine Vollweiler at Sharpe Hill—two high-quality, boutique-style estates in Connecticut. Although New England wine growing is still in its infancy, the future appears bright. Recent scientific research in cool-climate clonal selection and canopy management has brought *vinifera* grape growing to areas that previously could grow only native or hybrid varieties. At Chamard, winemaker Larry McCulloch began producing small lots of exclusively *vinifera* wines in 1989. "We've proven," he says, reflecting on a decade's worth of work, "that if you pick the right site and put your mind and money into it, you can make nice wine. It may not be easy, but it can be done."

It can be done in Virginia as well, where an influx of private capital has joined with the state-funded programs of public support to jump-start the previously moribund wine industry. People like Archie Smith at Meredyth Vineyards and Charles Raney at Farfelu had planted hybrid grapes in the late 1960s, but everything was on a small, largely experimental scale until 1978, when Gianni Zonin, an Italian wine magnate, purchased an 830-acre estate north of Charlottesville called Barboursville. This property, the historic former plantation of Governor James Barbour, a close friend of Thomas Jefferson and an admirer of fine wines, was being used as a horse farm. Zonin, however, wanted to make wine. He hired a gifted young Italian agronomist, Gabriele Rausse, to manage the property, instructing him to plant European vines. Although a few Virginians already had experimented with *vinifera* (notably Elizabeth Furness at Piedmont Vineyards), the prevailing wisdom was that the intense mid-Atlantic humidity would rot the grapes. Rausse did not agree. When he compared conditions at his family's farm north of Venice with those in central Virginia, he found a host of similarities. "We have high humidity where I come from," he explains. "The data I gathered showed that the average rainfall is the same and the temperatures are similar." Rausse determined that the major reason why people had failed with *vinifera* in Virginia was that they treated these grape varieties much like hybrid or native ones. "The problem is that they were following the wrong rules," he says. "The skin of the Chardonnay grape, for example, is probably the thinnest of any grape in the world, while the Concord is probably the thickest. Obviously it's much easier for fungal disease to enter the Chardonnay . . . [The growers] never looked at the grapes the right way." Rausse started a nursery, planted Cabernet, Chardonnay, and Riesling, and immediately initiated a program of careful spraying and canopy management. When Barboursville's 1979 wines were released, people throughout the state took notice. The very next year, Rausse sold 100,000 *vinifera* vines to other Virginia wine growers. The boom was on. Three years later, *vinifera* acreage in Virginia surpassed that of hybrid and American grapes combined. "It was," he remembers, "a very exciting time."

Gianni Zonin's money made Gabriele Rausse's experiments with *vinifera* possible. In turn, Rausse's accomplishments spurred a new wave of investment in Virginia wine. Two of the more important investors were European businessmen, Jean Leducq, who started Prince Michel Vineyards in 1983, and Patrick Doffeler, an executive with Phillip Morris in New York, who began converting a farm near Williamsburg into a vineyard that same year. Doffeler's Williamsburg Winery has since grown to become the largest and one of the most respected in the state. "I'd lived as a corporate mercenary for twenty years," he recalls. It was time "to do something intelligent." Planting grapes and making wine in Virginia proved intelligent indeed. Because the state lies south of the sometimes brutally cold winters of the Northeast, but north of the oppressive heat of the South, it is probably the East Coast's most promising viticultural region. Since 1980, nearly fifty Virginia wineries have opened for business, and production has increased twentyfold. Most of these wineries are small, and most are owned by people who have had to borrow the money they needed to get started. But the success of self-sufficient estates like Barboursville, Prince Michel, and Williamsburg is at least in part what led them to even think about premium winemaking. Deep pockets led the way.

In New York, the story was more complicated, as big money both entered and left the Empire State wine business, a business that underwent a period of tumultuous change in the 1980s. First, corporate investors who were looking to profit from the national wine boom purchased a number of large-volume New York wineries, including Taylor, Great Western, and Gold Seal. These wineries used primarily native grapes, and with consumer tastes changing, the market for their cheap, sweet wines was drying up fast. The New York wine industry soon fell into an economic depression. In one year alone, Taylor, then owned by the liquor giant Seagram, had to cut its grape purchases by nearly 90 percent, from 15,000 tons in 1984 to 1,800 tons in 1985. New York vineyard acreage declined by nearly a third during the decade, and soon the corporate money fled.

Some people had presciently predicted the decline of New York wine. As far back as the 1960s, for instance, Walter Taylor had urged his family to raise the quality of their wines by switching from *labrusca* to French-American hybrid grapes. After a series of heated exchanges, the company's board of directors bought out Taylor's interest in the business, and in 1970 he started his own winery in his grandfather's old horse barn atop

Bully Hill in the town of Hammondsport. His troubles were just beginning. When Coca-Cola purchased Taylor a few years later, it filed a lawsuit forbidding Walter to use his family name on his wines. He responded by inking out "Taylor" with black marker on thousands of bottles and designing new labels that featured masked pictures of his ancestors. Coke sued again, and eventually Taylor was ordered to turn over everything he owned that related to the family business. He complied by dumping truckloads of files, books, family portraits, and all sorts of other paraphernalia on the winery's front lawn, and then posing his pet goat atop the heap. "They got my name and heritage," ran his now legendary quip, "but they didn't get my goat."

Bully Hill wines, featuring various drawings of goats on the labels, went on to achieve a modest popularity, and the winery survived both Coca-Cola's investment and the Taylor Wine Company itself. The irony is that Walter Taylor had not been prescient enough. The future of New York wine lay not with hybrids but with *vinifera*. Today, Bully Hill wines, though still popular, are little more than curiosities, while premium New York *vinifera* wines are the ones garnering ever-increasing renown. Riesling and Gewurztraminer from the Finger Lakes, Merlot and Cabernet Franc from Long Island, Chardonnay from the Hudson Valley—these are among the contemporary New York wines that win medals in international competitions, sell out upon release, and are featured on some of the country's best wine lists.

The shift to *vinifera* in New York was, as in many parts of the country, led by moneyed investors who came to wine from other occupations and who could afford the risk inherent in trying something new. The one exception was in the Finger Lakes, where the growers themselves saw the market for their Concord and Niagara grapes getting smaller with each passing vintage. To stay in business, they reasoned, they would have to replant. Led in part by the descendants of these old-time grape growers, the Finger Lakes is now becoming a strong *vinifera* wine region. Because it had an ongoing history of wine growing, outside money did not have to show the way. But in all the other New York wine regions, new investment proved critically important. In the Hudson Valley, for example, John Dyson, a former state commissioner of agriculture and heir to a family fortune, purchased an old dairy farm in 1979 and converted it into a state-of-the-art winery. (He has since gone on to purchase vineyards and wineries in California and Italy.) The wines from Dyson's Millbrook Vineyards rank among the state's best, and their high quality has begun to persuade other Hudson Valley growers and winemakers that *vinifera* represents the future. Similarly, on Long Island, a flood of investment in the 1980s financed winemaking that impressed farmers and consumers alike—farmers because they realized that growing wine grapes could be profitable, consumers because the wines tasted surprisingly good. There were only a few wineries in operation on Long Island in 1979 when Dr. Herodotus Damianos used profits from his medical practice to found Pindar Vineyards. Today, nearly a score of wineries are open for business, all producing almost exclusively *vinifera* wines. Palmer Vineyards, started in 1983 by a wealthy New York advertising executive, is one of the best known. With one hundred acres under vine, its wines are available for sale in twenty-three states and five foreign countries. Winemaker Dan Kleck was responsible for

Palmer's first award-winning Chardonnays and Merlots. Then, in 1998, Jess Jackson of Kendall-Jackson hired Kleck away. Even Californians recognized that money had changed things back east.

The most spectacular example of the role played by big money in the rise of American wine beyond California can be seen in Washington State. The key player there was a young financial manager, Wally Opdycke, who in 1972 organized a group of investors to purchase American Wine Growers, by far the state's largest producer. Opdycke renamed the company Ste. Michelle Vintners because the Ste. Michelle label, which represented a tiny percentage of the company's total sales, was the only one he really cared about. The vast majority of the wines produced by American Wine Growers, under labels such as Pommerelle and Nawico, were cheap, sweet, and often fortified. Opdycke, who knew how to read sales figures, recognized that their days were numbered. He wanted to reposition Ste. Michelle to lead Washington into a new era of world-class *vinifera* wine growing. To do so, however, he needed money, lots of money. So he went looking for help, and in 1974 sold the company to U.S. Tobacco, which proceeded to pour millions of dollars into vineyard expansion and winery development. Unlike so many corporations that invested in American wine in the 1970s, U.S. Tobacco "really had the conviction to stick with it," recalls Opdycke. The company understood that to be successful it needed to build not only a brand but an image — the image of first-rate Washington State wine. That was what had gotten Opdycke interested in wine to begin with, and U.S. Tobacco retained him to implement his original business plan. Over the next twenty-five years, Ste. Michelle, later renamed

Stimson Lane, would become the most successful American wine producer outside California—successful in terms of both profit and the high quality of the wines themselves.

Wally Opdycke became interested in wine in part because he envisioned a bright future for it and in part because he simply liked it so much. He had often visited the northern California wine country, and he sensed early on that American wine was about to skyrocket in popularity. Living in Seattle, he followed the legislative debate about repealing Washington's protectionist wine laws, and he took note of the man whose testimony seemed to carry the day. So when Opdycke began to think seriously about investing in wine, he wrote to Walter Clore at the Prosser Station, asking for more information about the Wine Project and Clore's experiments with different *vinifera* varieties. Instead of answering by mail, Clore came to Seattle in person. "We had a great visit," Opdycke remembers. "He gave me a lot of information about the potential for investing in grapes and wine. He said, 'Look, someone should really do something here.'" When Opdycke outlined his ambitions, Clore offered to help. That was in 1970. Three years later, Wally Opdycke, now in control of Ste. Michelle, took Walter Clore's advice and bought five hundred acres of land in a place called Cold Creek in the Columbia Valley. He could afford to plant only two hundred of them right away (with Cabernet and Riesling, again on Clore's recommendation), but the next year, thanks to U.S. Tobacco, he planted the rest, thereby doubling the amount of *vinifera* in all of Washington State.

U.S. Tobacco's resources and Wally Opdycke's vision radically changed Washington wine. Opdycke was not the only visionary, just as Ste. Michelle was not the first company to produce *vinifera* wines. Nonetheless, this combination of big money and a commitment to high quality was what allowed Walter Clore's predictions to come true. "We can compete very favorably in producing top table and varietal wines with any other region in the United States," Clore had told the legislators during the debate over House Bill 100 back in 1969. Hardly anyone then drinking Washington wine would have believed him, but millions of Americans do now, as wines sold under Stimson Lane's Chateau Ste. Michelle and Columbia Crest labels rank among the country's most popular. Much the same thing happened, though on a much smaller scale, elsewhere. No matter whether in the East or the West, and no matter whether in areas that had to overcome a history of poor-quality wine production or in areas that were new to wine, daring ambitions coupled with serious capital investment changed the very character of American wine — taking it from sweet and cheap to dry and chic, and from a butt of jokes to an object of respect.

The same factors that propelled the rise of California wine led to the rise of American wine elsewhere: changing consumer tastes, advanced viticultural and enological research, moneyed investment, and perhaps most important, individual artistic vision. Yet beyond California, the climate — economic and political as well as meteorological — proved less hospitable. Because the prospect of high-quality local wines seemed for so long to be nothing more than fantasy, the wine growers who dreamed of making such wines were by necessity rebels as much as artists. They too wanted to craft wines that could challenge Old

World supremacy, but to do so they had to go against the grain of history and current practice.

In 1962, when Lloyd Woodburne organized a group of University of Washington professors to make small lots of commercial *vinifera* wine, many of his friends and colleagues thought he was crazy. Similarly, two years later, when David Lett, then a student at UC Davis, first proposed making wine in Oregon, Maynard Amerine advised him not to do it. Oregon, Amerine said, was so cold and wet that the vines were bound to be hit by frost in the spring and then rot in the fall. But Lett and Woodburne paid no attention. Maverick pioneers, they made wines in extremely small volume that attracted the attention of other would-be vintners and thus helped inspire the rise of premium wine growing in the Pacific Northwest. Twenty years later, much the same thing was happening farther east. Visionary winemakers, often working in isolation, produced handcrafted gems that began to change people's perception of American wine, its twenty-first-century potential even more than its twentieth-century reality. These artisanal vintners came from a variety of professions and were motivated by a variety of desires. They worked in basements and rented warehouses, farm outbuildings and renovated barns, but they shared a simple and at times apparently audacious goal—to make nothing less than outstanding American wine.

Some of them started as home winemakers. After all, in the dark decades following Prohibition, Americans interested in quality table wine often had little choice but to try to make it themselves. Lloyd Woodburne began doing so in the early 1950s. He bought grapes shipped north from California and, using a hand crusher and a screw press, made wine in his Seattle garage. Soon he recruited friends to help him, mostly fellow academics, and for nearly a decade this group of dedicated amateurs made what were by all accounts the best wines in Washington State. They took considerable pride in what they produced, and from time to time sent samples to select people to solicit comments. In 1961, they shipped a few bottles to André Tchelistcheff in Napa, who wrote back saying that he liked the wines very much — especially a pink sparkling wine that he said was as good as the "champagne" he made at Beaulieu Vineyards. (Five years later, he would declare the group's homemade Gewurztraminer "the best in the United States.") This sort of encouragement, coupled with the fact that it was getting harder to find high-quality grapes, enabled Woodburne to persuade nine members of the group to join him and form a small commercial winery, which he called Associated Vintners. Its first wines were not released until the summer of 1969, a few months after the passage of House Bill 100. When Stan Reed, the *Seattle Post-Intelligencer*'s food columnist, tasted these wines, he waxed rhapsodic. "They are of a stature so high that a Washington Wine Month should be declared in their honor," he wrote. "To add to the wonder . . . [they were] created by ten dedicated vintners who started out eighteen years ago not knowing winemaking from carpentry. Amateurs bore the torch for the professionals, and we hope that the light has been seen." One person who clearly saw that light was Wally Opdycke, who read Reed's articles and began to envision even greater change. Within a few months, he wrote to Walter Clore, asking for advice on how to get started. The rest, as they say, is history.

Along with the entire Washington wine industry, Associated Vintners expanded in the 1970s. Before long, new investors and stockholders came aboard. Building on Clore's work with the Wine Project, the company managers purchased new vineyards and planted new grape varieties. In 1983, they renamed the company the Columbia Winery, and five years later, with production at the 100,000-case mark, they moved its operation to Woodinville, across the street from Chateau Ste. Michelle—a long way in size and scope, if not actual miles, from Lloyd Woodburne's garage. Nonetheless, what happened in that garage had been just as formative as anything that happened at Ste. Michelle, for the artistic vision of the professors who formed the original Associated Vintners group produced the first commercial Washington wines to turn heads and inspire change. And although Washington today is unique among the wine-producing states beyond California in that its production is dominated by large wineries (Hogue Cellars in addition to Chateau Ste. Michelle, Columbia Crest, and the Columbia Winery group), some of the best wines in the state still come from small, artisanal producers whose wineries remain little more than renovated garages. These include Gary Figgins at Leonetti Cellar and Rick Small at Woodward Canyon, two of America's most esteemed boutique winemakers.

But it was in Oregon, more than any other important wine-growing state, that an artistic spirit led the way. Even today, the Oregon wine industry is characterized more by small, fairly low-key, family-run enterprises than by large, multimillion-dollar estates. David Lett, so much the perfectionist craftsman that during fermentation he would sleep in his winery with an alarm clock set to go off every two hours, became known as "the father of Oregon wine," largely because his Pinot Noir performed so spectacularly at the 1979 Gault-Millau Wine

Olympiad in Paris. Lett, however, was not the state's first artisanal winemaker. That honor goes to Richard Sommer, also a
Davis refugee, who in 1961 bought a farm near the town of
Roseburg in the Umpqua Valley, where he soon started growing grapes. Sommer concentrated on white varieties, especially
Riesling, and before long, bottles sporting his Hillcrest Vineyard label were being featured in Portland restaurants and wine
shops. Few people followed Sommer to Umpqua, for by the
1970s the buzz had it that the cooler Willamette Valley was a
better wine-growing area. Lett's Eyrie Vineyards was the first
post-Prohibition operation there. He planted a vineyard in the
red hills of Dundee, and bonded his winery in a former poultry
processing plant in the nearby town of McMinnville. Within a
year, he was followed by two San Franciscans, Dick Erath and
Dick Ponzi, and a small Willamette wine boom was under way.
That boom exploded in the 1980s, when Oregon vineyard
acreage more than tripled. Two things motivated these winemaking pioneers. The first was the promise of fine, northern
European–style wines, a promise that in the beginning was as
much fiction as fact. The second was the lure of a back-to-na-
ture lifestyle. Erath was an electrical engineer by trade and a
home winemaker by passion. He decided to make a change in
his life when he realized that he wanted to get out of the city
and make that passion his life's work. When he moved to the
valley in 1967, he lived with his family in an unheated logger's
cabin as he planted his first vineyard and built his winery—a
cedar log structure that doubled as home. Similarly, Dick Ponzi
left California (where he was designing rides for Disneyland)
because he wanted "to go back to the land." As he puts it, "That
was a period of unrest. People were looking for alternatives."

For Ponzi, as for Erath and Lett, the alternative was wine—specifically, red wine made from Pinot Noir.

Much as with Josh Jensen and Richard Graff in California, the first wave of Oregon wine growers planted Pinot Noir because they were in love with Burgundy—both the wines and the romanticized lifestyle of the Burgundian *vigneron*. Unlike Graff and Jensen, they were not fanatical about limestone. They were, though, interested in climate. One reason they chose Oregon was that it lies roughly on the same latitude as Burgundy and has similar weather patterns. Another reason was that land was cheap. Dick Ponzi, for example, looked first at property in California's Mendocino County but could not afford to buy there. The most important reason, however, was that the Willamette Valley seemed to have the potential to become America's Côte d'Or, a region where small-volume, hands-on winemakers could produce high-quality wines. The artisanal Burgundian model held great appeal because it represented a European version of the alternative lifestyle that so many Oregon wine growers, themselves urban refugees, wanted. Not surprisingly, they copied Burgundian styles and aimed to make their wines in a Burgundian image. When Lett's Pinot Noir performed well in Paris, people elsewhere took note and a new wave of planting began. Between 1979 and 1991, Pinot acreage increased tenfold. The wines continued to do well in comparative tastings, notably in a 1985 event at the International Wine Center in New York. Two years later, the influential critic Robert Parker declared that "the best Oregon Pinot Noirs . . . have an amazing similarity to good red Burgundies." He went on to note that "most Oregon wineries started as underfinanced, backyard operations where the owners [and] winemakers learned as they went along," and that "wonderful wines have emerged from winemakers who have had little textbook training, but plenty of hands-on experience."

The Oregon vineyard boom of the 1980s eventually brought new investment into the state. Some, paradoxically enough, came from California. Well-heeled Napa vintners such as Steve Girard, William Hill, and Gary Andrus purchased land and started growing vines. Other money came from abroad, especially once the Burgundy *negociant* Joseph Drouhin purchased 180 acres in the Willamette Valley and constructed his state-of-the-art winery. But the most spectacular investment came when Ed King III, whose father had made a fortune in electronic aviation equipment, purchased 550 acres south of Eugene and began designing the state's largest winery. King had no experience in the wine business, but he had very deep pockets. He spared no expense in building a modern and lavish winery, King Estate, where his ambition quite clearly was to become the biggest and the best. By the 1990s, Oregon wine growing, though still dominated by small producers, had entered a new phase, one in which scientific research and capital investment went hand in hand with artistic vision. In the process, Burgundy, still a source of inspiration, became less an obvious model, and the wines began to acquire an identity of their own. As Ken Wright, winemaker at Panther Creek and later at his own Ken Wright Cellars, puts it, "I don't really care what the Burgundians do. The only thing that matters is attention to detail."

Detail mattered wherever people labored to produce handcrafted wines. In Texas, Kim McPherson, son of one of the founders of Llano Estacado, made small lots of high-quality *vinifera* wines at Cap Rock, where he was assisted by the respected California consultant Tony Soter. Much the same was true at Fall Creek Vineyards, where Susan and Ed Auler produced some of Texas's best wines. Elsewhere in the South and Southwest, quality table wine production existed only in isolated pockets — for example, at Callaghan Vineyards in Arizona, Gruet Winery in New Mexico, and Biltmore Estate in North Carolina. Farther north, artisanal winemakers such as Hamilton Mowbray, Brett Byrd, and Bert Basignani in Maryland, Richard Moersch and Doug Welsch in Michigan, Frank Salek in New Jersey, Anthony Carlucci and Ted Moulton in Ohio, John and Tim Crouch in Pennsylvania, and Bob Wollersheim in Wisconsin fashioned award-winning wines in all but local obscurity. They often did so as a second job, or after early retirement, since quality wine growing in these largely untested regions was a labor of love far more than a way to wealth. Salek operated Sylvin Farms in Germania, New Jersey, for some twenty years as a sideline, his principal source of income being his work as a university professor. All the while he produced anywhere between five hundred and one thousand cases of some of the best wines in the East. When asked why he did it, he offered a simple but revealing answer: "Look, this is an endeavor that requires a great deal of personal interest. When you get right down to it, it's madness. But it's a hell of a lot of fun."

In states with a more viable premium wine industry, artisanal production required just as much personal interest and attention to detail, but perhaps a little less madness. Although selling wines grown anywhere east of the Rockies always proved difficult, it was easier in New York or Virginia than in states like New Jersey, where customers tended to expect the wines to taste sweet and unsubtle. Salek stopped making Blanc de Noirs sparkling wine in 1999 because hardly anyone believed that a dry, champagne-style wine from New Jersey could be any good. "It's too hard a sell," he explained. "It isn't just the money. The way I make wine and the prices I can ask for it—well, let's put it this way, I'm never going to make much money on this. But there's not much point in making a wine like the Blanc de Noirs and not be able to sell it." By contrast, winemakers like Kip Bedell on Long Island and Dennis Horton in Virginia have customers who expect quality. At the turn of the century, they are among the handful of artisanal vintners who are leading American wine's renaissance in the East.

Like so many East Coast winemakers, Kip Bedell came to wine from far afield—in his case, the fuel oil business. He was running a small oil company near New York City when in 1980 he purchased a potato farm in the town of Cutchogue, on Long Island's North Fork, largely because he wanted to get away from the rat race. For the next ten years, he and his wife, Susan, commuted back and forth. He continued to sell heating oil, but on the weekends and summer evenings he cleared the property and planted vines. In 1985 he bonded Bedell Cellars. Five years later he sold the oil company and became a full-time wine grower. "I'm still in a business that depends on the weather," he jokes. "And I'm still just pumping liquid from one container to another." Bedell's self-effacing manner belies his achievement, for he produces what most tasters agree are Long Island's finest wines—Merlot, Cabernet, and a red Bordeaux-style blend called Cupola.

Along with Bedell, small-scale winemakers such as Eric Fry and Larry Perrine raised the quality level of Long Island wines. In the beginning, they worked mostly by trial and error, emulating European techniques without necessarily knowing why. "There's no doubt that some of our earlier wines weren't great," Bedell acknowledges. "Our vines were young and we made some mistakes." One of the mistakes was following a Bordeaux model too closely, a mistake that ironically enough became apparent only after a number of celebrated Bordeaux winemakers and viticultural scientists came to the North Fork in 1988 to give a master class on winemaking. Their biggest piece of advice was to not necessarily adopt French methods and practices. "In winemaking one must be neither too theoretical nor too dogmatic," Paul Pontallier of Château Margaux explained. "A good wine is the result not of just a few broad decisions, but of close attention being paid to many small ones." No one took that advice more to heart than Kip Bedell. "They got [me] thinking," he says. "I'm more conscious now of what I do and of the effect it has . . . I'm paying much closer attention to the details." To Bedell, whose wines today are featured at some of Manhattan's finest restaurants, the future looks rosy. "The Long Island style is just beginning to evolve," he notes. "We'll be able to define it better when our region gets a little more time under its belt. We're poised right on the edge of a very exciting time."

At Horton Vineyards in Gordonsville, Virginia, Dennis Horton, a former office equipment salesman, takes a similar view. "We've come a millennium in almost no time," he says, "but we have much more to do." Horton, who planted his vineyard in 1988, realized early on that the key to success would come from matching grape variety with location. While most of Virginia's other *vinifera* pioneers planted the classic Bordeaux and Burgundy varieties, he decided to emphasize Mediterranean grapes with thick skins and loose clusters that would better tolerate the humid summer heat. Along with his wife, Sharon, he planted Viognier, Mourvedre, and Marsanne from the Rhône, and later Touriga Nacional and Tinta Cão from Portugal. It was a gamble. "In trying to find something that is absolutely suited for the environment," he admits, "marketing can be a problem." In 1995, the gamble paid off. Horton's Viognier was named one of the "top 100 wines in the world" by the *Wine Spectator*, and then received three stars, the highest rating, from California writers Charles Olken and Earl Singer in their influential *Connoisseurs' Guide*. "Consider the temerity," wrote Olken and Singer. "Consider the inconvenience. Consider the results . . . Who's heard of Horton?" Soon many people had heard of Horton, as the wines began to show up on restaurant wine lists and in retail shops across the country. "Our wines now are even sold in Napa," says the iconoclastic Dennis Horton, a big grin on his face.

In addition to Mediterranean grape varieties, Horton planted Norton, a little-known native grape variety that is surprisingly devoid of foxy flavors. He did so in part because he thought it would grow well, and in part because he wanted to pay homage to the past. That past was local, Norton having been first propagated in Virginia (by Dr. D. N. Norton) in the 1830s. It also was personal. Dennis Horton had grown up in Hermann, Missouri, just down the street from George Husmann's old house, where in the mid-nineteenth century some of America's most highly regarded red wines had been made from Norton grapes. Today his Norton wins medals and plaudits in international competitions, as do Nortons that once again hail from Missouri—notably those produced at the Stone Hill Winery back in Hermann.

Stone Hill, an imposing brick structure built by German immigrants in 1847, was once the second-largest winery in the United States. But in 1965, no one had made wine in it for fifty years, its vaulted cellars being used instead to cultivate mushrooms. Then Jim and Betty Held reopened it. Family farmers, the Helds knew little about wine. They grew corn and raised hogs, and a few years earlier had planted four acres of grapes, largely on a whim. The grapes fetched a fair price, so when Stone Hill became available, they decided to go into the wine business. That summer they moved into the second floor of the old building and began the long, laborious job of restoring the winery. "It took two years just to get rid of all the mushroom compost," Jim recalls. Meanwhile, they had to make wine. Jim purchased equipment through the State Experiment Station in Mountain Grove, spent $27 for a book titled *Technology of Winemaking*, and got to work. From the beginning, it was a family affair. Seven-year-old Jon turned the crank on the crusher, while five-year-old Patty kept two-year-old Thomas and baby Julie out of the way. Betty served as barrel cleaner, janitor, and accountant. By mid-October, the Helds had made fifteen hundred gallons of Stone Hill wine—the first legally produced, commercial wine in Missouri since before Prohibition.

Over the next thirty years, Stone Hill grew to become the Midwest's most successful winery. And it stayed very much in the family. The Held children all grew up working in the vineyards and cellars. Jon went on to study enology at UC Davis. Patty did much the same at Fresno, and Tom earned a degree in viticulture at the University of Arkansas. (Julie was the only member of the family not to go into the wine business. "We may have started her a little too early on the bottling line," explains her father. "She was two.") Jim Held made all the wine until 1977, when, with production doubling almost every year, he hired a full-time vintner—Dave Johnson, who since has gone on to become the most awarded American winemaker outside California. Stone Hill grows native American and hybrid grapes on the bluffs overlooking the Missouri River. Many of the Helds' wines are sweet and sappy, but their pride and joy is their Norton, which Johnson calls "*the* Missouri red." Until the American wine boom of the last few decades, only a handful of small plots of Norton remained in all the United States. Today, led by Stone Hill, Hermannhof, and other Missouri wineries, as well as by Horton in Virginia, it is enjoying a revival—what Gerald Asher in *Gourmet* magazine wryly calls "the return of the native." As Asher notes, the Helds well understand "that if there is to be more than just folklore in their future, they have to produce wines with more than popular appeal. They have to restore if not the glory then at least the former good standing of Missouri viticulture." Tasting Stone Hill's Old Vines Norton provides ample evidence that they are succeeding. In Missouri, much as in Michigan and Texas, New York and New England, the Mid-Atlantic, the Pacific Northwest, and the other wine-producing regions beyond California, local American wine has changed tremendously for the better, all in a remarkably short time.

8

The Rise of
American Cuisine

AMERICAN FOOD changed too. Over the span of a generation, in both restaurants and home kitchens, millions of Americans discovered the delights of fine cooking, much as many of them discovered the joys of fine wine. In the process, a new American cuisine emerged to challenge, and in some places replace, the tired American traditions of dowdy home cooking and "continental" restaurant fare. At the same time that many Americans began to look at wine as something more than alcohol, they also began to look at food as something more than sustenance. Gradually, a significant number of people came to think of the two together, each an integral part of a meal, each incomplete without the other, each part and parcel of a cultured, civilized life. Never before had Nicholas Longworth's and George Husmann's old dream, to bring wine home to the American table, seemed so close to reality.

Of course, what was on the table was a far cry from what those two distinguished nineteenth-century gentlemen ate. For nearly two hundred years, American cooking had consisted largely of regional adaptations of immigrant cuisines. By contrast, this new American cuisine was global, combining ingredients and techniques from a host of different cultures and traditions. *Combination*, in fact, became its hallmark, which is why some of today's versions carry the sobriquet "fusion." Whether hailing from California or the Caribbean, the Pacific Rim or the new South, these American culinary styles integrate disparate flavors, ingredients, and traditions in innovative, often offbeat ways. They combine classic French culinary techniques, regional American products, and diverse ethnic influences to produce a cuisine that, much like the country itself, functions as a modern melting pot—cross-cultural food for a cross-cultural land. And just as the democratic veneration of individual liberty gives the political melting pot its distinctive shape, a newfound respect for genuine ingredients and authentic flavors is what prevents the new American cuisine from becoming a hopeless hodgepodge. Over the past thirty years, its emergence has paralleled the rise of American wine. Neither development caused the other, but each inspired and profoundly influenced the other. As a result, for the first time in the country's history, American food and wine truly go together.

The changes in American cuisine have been only partial. After all, the United States is the homeland of McDonald's and Coke, Pop Tarts and Tang, a country whose citizenry has a well-documented penchant for eating quickly and haphazardly. Nonetheless, the changes have been real. One need only survey the ever-expanding selection of prepared foods in any suburban supermarket to see it. Fusion items vie for attention alongside old standbys like roast beef and fried chicken, as do an increasing number of salads, pastas, and ethnic dishes. Many of these are strongly seasoned and were unknown a generation ago. Although an Asian noodle salad from the Safeway bears little resemblance to what people eat in Bangkok (or for that matter in a Thai restaurant in America), its very existence signals an important cultural shift in the country's taste. That transformation began in the 1960s, when large numbers of people started to explore new tastes, flavors, and styles. Along the way, they came to regard food and wine as valuable entities in their own right.

Much as with the changing profile of American wine at the time, this exploration began on a distinctly French note. One person's vision proved revolutionary. Julia McWilliams first became interested in food as an offshoot of romance. While working for the Office of Strategic Services during the Second World War, she fell in love with Paul Child, a painter turned OSS officer who had been raised in France. After they married in 1946, she worked on mastering the typical American fare of the day—meatloaf, tuna casserole, and the rest. A few years later, Paul was transferred to France. The couple's first meal there was inspirational. A plate of fresh oysters, followed by sole meunière and accompanied by a bottle of pale Chablis— "the whole experience was an opening up of the soul and spirit for me," she recalls. If she first had wanted to learn to cook to please her husband, now she decided to try to please herself. So at the age of thirty-seven, Julia Child enrolled in the world's most famous culinary school, Le Cordon Bleu in Paris, where she was the lone woman taking classes with Max Bugnard, a disciple of Auguste Escoffier, the high priest of haute cuisine. What she learned would forever alter America's appetite.

Julia practiced her lessons from Le Cordon Bleu on her

husband and his colleagues. When people who dined at her home started asking her for recipes, she invited them into her kitchen, told them to roll up their sleeves, and showed them what to do. That happened so often that she enlisted the help of two French friends, Simone Beck and Louisette Bertholle, and the three women started an informal cooking school of their own—L'École des Trois Gourmandes. Eventually they began working on a cookbook. Designed from the start to introduce sophisticated French food to an American audience, the book started small but grew ever larger and ever more detailed over the years. Julia was the one who insisted on the detail. She wanted to provide not only recipes but also instruction on technique, so that readers truly could learn from it. She came to do an increasing amount of the work herself, testing the recipes and writing most of the copy—much of it long distance, since Paul's job required them to move every few years. Finally, in late 1961, *Mastering the Art of French Cooking* was published. Although the title page listed the names of three authors, it was predominantly Julia Child's book.

Mastering the Art sold like proverbial hotcakes—or in this case, crêpes—leading the host of a book-review program on public television in Boston to invite Julia to go on the air to discuss it. She went to the station carting an electric hotplate, a bowl, a whisk, a copper pan, and two eggs. Instead of just talking for half an hour, she made an omelet and, most importantly, showed the astonished host how to make one himself. The station management thought she was crazy, but viewers loved her, and in 1963 WGBH created a show for her, *The French Chef.* Cooking in America would never be the same.

Through her books, but even more through her television

programs, Julia Child brought a new awareness of food into American homes, gently but effectively changing how millions of people thought about themselves and their kitchens. She demonstrated that cooking could be fun and exciting. Part of her success came simply as happenstance. She had worked on *Mastering the Art* for nearly a decade, and by luck saw it published amid the Kennedy-inspired Francophile craze. "I happened to come along just at the right time," she says. "If it had been a bit earlier, it wouldn't have gone over." Even more significant was the woman herself—a Californian in New England, thoroughly American, ungainly and unpretentious, clearly knowledgeable but also clearly down-to-earth. No actress, she nonetheless proved captivating, if only because she so obviously relished being herself and did not fear the camera. She had a funny voice, said funny things, sometimes dropped a chicken or spilled a sauce, but she turned out culinary masterpieces, all the while showing viewers exactly how she did it. As she herself acknowledged, "People look at me and say, 'Well, if she can do it, I can do it.'" Her *French Chef* set, which replicated a typical suburban kitchen, not a Parisian bistro, served as a symbol of the most crucial aspect of her success: her ability to demonstrate that fine food had a place in American homes.

The French Chef democratized an authentic cuisine, bringing traditional French food to a primarily middle-class audience at a time when a taste for it was the province of a privileged few. Hers was the first national cooking show, but it soon was followed by scores of imitators. Today, television talk shows routinely feature cooking segments, and an entire national network features only food programs. The audience for these shows, while largely female, includes men too—yet another of

Julia's legacies. She subverted accepted gender roles—first because she was a woman in the previously almost exclusively male world of professional cooking, and second because she redefined cooking for American housewives. The original *French Chef* aired from 1963 to 1973. It would take a bit longer before a substantial number of men rolled up their sleeves and joined her behind the stove, but she was the one who first invited them to do so. In addition, she changed how many women thought of themselves in the kitchen. While Betty Friedan and Gloria Steinem were telling American women to get out of the kitchen, Julia Child showed them how to change their role in it. For millions of them, her nonconfrontational message proved equally liberating.

Julia Child's influence on American culture was less a matter of recipes and menus than a matter of attitude—an attitude of comfort and confidence, comfort in that she treated the kitchen as a place of joy rather than toil, and confi-dence in that she showed ordinary Americans that they had the ability to master culinary art. In 1965, *Time* featured her on the cover, with the headline "Everyone's in the Kitchen." It may have been an exaggeration, but it was a sign that things were changing.

Things had to change. Like American wine, then dominated by skid-row fortifieds, American food had fallen to its lowest point in the 1950s. Earlier in the century, the country had shifted from a primarily agricultural society to one that was largely urban, so fewer and fewer people were eating food that they grew or raised themselves. Then, following the Second World War, America shifted again, this time to suburbia, where by 1960 a full quarter of the population lived. Unlike compact cities, which could support butchers, fishmongers, and green-grocers, America's suburbs were diffuse, scattered places. Since people had to drive to get just about everywhere, one-stop shopping became all the rage. Urban markets (Pike's Place in Seattle, for example, or the Reading Terminal in Philadelphia) had attracted customers by offering variety and freshness. By contrast, much of the food in suburban supermarkets was standardized and, because it had to be trucked in from distant places, often treated with chemicals and preservatives. And while supermarkets attempted to carry some of almost everything, they were not big enough to stock a lot of anything—certainly not different varieties of apples or lettuces, or a wide selection of meats, or different kinds of fish. But for a generation that had grown up with shortages, first in the Depression and then during the war, none of this much mattered. Suburban America valued convenience rather than variety, ease rather than authenticity, and speed rather than freshness.

The move from farm to city to suburb meant that cooking skills no longer were automatically being handed down from mothers to daughters. Many a 1950s suburban cook scarcely knew how to make a pot roast, let alone how to pluck a chicken. Because she (and the home cook back then invariably was a woman) tended to think of cooking as drudgery, she often looked to technology for help. She used a bevy of electrical appliances—can openers, plug-in carving knives, mixers, blenders, toasters, crock pots—to cut down on the time she had to spend in the kitchen. In the same spirit, she seldom strayed into the dining room, which one survey revealed to be the least frequented room in the American home. After 1953, with the advent of the TV dinner, many people ate in the den or family room, eyes glued to the set, dinner conversation a relic of the past. It was the era of open-the-can, defrost-the-package, and stir-the-mix cooking, the age of Jell-O salad, Salisbury steak, and tuna casserole (made with canned tuna, canned cream of mushroom soup, processed American cheese, and crushed potato chips). Not surprisingly, this also was when American cuisine became the object of jokes abroad and acquired an international reputation as something dull, if not vulgar—a reputation it has never entirely shaken.

Dining out in the suburbs in the 1950s and 1960s was only marginally better than eating at home. Convenience there also often proved more important than taste. The first McDonald's franchise opened in 1955, but fast food already was well established—most famously at the local drive-in, where people did not even have to get out of their cars. Italian and Chinese restaurants were popular, but the food in both tasted remarkably homogenous. More upscale restaurants tended to serve "continental" fare, which meant things like Veal Cordon Bleu or Chicken Kiev, everything accompanied by a medley of frozen vegetables, leading more than one wag to wonder what continent was being implicated so cruelly. The fanciest restaurants usually served a predictable sort of supposedly haute cuisine—Duck à l'Orange, Steak Diane, Tournedos Rossini, all distinguished primarily by the use of rich, heavy sauces. As food historians John and Karen Hess complained, such food was "fancy for the sake of being fancy." The Hesses lambasted the state of cuisine in the United States. "How shall we tell our fellow Americans," they asked, "that our palates have been ravaged, that our food is awful, and that our most respected authorities on cookery are poseurs? . . . Good food in America is little more than a memory, and a hope."

Julia Child on the set of *The French Chef* provided the hope, but the memory was more native. It focused on American, not French, food—food that had been and sometimes still was being made in small towns and big-city immigrant households, where cooking reflected regional origins. The author and bon vivant James Beard was its great champion, and many of the distinctly American dishes he admired have survived unchanged—crab cakes from the mid-Atlantic states, cedar-planked salmon from the Pacific Northwest, sour cherry soup made by midwestern Germans, spicy sausages cooked by Italians in New York. The next stage in the rise of American cuisine involved broadening and refining America's culinary heritage. The local or regional became national, a transformation that changed it in subtle but significant ways and resulted in the gradual emergence of a new American cuisine. Yet even here, the changes were inspired by French models. After all, in most people's minds, fine food *was* French food. That was what Julia Child had taught them.

In 1966, the same year that Robert Mondavi opened his winery and announced that he would make wines to compete with the French classics, a young American from New Jersey, by way of California, was living in Paris. She ostensibly was studying literature as part of the French major that had sent her abroad for her junior year of college, but by her own admission she actually was spending most of her time "eating all over." Her name was Alice Waters, and like many students in the 1960s, she was rebelling against bland American conformity—including bland suburban American food. She admired writers like Simone de Beauvoir and Françoise Sagan who refused to follow social or literary conventions, and she thought of French food as itself somehow countercultural. She could not afford to go to fancy Michelin-starred restaurants, but then the haute cuisine served there would have satisfied neither her politics nor her palate. Instead, she delighted in the unpretentious fare offered in local cafés and bistros, food enjoyed by working people who often made their living off the land. France beyond Paris was still a predominantly agricultural country, and Waters spent much of her year abroad traveling through the provinces, savoring and romanticizing the way of life she found there. In doing so, she experienced what she calls "a major realization"—namely, that food and wine can nourish the heart and soul even more than the body.

The realization crystallized after an especially memorable dinner at a small country inn in Brittany, when after dessert Waters and the other patrons stood as one, applauding the cook and crying out, "*C'est fantastique!*" It was, she thought, a communion of love:

> I've remembered this dinner a thousand times: the old stone house, the stairs leading up to the small dining room, which seated no more than twelve at the pink cloth-covered tables and from which one could look through the opened windows to the stream running beside the house and the garden in back. The chef, a woman, announced the menu: cured ham and melon, trout with almonds, and raspberry tart. The trout had just come from the stream and the raspberries from the garden. It was this immediacy that made those dishes so special.

Back home after graduation, Waters couldn't get that experience out of her head. Food—or more precisely, a lifestyle that valued food as more than fuel—had become a passion. She was training to become a Montessori teacher, but found that she cared more about teaching her friends and neighbors about food than about teaching children. Like so many Americans at the time, she wanted to make a difference, but unlike most everyone else, she wanted to do it in the kitchen. So in 1971, she opened a restaurant called Chez Panisse in a shingled Victorian house in Berkeley. Her goal was simple enough—to share some of what she had first learned in France, by making meals like the one she remembered from that old stone inn in Brittany.

Alice Waters often is called the mother of the new American cuisine. Yet few chefs and restaurateurs, even those who cut their culinary teeth working for her, have imitated her menus. Her influence, then, is less a matter of recipes or ingredients than of vision. That vision can be summed up in one word—her own word, *immediacy*. From the beginning, Waters wanted to provide her guests with an experience akin to her seminal supper in Brittany. She could not transplant the stream or the garden, so she did not try to replicate specific dishes. Instead, she tried to reproduce what had made those dishes so special. And she soon became convinced that in order to provide her customers with culinary immediacy, she had to do two things: use the freshest and finest ingredients possible, and cook so as not to disguise those ingredients' natural flavors.

More than anything else, immediacy defines the new American cuisine in its many guises. Not that long ago, sophisticated cooking in America aimed for just the opposite effect. The classic French sauces, like the complicated dishes to which they contributed, were a series of tricks and mystifications, sleights of hand in which basic ingredients got transformed into new and delicious concoctions. A béarnaise sauce, for instance, was not supposed to taste like tarragon, its most flavorful ingredient, just as quenelles were not supposed to taste of river fish. The goal was to turn raw nature into something elegant and sublime, with the chef functioning as an artful magician. Much the same was true of continental cooking, although in a blander, watered-down form. But the new American cuisine has a different goal — to use the finest ingredients and to cook them so that they taste first and foremost of themselves.

Waters opened Chez Panisse with a vision, even a dream, but absolutely no experience in the restaurant business. Because she did not know how other restaurateurs purchased food or composed menus, and because she had no mentors in the trade to instruct her, she did things her own way. Rather than purchasing foodstuffs from wholesale sources, she went directly to farmers, searching all over the Bay Area for what was freshest and most flavorful. She bought ducks in Petaluma, lamb in Carneros, produce from East Bay growers (including plenty of home gardeners), and fruit from local orchards. In the beginning, she even traded meals in the restaurant for ingredients she needed. Gradually she developed relationships with farmers who were willing to grow exactly what she wanted, as she wanted it. Her food was wholly local, even though much of it (say, mesclun salad) had little or no local history. She bought wine from young producers who were just getting a foothold in Sonoma and Napa. They, in turn, excited by her wine-friendly food, brought their friends, their colleagues, and their customers to the restaurant. "We tried from the start to do things the way we would like to have them done at a dinner party at home," Waters remembers. "We wanted the restaurant to be popular and inclusive, but at the same time we wanted the food to be nothing but the very, very finest obtainable." Soon enough, Chez Panisse became very popular indeed. Helped by a number of laudatory reviews, including one from James Beard in his nationally syndicated column, it became *the* chic California restaurant—all the while serving decidedly unchic country French food.

Make no mistake, Chez Panisse at the start was unabashedly French. The menu was written in French, the wine list featured lots of French wines (many soon to be imported by Waters's friend and neighbor Kermit Lynch), and the recipes came from French cookbooks. It wasn't at all, however, the kind of French restaurant with which Americans were familiar. The waiters didn't wear tuxedos; there were no red velvet banquettes or crystal chandeliers; the menu wasn't full of complicated creations and super-fancy sauces. Instead, the food quite literally was down-to-earth. Waters offered a single menu, giving her customers the ingredients she had been able to forage that particular day. If people wanted choices, they could go elsewhere and select from the same tired haute cuisine options. But if they wanted to savor the freshest and the best, she found a place for them at her table.

Yet because she cared more about creating the "*c'est fantastique*" feeling of culinary immediacy than about replicating specific dishes, the food Waters served slowly but inevitably asserted an identity of its own. Her insistence on using local ingredients meant that dishes at Chez Panisse simply had to taste different from their original French models. Pacific shellfish were not the same as those in the Mediterranean, for example, so a Berkeley bouillabaisse could never be the same as one in Marseilles. When Waters realized as much, she dropped the name and called the new dish a stew. Then she started printing her menus in English. And because she kept highlighting native, locally procured ingredients, her food gradually began to seem more northern Californian than anything else.

Waters challenged conventions, and that challenge became her most important legacy. She became an ardent advocate of farmers' markets, an eloquent spokesman for community-supported, sustainable agriculture, and the founder of a children's gardening project called the Edible Schoolyard. Although few restaurateurs copied either her menus or her politics, more and more of them took up her original challenge — to try to change Americans' attitudes toward food, to compel people to care about it by enticing them with authentic, immediate flavors. In 1992, Waters wrote to President-elect Bill Clinton, urging him to hire an American rather than a French chef at the White House. (He did.) Four years later, she asked him to initiate a public dialogue about food's place in American culture, and to plant an organic garden on the White House grounds. (He didn't.) "How can we teach basic human values — such as courtesy, civility, honesty, and generosity," she asked, if "eating [is] little more than refueling, devoid of any seasonal, agricultural, or social context?" By that point, Waters's vision, originally wholly French, had become truly American — but American as melting-pot fusion, Jeffersonian agrarian ideals enlivened with provincial French flair.

In the 1980s, a new generation of restaurant chefs began to promote and popularize the new American cuisine. Some of them — Jeremiah Towers, Joyce Goldstein, Mark Miller — had cooked at Chez Panisse. Others had different backgrounds, but

they all shared Waters's commitment to immediacy. Larry Forgione, who became the executive chef at Brooklyn's River Café
in 1979 and then the chef-owner of Manhattan's An American
Place in 1983, was one of the most influential. Forgione believed in American food, so he used only American ingredients:
wild mushrooms from Michigan, shrimp from Key West, eggs
and chickens from a New York farm (where he insisted that the
birds not be kept in coops, leading him to coin the term "free-
range"). Some items on his menu were traditional. Dishes such
as New England Cod Cakes or General Robert E. Lee's Favorite Soup (a tomato-based vegetable soup enlivened with
sherry) proudly proclaimed a regional or historical identity.
Much of the menu, however, bespoke innovation. Oyster and
Ginger Bisque, Chile Duck Pilaf, Grilled Mahi-Mahi with
Pineapple-Chile Barbecue Sauce, Spring Lamb with Rhubarb
and Dandelion—these were among Forgione's fusion-style
dishes that seemed unusual and surprising. They clearly were
American, but they also clearly were new.

Forgione's cooking was inspired both by his respect for regional American ingredients and by his admiration for French
cooking, specifically the nouvelle cuisine movement of the late
1960s and 1970s. Itself a product of that politically charged era,
nouvelle cuisine challenged French tradition by bringing the
best of the provinces into some of France's most sophisticated
dining rooms. Its adherents rejected complicated preparations
in favor of simple, direct ones. They advocated using fresh, seasonal ingredients, and added texture to dishes with stock reduc-
tions in place of heavy doses of butter and cream. So too, they
tried to retain natural flavors instead of creating something allegedly more refined. At first, nouvelle cuisine sparked heated

debates in France. Traditionalists viewed it as a debasement of culinary art, a conspiracy against good taste, while supporters argued that it marked renewal and renovation. Over time, it carried the day, so much so that it eventually became somewhat traditional itself. Christian Millau, the cofounder of the Gault-Millau magazine and restaurant guide that became the movement's bible, predicted as much. "Be creative and open-minded," he told the chefs on the gastronomic front lines. "You are the only one who knows. People want to come to eat your cooking and experience your taste, not the contrary."

In France, noted chefs like Paul Bocuse, Michel Guérard, Joël Robuchon, and Alain Senderens heeded Millau's advice. But his words had an equally strong effect in America, where creativity as he described it became a primary ingredient in the new American cuisine. He addressed American chefs in person at a New Orleans symposium on American food in 1983. "Trust yourself," he told them. Feel free to "experiment" with "new taste combinations" and "new ingredients, not only from your own country, but from all over the world." While he promoted the principles of nouvelle cuisine, he urged Americans not to fashion explicitly French menus. "The real problem for a nation is to express its true genius in its own language," he argued. "The extraordinary diversity of this country has not [yet] been reflected in its cuisine." But when that happens, he prophesied, the United States will become "a major gastronomical power in the world."

Over the next two decades, Millau's predictions came true. More and more American chefs used fresh, seasonal ingredients. They emphasized natural as opposed to concocted flavors, and experimented through combination. Asian and Latin

American elements became commonplace as their cuisines became ever more global. In addition, these chefs used traditional, regional American ingredients, many of which earlier cooks had dismissed as being too provincial for fine dining. Some restaurants had distinct regional identities — Mark Miller's Coyote Café in Santa Fe, for example, which put a new spin on southwestern cooking, or Paul Prudhomme's K-Paul's Kitchen, where traditional New Orleans cuisine was tweaked in nouvelle fashion. Others offered a broader range, serving up global fare with the taste of immediacy — Danny Meyer's Union Café in New York, Wolfgang Puck's Spago in Los Angeles, Joyce Goldstein's Square One in San Francisco, and the eponymous Charlie Trotter's in Chicago. Still other chefs cooked in a fusion style that combined a single country's culinary traditions with American tastes. Roy Yamaguchi's cooking was Japanese with an English accent, Michel Richard's French in California garb, and Susan Fenniger and Mary Sue Milliken's Mexican but simultaneously very American. Fenniger and Milliken called their West Hollywood restaurant Border Grill, a name that expresses well what this new cooking was all about. American cuisine became revitalized and redefined when chefs began to cross (and recross) culinary borders.

No one person invented the new American cuisine. It developed from a host of sources, different elements of which different people combined in different ways. One crucial factor in its development was product availability. Overnight air shipping allowed chefs to feature farm-fresh ingredients from sources thousands of miles away. As a result, restaurateurs could broaden their range of offerings without sacrificing quality, and regional ingredients from far and near started showing up on menus nationwide. Another crucial factor was that Americans took to this new cooking right away. People were literally hungry for it—ironically, not so much because they wanted change, but because this particular change proved so comfortable. After all, fusion cuisine was nothing new. Traditional American cooking had always been something of a hybrid, the product of colonies and outposts with heterogeneous, transient populations. The new American cuisine took the melting-pot principle to a new, rarefied level, but the principle itself was well established. Larry Forgione and the other pioneering chefs were not doing something all that radical when they combined elements from different culinary traditions. The big difference came in their attempt to elevate those combinations to the level of fine dining. As Forgione himself argued, the new American cuisine marked an evolution more than a revolution. "To evolve is to move forward, to grow, and to change continuously from a simpler to a higher and more complex state," he said. "It is this that I believe we are experiencing."

Precisely because these new restaurant chefs aimed to elevate American cuisine to a higher state, wine played an important role in their thinking. In keeping with his philosophy, Forgione's wine list was American. Other restaurateurs took a more global approach, and in the early days some were unabashedly Eurocentric. Yet regardless of what went on their lists or of the depth of their own wine knowledge, they all wanted their customers to drink wine. Back in the 1950s and 1960s, Americans frequently drank spirit-based cocktails before and even during meals. At home, wine often was viewed as something cheap and tawdry, while in restaurants it seemed effete and pretentious. No matter whether eating in or out, few people thought of it in connection with American food. But then this new generation of American chefs appeared on the scene, trying to elevate American cooking to a new standard of sophistication — to take it from the home kitchen, give it class and style, and introduce it into the world of linen tablecloths, polished silver, and crystal glassware. In other words, they wanted to make it as chic and sophisticated as fine French cuisine. And high-class French dining always included wine. If American cooking was to reach that level, it needed to follow suit. Wine had to replace cocktails on the American restaurant table.

It did. By the 1990s, wine had become a regular part of restaurant dining for millions of Americans, including many who did not often drink it at home. Increasingly, these people drank American wines, ordering from lists that bore little resemblance to the *cartes des vins* of two or three decades earlier, when the lists at exclusive restaurants had been dominated by French bottles, especially red Bordeaux and white Burgundies. (Italian restaurants had been the one notable exception, but they also offered few American wines.) Now California Cabernets and Chardonnays were the biggest sellers. And now the food as well as the wine was apt to be American, although much of it would have been unrecognizable to anyone dining out a generation earlier. The melting pot of American cuisine had changed. It now included spices from India, chilies from Latin America, sashimi from Japan, and all manner of other ethnic ingredients. American cooking had become truly international. It also had become lighter and fresher, less dependent on heavy, cream and butter-based sauces. And because the food so vibrantly expressed natural flavors, no matter what regions or nationalities those flavors fused together, it tended to be extraordinarily wine-friendly. While it might not pair all that well with an old-fashioned, tannic red Bordeaux, the new American cuisine proved ideal for wines that themselves had been made on the American-style varietal model. And well it should, since those wines stressed natural fruit flavors above all else, flavors that echoed the bold, fresh elements in the food. Indeed, one thing that links the rise of American wine with that of American cuisine is a shared emphasis on primary flavors, letting the wine and food taste of themselves.

Over the past twenty years, the new American cuisine has become the most popular style of fine restaurant dining in the United States. Ingredients previously unknown outside specific regions are now ubiquitous all across the country—seared yellowfin tuna, for instance, or soft shell crabs, both enhanced through the addition of ingredients foreign to the regions. (The tuna might be coated with a ginger and sesame seed crust, and the crabs might be topped with a tropical salsa.) This sort of combination is no longer countercultural, no longer especially daring, no longer all that new. Now it is part of the mainstream. The combinations do not always work, as some zealous chefs take the fusion notion to absurd extremes, but they work often enough—and not only in New York, Los Angeles, or San Francisco, but throughout the country (although rarely, as yet, in small towns). Moreover, to the degree that it represents an evolution from old-fashioned American food, this new cuisine seems natural, almost expected. American food has gone upscale, but it has not forgotten its roots.

The prevalence of American wines in American restaurants to-day is due in large measure to their improved quality. Yet quality by itself does not get any wine onto a restaurant list, let alone ordered by a customer. The wine first has to be marketed and sold, and an important factor in the changing image of American wine over the past thirty years was its acceptance and promotion in restaurants. Even more than retailers, restaurateurs convinced previously loyal French wine drinkers to associate fine dining with American wine. Probably the most influential single restaurant was New York's Windows on the World, which opened atop a World Trade Center tower in 1975. Windows placed a great deal of emphasis on wine, going so far as to have a separate "Cellars in the Sky" annex that featured an elaborate tasting menu in which course after course was paired with wine after wine. Its wine director, Kevin Zraly, put together a list that, while international, featured California wines prominently. This was in part because the weak dollar of the mid-1970s made investing in a wholly French cellar prohibitively expensive, but also because the restaurant's management believed in the future of American wine. To the surprise of many in New York's self-contained restaurant trade, the California wines sold well, and soon other restaurants, especially those featuring new American cuisine, followed suit. It was not long before a list without American wines seemed hopelessly out-of-date. The East Coast, long a bastion of Francophile wine appreciation, was changing fast.

The West Coast was changing even faster, as San Francisco and Los Angeles dueled to be the trendiest, hippest American culinary city. One of the most important restaurants in California, though, was Domaine Chandon in the Napa Valley, which opened in 1977 under the direction of a French chef, Philippe Jeanty. Because it offered the valley's first and, for a time, only fine dining experience, Domaine Chandon played host to virtually everyone with an interest in food and wine who visited Napa. The cuisine was nouvelle-inspired French, the wines largely (but not wholly) Californian. Diners came away from a meal there armed with a crucial bit of new knowledge: American wines really could pair well with sophisticated food. They took that knowledge home with them, and soon fine restaurants all over the country began to include American wines on their lists.

The format of those lists was changing as well. Before the rise of American wine, most upscale restaurant lists, being predominantly French, were organized by geographical region. Under "Red Wines," for example, came Bordeaux and Burgundy; under "Whites," those two regions as well as the Loire and Alsace. If the restaurant deigned to include non-French wines, it likely lumped them together as "Other"—a California Chardonnay side by side with a German Liebfraumilch, a Zinfandel next to an Italian Lambrusco. The demand for varietally labeled American wines changed all that. At first, many restaurants just added more categories—"Red California," for example. But with the emergence of wines from other states, as well as internationally styled wines from other countries, geographical organization became unwieldy and confusing. Many lists then began to be organized varietally, with red Bordeaux placed under "Cabernet," and white Burgundies under "Chardonnay." Other lists were reconfigured according to wine style—"light, crisp whites," "full-bodied reds," and so on. Some restaurateurs went a step further, helping their customers by matching dishes on the menu with specific wines on the list. Twenty-five years ago, unless a customer was fluent in French (vintages and appellations as well as the language), ordering a bottle of wine in a restaurant could be an intimidating experience. Even though restaurants today offer many more high-quality wines from many more places, the experience has become much friendlier —all because, from the list to the table, wine has become a regular part of dining out.

One other factor proved crucial to consumer acceptance of wine. In 1991, the popular CBS television program *60 Minutes* aired a segment on the so-called French paradox, bringing to a wide audience for the first time medical research demonstrating the health benefits of wine consumption. Viewers learned that the French, despite a diet high in fat and cholesterol, have a significantly lower rate of heart disease than Americans. Researchers at Harvard and Boston University identified a possible cause—the flushing effect of red wine on platelets that cling to fatty deposits on the artery walls. Consumers reacted enthusiastically to the news, and red wine sales skyrocketed. People began ordering a glass of red wine in lieu of a cocktail, and doctors even began advising their patients to drink a glass or two of wine a day.

The *60 Minutes* story was just the beginning. More and more research, some American but plenty coming from abroad, suggested that alcohol in general and wine in particular have positive medicinal effects. Even the federal government concurred. First the Departments of Agriculture and Health and Human Services declared that moderate alcohol consumption could be part of a healthy diet. When they revised the federal dietary guidelines, they referred specifically to wine's having enhanced "the enjoyment of meals by many societies through-out human history." Then the two departments approved bot-tle labels directing consumers to "learn the health effects of wine consumption." This may sound like an endorsement that damns with faint praise, but because only sixty years had passed since selling wine had been a crime against the United States Constitution, it represented a big change. Wine in America was becoming more than acceptable. It was desirable. At least in fine restaurants, a bottle on the table is now a fact of American cultural life.

That same bottle, however, has not necessarily come into the home. Many Americans continue to view wine as some-thing appropriate only for special occasions, suitable for dining out but not really part of daily fare. Elsewhere in the wine-pro-ducing world over the past thirty years, it has become an in-creasingly democratic drink, with bottles previously the province of a privileged few being enjoyed by people from all social and economic backgrounds. Ironically, in America, the world's leading democracy, many people continue to regard wine as an elitist, even an aristocratic beverage. The prevalence of this view helps explain why per capita wine consumption, af-ter the sharp rise of the initial boom years in the 1970s and early 1980s, leveled off and, for a time, actually declined. A small, mostly well-heeled minority does drink wine regularly at home, but while consumers spend more money on wine today than they did twenty years ago, neither the amount of wine they purchase nor the number of them purchasing it has in-creased. The legacy of Prohibition lingers, as does the popular association of wine with snobbery and pretension.

Prohibition's still potent legacy is most evident in the

thicket of state laws and regulations that link wine with spirits everywhere in America in a three-tier system of producer, wholesaler, and retailer, with wholesalers as the linchpin. Liquor wholesalers dictate which wines do and do not get into the market, and ever since Repeal they have been loath to relinquish any of their control. In state after state during the 1970s and 1980s, they opposed laws that would permit farmers to sell wine directly to consumers. And more recently, since the advent of e-commerce, they have lobbied long and hard to prevent wineries from selling directly to customers across state lines. Because wine remains linked with spirits in terms of distribution and regulation, it cannot be sold in supermarkets or other food stores in most parts of the country. Antiquated blue laws force people to purchase it in (sometimes state-run) liquor shops, at times from a clerk behind a barred window, and just about never on Sunday. Wine in the United States is, as ever, overseen by the Bureau of Alcohol, Tobacco, and Firearms, not the Department of Agriculture. In myriad ways, it still carries the stigma of being something dangerous and even sinister.

Yet the potential for broad public acceptance of wine has never been greater. One reason is the high quality of today's wines. Another is the fact that wine's popularity in restaurants has brought it to the attention of millions of new consumers. At the dawn of the twenty-first century, the challenge for American wine producers no longer involves getting their bottles on exclusive lists alongside French classified growths. The challenge now comes at home, on the supper table, where wine too often remains unknown.

In the heady early days of what he called "the wine revolution," Leon Adams confidently predicted that table wine soon would become America's "national mealtime beverage." Writing in the 1978 edition of *Wines of America*, he foresaw per capita consumption reaching five gallons sometime in the next decade. He also thought that Americans would move away from label-drinking snobbery, that young people would lead the increase in consumption, and that the popular acceptance of wine would help civilize drinking by encouraging a social intolerance of drunken behavior. "Today wine is being recognized as an integral, wholesome new part of the national diet," he declared. "The wine revolution has only begun." Nearly twenty-five years later, none of those predictions has come true. (With per capita consumption at about two gallons, almost 70 percent of wine purchases are made by people over forty, and they still pay a great deal of attention to the supposed prestige of the label.) This is not to denigrate Adams, who until his death in 1995 was American wine's most ardent champion, but rather to indicate how unpredictable the developments of the past three decades have been. Quality has reached unprecedented heights, and American wines have become international style setters, but table wine still has little to do with daily home life in much of the country. In this regard, the wine revolution still has only just begun.

Many factors have combined to hinder the widespread acceptance of wine as part of the American daily diet. These include lingering neo-prohibitionist sentiments, the three-tier distribution system, the enforced separation of wine and food in places where the two cannot be sold together, and the legal drinking age of twenty-one — raised from eighteen in most states during the 1980s, a move that paradoxically led to an increase in drunkenness and a perception among many young people that all alcoholic beverages serve but one function, intoxication. Equally problematic has been the wine industry itself, which instead of promoting wine to middle America, courts an affluent but stagnant market by advertising and selling it as a luxury product.

With few exceptions, American wine producers today are just as short-sighted as vintners were following Prohibition. Rather than trying to increase demand, they continue to play to an existing market, charging ever more money for wines that can make them a profit but that cannot attract new customers. As a whole, the industry has not yet learned the lesson of Robert Mondavi's historic gamble back in the 1960s—that producers should not be satisfied with simply giving people what they want, since when it comes to wine, many Americans do not really know what they want. When American wine producers do try to attract new customers, they tend to create products that they can promote like beer—wine coolers, carbonated pop wines, and most recently, fruit-flavored concoctions such as peach Chardonnay or blackberry Merlot. These beverages are advertised as something to drink at a party or while watching a ball game, and so at least implicitly as something with which to get drunk. They do nothing to help increase the national acceptance of wine as a civilized mealtime beverage. In terms of how wine is advertised, promoted, and sold in America, many wineries operate as though the changes of the past thirty years had not occurred.

But the changes did occur, and some of the most significant ones took place at home. Just as American restaurant cuisine has evolved in new directions, American home cooking has become more adventurous and more inclusive. Many of the influences were similar. Exotic herbs and spices added new flavors to food, and oils replaced butter and cream, resulting in lighter, fresher-tasting fare. This emphasis on fresh flavors led home cooks, like their restaurant compatriots, to pay more attention to seasonal produce, a change that contributed to the resurgence of farmers' markets around the country. Salads, made with a variety of lettuces rather than just the ubiquitous iceberg, became more popular, as did pastas in all shapes and forms. Foreign influences also played a role, as the home menu became more diverse, incorporating elements from Asian, Caribbean, and Mexican cuisines. Those influences changed even traditional American fare. Ground beef, once used principally for hamburgers or meatloaf, now fills tacos, and health-conscious cooks poach chicken breasts instead of frying drumsticks. Unlike restaurateurs, home cooks did not usually have ingredients airfreighted to their doors. But they did see their markets change, with better-quality fish, meat, poultry, and produce becoming available. Expensive specialty stores started the trend, but ordinary supermarkets soon followed. Today, three-quarters of the country's supermarkets have "gourmet" sections. They carry ingredients that no one had heard of thirty years ago. Moreover, cookware shops have popped up all over the place, most tellingly at that emblem of middle America, the shopping mall, where a Williams-Sonoma store has become almost as commonplace as Sears.

The change in what Americans eat at home extends even to foods they do not cook—prepared, packaged, and take-out products. Nearly every American supermarket now sells rotisserie chickens as well as an array of cooked dishes. These range from the familiar to the foreign, and they reflect all the influences of the past thirty years. Foods previously considered exotic are everywhere today. Americans buy ready-made designer pizzas and supermarket sushi, curries and calamari, all sorts of cheeses, pastas, and olives, which they take home and eat for dinner. So although the country as a whole may not be cooking more than it did before, it clearly is eating differently. For many Americans, food has become a more important part of their lives. It no longer is just fuel.

A generation ago, many Americans tried to get out of the kitchen as quickly as possible. Preparing daily meals was widely viewed as drudgery, and eating them was not much better. Today, plenty of people still buy primarily convenience and fast foods, but an increasingly influential minority now takes the time to care about what they make and eat. They think of cooking as an act to share with family and friends, and they consider food a source of fun. Although the wine industry often treats the home kitchen as if it were trapped in a 1950s suburban time warp, American home cooking has evolved apace with American restaurant cuisine. The changes have not been felt in every kitchen, but they have been sufficiently widespread to make the first decade of the new century wine's truly golden opportunity to, at long last, come home.

9

The World
Comes Knocking

THE MOST INFLUENTIAL figure in American wine has never planted a vine or crushed a grape. Robert M. Parker, Jr., does not make wine. Instead, he writes about it, and his writing has changed how people all over the world appreciate, consume, and even produce it. Parker wields tremendous power with his pen. For more than twenty years, he has been evaluating and rating wines in a bimonthly newsletter, *The Wine Advocate*, which he publishes privately from his home in Monkton, Maryland. His opinion can make or break the fortunes of an entire vintage, since millions of consumers buy wines according to the numbers he assigns to the ones he reviews, numbers that the wine trade publicizes prominently in order to promote sales. Parker's influence, however, is more profound than that of a mere critic. His taste affects not only sales but also production—specifically, the style of wines vintners make. And although he is a devoted Francophile, his palate remains unabashedly American. He values bold flavors over delicate ones, richness over austerity, power and concentration over finesse. Parker has strong opinions about how wine should be made and, especially, about how wine should taste. He favors low yields in the vineyard, minimal filtration and clarification in the winery, and most important, winemaking that begins with fully ripe grapes. "I'm a fruit fanatic," he says. "The taste of the grapes is all-important." In turn, he is most enthusiastic about wines that display "gobs" or "oodles" of rich, ripe flavor—or, as he puts it, "wines with personality."

That bold, fruit-forward style is American wine's hallmark. It comes naturally in California's sun-drenched vineyards, where, in Parker's words, the best wines exhibit "exuberance, flavor, ripeness, and, for better or worse, power." It increasingly also defines excellence beyond the Golden State, especially in the Pacific Northwest. As a style, though, it is not exclusively American. Indeed, over the past two decades, more and more wines coming from elsewhere, from vineyards in both the New World and the Old, have been fashioned so as to express this sort of exuberance. During this same period, consumers and producers the world over have come to view the bold, vibrant taste of fruit as a salient mark of quality. As a consequence, wine has become internationalized to an extent inconceivable a generation ago. Robert Parker is not responsible for the global prevalence of fruit-driven, personality-filled wines. Yet more than anyone else, he is responsible for the establishment of international rather than merely regional standards of wine quality, standards that are one of the main legacies of American wine's rise.

Parker first discovered wine as a college student, when he went to France to spend his 1967 Christmas vacation with his girlfriend, Pat, who was studying there during her junior year. On his first night in Paris, she took him for a reunion supper to a café, where he, surely jet-lagged, had his first glass of dry table wine. "It was a revelation," he says. At home, his beverage of choice with a meal had usually been a soft drink. "I'd never liked beer or hard liquor," he recalls, "but I found that wine tasted good. It was also the perfect accompaniment to food, and in those days it was even cheaper than Coke." He and Pat had little money, but they found that it was possible to eat and drink well in France on a shoestring budget. So they did just that for six weeks, traveling throughout the country, seeing the sights, and drinking wine every day, until each had to go back to school.

Parker returned home hooked. He joined a tasting group, started frequenting local wine shops in Baltimore and Washington, and read everything he could find about wine. He soon discovered that there was a dearth of reliable information concerning which wines were worth buying and which should be avoided. Most well-known wine writers worked in the wine trade as merchants or importers, and they wrote as if talking to each other—praising this wine for its resemblance to that one, and defining quality in terms of regional characteristics. Because they had obvious vested interests, their recommendations did not prove particularly useful. Parker also discovered that while there were many superb wines available for purchase, there were plenty of bad ones too, wines that often tasted sour and nasty. Many of these were praised by writers as being "typical" of a region or appellation, which led him to wonder why anyone would want to drink something typical if it did not first taste good. Much like the vintners who ignited the American wine boom in the early 1970s, Parker loved French wine. He did not love it, however, for its pedigree or renown. What he cared about—all he really cared about—was taste, and he couldn't understand why writers so often praised wines that tasted bland and unexciting. Ten years after that first glass of wine in Paris, his hobby had grown into a consuming passion. Now thirty-one years old, married to Pat, and working as a lawyer in Baltimore, he borrowed $2,000 from his mother and started *The Wine Advocate*. Although initially aimed at a local audience (and in fact called *The Baltimore/Washington Wine Advocate*), it was from the start geared to wine drinkers rather than to members of the trade. As the cover proclaimed, this was "the independent consumer's guide to fine wine."

Robert Parker saw himself as wine's Ralph Nader—a whistle-blower when something was made poorly because a champion of quality. For Nader, the criteria for determining quality were fairly obvious. Since automobiles should not explode in accidents, the Chevrolet Corvair that failed the crash test was defective. But for Parker, whose concern was taste rather than safety, things were more ambiguous. If a wine tasted sour but was said to be "typical," was its "design" really defective? His solution to this aesthetic conundrum was to posit a universal standard, a Platonic form of excellence against which particular wines could be measured. This form or ideal, which he defined with a number (the perfect 100), transcended all local or traditional criteria for assessing quality. No matter where a wine came from or how it was made, Parker measured it against that same unchanging standard. To do so, he evaluated it solely in terms of its sensorial composition—the depth and length of its bouquet, its weight and body on the palate, its assorted aromas and flavors. He paid little attention to pedigree or expectation, and so defined quality without reference to reputation or renown.

In Parker's view, the problem with using regional typicality as a standard was that it was both too narrow and too mundane, reflecting by necessity averages rather than benchmarks. The latter certainly existed in traditional regions, and the more Parker tasted, the more easily he could identify them. But he was convinced that certain wines existed as benchmarks precisely because they stood apart from other wines made in their region. They were better than those other "typical" wines because they approximated a universal ideal of perfection. This was a distinctly New World approach, much like the one adopted by the pioneering California vintners who first tried to make wines to challenge French supremacy but had no tradition of premium wine growing to guide them. For winemakers, focusing on a wine's composition meant analyzing it scientifically. For Parker, who had little interest in acid ratios or Brix levels, it meant concentrating exclusively on taste. And he was an intensely analytical taster. "That's what I do," he told an interviewer. "I'm a taster—and tasting is a matter of focus, of mental discipline. When a wine is in my mouth, I can taste it and smell it in all its dimensions—the full range of flower, plant, vegetable and earth, of red and black fruits. I don't let anything interfere."

Taste, of course, is always at least partly subjective, and the cover of *The Wine Advocate* advised readers, in small but boldface print, that "there can never be any substitute for your own palate nor any better education than tasting the wine yourself." Nonetheless, Parker's reviews, and especially his scoring system, represented an attempt to objectify taste. From the start, he employed the 100-point grading scale that he and his American readers knew from school. When people told him that wine was the drink of romance and poetry, not a test to be marked, he had this retort: "I know of no one with three or four different glasses of wine in front of him or her, regardless of how good or bad the wines might be, who cannot say, 'I prefer this one to that one.' Scoring wines is simply taking a professional's opinion and applying some sort of numerical system to it on a consistent basis."

In the early days of *The Wine Advocate*, hardly anyone knew who Robert Parker was, and hardly anyone paid much attention to his Platonic ideal of the 100-point wine. His breakthrough came five years after he started the newsletter, when after a trip to Bordeaux to taste barrel samples of wines from the 1982 vintage, he returned home and breathlessly described them as "voluptuous and ravishing," absolute must-buys. "From a purely hedonistic standpoint," he wrote, "this vintage has probably produced the most perfect and enjoyable wines in the post–World War II era." This was quite a limb to go out on, for these wines were not at all "typical." Because the growing season in 1982 had been especially hot and dry, the wines tasted riper, fleshier, and more intensely fruity than those from previous years. To Parker, whose only criterion for evaluating a wine or a vintage was taste, this made them better. But to many in the trade, including many respected writers, those same characteristics made the wines suspect. They were too rich, ran the argument, to be truly representative of Bordeaux. But when the bottled wines arrived in the United States, consumers began to vote with their wallets. Sales of 1982 red Bordeaux went through the roof. So did subscriptions to *The Wine Advocate*, and Parker soon had enough subscribers to quit practicing law and devote himself full time to wine.

A comment often heard about the 1982 Bordeaux vintage was that the wines tasted Californian. Parker never said that, and indeed, in the early days of *The Wine Advocate* he often was quite contemptuous of California wines, finding too many of them sterile and vapid, pale imitations of European classics. Nevertheless, the characteristics that so enthralled him about the 1982 Bordeaux were precisely the ones that the best California wines displayed—rich ripe fruit, a full body, and intense, concentrated flavors. Other wines, many from Burgundy and Italy for example, often came in a lighter, more restrained style. Restraint, however, had no place in Robert Parker's ideal of perfection. No matter whether reviewing red wines or whites, and no matter whether the wines in question came from the Old World or the New, he bestowed praise and awarded high scores to wines marked by exuberance, ripeness, and above all the rich taste of fruit.

Although it is difficult to know whether Parker's palate reflected or dictated consumer preferences, it is clear that he spoke to the emerging American market for wine as no one else did. His predilection for bold flavors mirrored the emergence of the vibrant new American cuisine. His lack of interest in whether a wine tasted "typical" rang true to people who, because they were new to wine, did not always know what to expect from it. And his notion of a standard of excellence that transcends varietals, regions, and types made especially good sense to consumers as well as merchants. In the 1980s and 1990s, every year brought more fine wines from more places into the American marketplace. Parker soon developed a receptive, sometimes even a fawning audience.

For Parker, who littered his reviews with references to rock music and approached his subject with passion rather than reverence, wine had nothing to do with snobbish pretension or effete posturing. It was first and foremost an object of sensual delight. As he freely confessed, "Wine is a beverage of pleasure, and I'm a hedonist." His scoring system was easy to grasp and hard to argue with. At first, he was the only person grading wines on the 100-point scale. But as his reputation grew, other critics and journalists adopted it, and digits began to replace adjectives as indicators of quality. Parker always insisted that his written commentary was a better source of information, but he knew that plenty of *Wine Advocate* subscribers saw only the numbers.

So did many winemakers, both at home and abroad. Robert Mondavi, for one, changed his winemaking methods because he was distressed by the numbers Parker was bestowing on his wines. "[When] I saw we weren't getting really good scores from Robert Parker," Mondavi says, "I began to taste our wines more carefully. [I found that] he was right. So I went back to making them without filtering and doing everything as naturally as I could." Parker advocated reduced yields and non-interventionist winemaking. He was not shy with his opinions, but the bottom line for him was always the wine itself. As David Shaw points out in an insightful *Los Angeles Times* profile, "He Sips and Spits, and the World Listens," he awarded 100 points to an American wine for the first time in 1990 even though the wine had been filtered and came from a vineyard harvested at "more than double the yield Parker generally recommends." The wine was Groth Vineyards' 1985 Reserve Cabernet from Napa. Parker described it in *The Wine Advocate* as "utterly compelling and magical . . . sumptuous on the palate, with mind-boggling richness . . . a tour de force in winemaking!" In the long run, then, how a wine was produced didn't much matter. What counted was what was in the glass, which he evaluated in universal rather than particular or regional terms.

Parker has had a similar influence in Europe. When Angelo Gaja started crafting new-style Barbarescos in Piedmont, for example, Parker's enthusiastic response and high scores provided an important form of outside validation. Wines that might otherwise have acquired only local renown became international stars. Other winemakers soon followed suit, and before long a stylistic revolution was under way. Much the same thing happened elsewhere. Led by such diverse figures as Jean-Michel Cazes in Bordeaux, Miguel Torres in Spain, and Piero Antinori in Tuscany, wines from the most tradition-laden regions began to change. They became richer, riper, more accessible when young, and above all fruitier. Was Robert Parker responsible? Not directly. But the criteria of quality he championed so passionately began to be accepted worldwide. "Tastes have been changing throughout the world," acknowledges the Italian winemaker Tino Cola. "To some extent, the American palate is becoming the international palate. Most people everywhere now want richer, fresher, fruitier wines, and Parker has captured that shift."

Wine's internationalization has not come because, as happened with Coca-Cola and McDonald's hamburgers, people everywhere started to consume the same thing. While it is true that global plantings of Cabernet, Chardonnay, and Merlot have increased significantly over the past thirty years, these varieties have tended to replace ones previously used mainly for the sort of cheap *vin ordinaire* whose market is shrinking everywhere. Even in European countries where wine traditionally has been an everyday beverage, quality has become more important than quantity. The average Frenchman today drinks half as much wine as his father did, but he spends twice as much money on it. Moreover, the success of the so-called international varietals has inspired vintners to upgrade the quality of other wines made from more indigenous grapes. "Super Tuscans," made primarily from Cabernet and Merlot, have paved the way for an upsurge in quality in Chianti, just as Chardonnay's success in Piedmont has led to better Arneis, and Cabernet's achievements in Catalonia have inspired vintners to improve the wines they make from Grenache and Tempranillo. These new wines do taste richer, riper, and fruitier than wines made in these regions did a generation ago. Yet while they tend to share a stylistic profile, they do not at all taste the same. Idiosyncratic regional standards of quality simply have taken a back seat to global ones.

Advances in communication and travel, the advent of the "flying winemaker" (and the flying viticulturist), increased competition, and a growing world market for fine wine have all played key roles in wine's internationalization. No factor has been more significant, though, than the emergence of criteria for assessing quality that can be recognized and employed worldwide. Whether expressed in numbers, adjectives, or exclamations of delight, for the first time in history wine quality is being recognized in much the same fashion all over the globe. One upshot of this is that no region sets a single standard anymore. This does not mean that Bordeaux and Burgundy have become unimportant, but rather that even there quality has been redefined. Another upshot is that wine everywhere is better. Not every producer's, to be sure, and not in every vintage, but the world's vineyards produce more truly fine wine today than ever before. As Hugh Johnson notes, "In the end it is the market that decides, and the message that it gives today is unambiguous: the days of the nondescript are numbered."

At the start of the twenty-first century, first-class wines are coming from both the New World and the Old. And in Europe, many such wines are being made in new styles, in new regions, and often from new grape varieties. The rise of American wine has coincided with—indeed gone hand in hand with —the rise of the world's wine. It is impossible to say what would have happened elsewhere if wine and wine appreciation in the United States had remained in Prohibition's dark shadow. Perhaps great wine would have emerged just as quickly from Australia, Argentina, Chile, New Zealand, and South Africa. Perhaps too, just as many new-style wines would have been produced in Italy's Piedmont and Tuscany, Spain's Ribera del Duero, and Germany's Pfalz. Yet given the power of the American dollar and the global influence of American tastes in other fields, one suspects not. In the twenty-three years since Robert Parker founded *The Wine Advocate*, the amount of money Americans spend annually on wine has increased more than fivefold, even though per capita consumption has remained relatively stable. That money has helped winemakers all over the world build new facilities and plant new vineyards. American consumers, like American wines, have made a global difference.

Only a small percentage of those consumers actually read *The Wine Advocate*, which is available solely by subscription and which, save for an occasional editorial, contains nothing but reviews and ratings. The *Wine Spectator*, a glossy biweekly with more than six times as many subscribers and an estimated readership of roughly 800,000, is a more popular source of general consumer information. The *Spectator* started in 1976 as a tabloid covering mostly California wine, but after former investment banker Marvin Shanken purchased it three years later, the magazine's focus gradually expanded to include wine from other countries as well as what Shanken calls "wine lifestyle." He explains: "I thought that wine in and of itself was too narrow. If you add the components of dining, cooking, travel and collecting, among others, then you really are inside the mind, the heart and soul of a typical wine lover who wants to enjoy many of the pleasures of life." The *Wine Spectator* adopted the 100-point scoring system in 1985, but the magazine's real significance is less as a forum for reviews than as a mirror in which to view wine's evolving place in American culture. Shanken not only reports on "wine lifestyle" but also helps promote it—notably through The Wine Experience, an annual weekend of seminars and tastings. Vintners from around the globe come to see and be seen at an event that itself symbolizes wine's internationalization. As Shanken notes, it "brings the wine world together."

As recently as thirty years ago, that world was fragmented. Producers in different countries and regions were mainly isolated from one another, and save for connoisseurs who collected a few recognized superstars (top Bordeaux growths and Burgundy crus), most of the world's wine drinkers consumed local wines. Since winemakers had little contact with their peers in other regions, they followed tradition largely for tradition's sake. The picture was especially bleak in the United States, where American wine was just getting off skid row and wine drinking in general was still regarded as something suspect. No one chronicled anything like a "wine lifestyle." Today, all that has changed. As wine has become internationalized, it also has become respected, even desired, with high-class wines from many different places being sought after by consumers from many different countries. Although internationalization does not mean Americanization, it is a phenomenon that has been inspired and often led by Americans—by vintners and researchers whose insights have been adopted worldwide, by

Robert Parker and the now widely accepted notion of global quality, and by consumers who include wine as part of their daily lives. The world has come knocking at America's door, and the result has been a cross-fertilization of ideas benefiting wine producers and wine lovers everywhere.

America's rise to a position of prominence in the international world of wine has brought foreign vintners to the United States as well as sent Yankee winemakers overseas. Ernest Gallo and Robert Mondavi both purchased European operations in the 1990s, Gallo in Italy and Mondavi in France. (Mondavi also became involved in joint ventures in Chile and Italy, in addition to his partnership with Mouton-Rothschild at Opus One in Napa.) Similarly, Jess Jackson of Kendall-Jackson purchased wineries in Argentina, Chile, and Tuscany, and Beringer Wine Estates began to import wines from Europe and South America. In each case, the company sent its own winemakers and viticulturists abroad, to teach but also to learn. The Americans sometimes created an overseas replica of a California winery, but they more often worked in partnership with local winemakers and grape growers, serving as consultants rather than colonizers.

Consultants have become a major force in wine over the past ten years, and so represent another important factor in its internationalization. Because they work at multiple properties, they have to be true to their own vision or style rather than to any one regional tradition. No one does that better than Michel Rolland, a Frenchman from Bordeaux, who advises winemakers at scores of chateaux and whose work has contributed to the changing style of that region's red wines, which over the past decade have become softer, richer, and more clearly fruit-driven. But Rolland's work in other countries is what sets him apart from other leading consultants (including Americans like Tony Soter and Helen Turley). His clients have included Trapiche in Argentina, Casa Lapostolle in Chile, Marqués de Cáceres in Spain, Ornellaia in Italy, and highly regarded wineries such as Cuvaison, Harlan, Merryvale, and Newton in California. Rolland's declared philosophy is that wine should provide maximum pleasure, and wherever he works he fashions wines in a ripe, supple, fruit-forward style. "The essence of what I love in a wine," he explains, is flavor that is "intense, generous, and bursting with fruit." Not surprisingly, his wines regularly receive scores of 90 and above in *The Wine Advocate*.

For American wine, even more significant than the role played by foreign consultants has been the influence of foreign investment—individuals and companies from abroad who have recognized the potential for great wine to be produced in the United States, and who then have purchased vineyards and constructed wineries in order to help that potential become realized. The Pinot Noirs made by French-owned Domaine Drouhin in Oregon and the *vinifera* varietals made by Italian-owned Barboursville Vineyards in Virginia, for instance, inspired other vintners in those states to reach for new, loftier goals—some of which already have been reached. But no wine has been more affected than sparkling wine, the quality and image of which has been utterly transformed over the past two decades. Almost all domestic "champagnes" used to be coarse and crude, their only connection to the classic French model being the name. Today, while most serious producers have stopped using the name, their best sparkling wines have become elegantly sophisticated—New World classics in their own right. This sea change mirrors in miniature the renaissance of American wine as a whole. Yet while native-born visionaries were responsible for the vast improvement in the quality of American table wine, foreigners, particularly Frenchmen from Champagne, led the rise with American sparklers.

With only a few exceptions, American sparkling wines lagged behind table wines when the country's vinous revival began in the 1960s and 1970s. There were two reasons for this. First, when growers began to replant premium vineyards with premium grape varieties, sparkling wine became a convenient outlet for fruit that no longer was considered good enough for quality still wine. This was because sparkling wine was viewed as something cheap—a legacy, perhaps, of the Cold Duck craze. The second reason was that sparkling wine indeed *was* cheap, both to make and to buy. Most producers created the bubbles either by injecting finished wines with carbon dioxide or by inducing a second fermentation in large tanks of still wine —two inexpensive methods that inevitably yield inferior results. Save for a few wineries in California (Schramsberg and Hanns Kornell in Napa, Korbel in Sonoma), no one used the more costly and labor-intensive *méthode champenoise*, in which the second fermentation is induced in each bottle. As Tom Stevenson notes in his *World Encyclopedia of Champagne and Sparkling Wines*, "American 'champagne' simply meant any wine that had bubbles, and the more the technology was applied, the cheaper the price became and the lower the quality dropped." Then in 1972, Moët et Chandon, the largest French Champagne house, purchased eight hundred acres near Yountville, in the Napa Valley, with the express intention of making premium, *méthode champenoise* sparkling wines. The first bottles of Domaine Chandon were released four years later, and in the decade that followed a host of other Champagne producers opened outposts in California. These included Piper-Sonoma (started in 1980), owned by Champagne Piper Heidsieck; Roederer Estate (1982), a subsidiary of Champagne Louis Roederer; Mumm Napa Valley (1985), owned jointly by Seagram and Champagne Mumm; and Domaine Carneros (1987), a partnership of Champagne Taittinger and its American importer, the Kobrand Corporation. American bubbly would never be the same.

The Champagne producers came to California because they knew that they could not satisfy the rapidly growing demand for quality sparkling wine with Champagne alone. By definition, Champagne comes exclusively from the region of that name, a *département* of rolling hills east of Paris where almost all of the plantable vineyard land is under vine. Moët et Chandon could have expanded by purchasing more property, but doing so would have been prohibitively expensive. So Count Robert-Jean de Vogüé, chairman of the luxury goods empire Moët-Hennessy, authorized the creation of Domaine Chandon as a way to maintain market share. Because Champagne had been an international favorite for so long, the Champagne houses often had taken a multinational approach to their product—fashioning, for example, different cuvées, or blends, for different markets. It is not surprising, then, that they were more willing than their colleagues in Bordeaux and Burgundy to accept the possibility that quality wine could be made elsewhere. Count de Vogüé never thought that the wine from Napa would equal Dom Perignon, but he knew that his winemakers could improve on most American "champagnes." Moët's *chef de cave*, Edmond Maudière, supervised the winemaking, which took place at Trefethen Vineyards while the Chandon facility was being built. He decided early on not to date the wines by vintage, and included wines from the 1973 and 1974 harvests in the first commercial cuvées—10,000 cases of Brut and 3,000 cases of Blanc de Noir, released in December 1976 for the holidays. Priced below Champagne but above almost all American sparkling wine, they were an immediate hit with consumers looking for something new. The winery, along with its ground-breaking restaurant, opened a year later. By 1983 production exceeded 200,000 cases, and Domaine Chandon was an unqualified success.

The boom in premium California bubbly made by the *méthode champenoise* proved spectacular. Between 1975 and 1985, production rose tenfold. No wonder other Champagne houses decided to follow Moët's lead. And the French were not alone. Two large Spanish sparkling wine producers, Freixenet and Codorníu, followed suit, opening Gloria Ferrer in Sonoma and Codorníu Napa in Carneros. During the 1980s, demand for sparkling wine kept growing, and it looked to some as though the upsurge would never stop. Sales slowed in the 1990s, though, largely because Americans have never accepted sparkling wine as a mealtime drink. They view it almost exclusively as a beverage for celebration, and with only a limited number of birthdays or anniversaries (and only one New Year's Eve) to celebrate, consumption is limited. Some sparkling wine producers have shifted to still wine, while others have moved aggressively into the export market—notably Mumm Napa, which is a leading brand in Great Britain.

Despite their initial success, the winemakers at the Champagne outposts in California all faced a steep learning curve. Their early releases, while clearly superior to the vast majority of what had come before in California or New York, often tasted thin, green, and clumsy. They lacked the elegance and finesse of world-class bubbly. The problem was that the winemakers aped a Champagne model, even though they were working with very different fruit. Grapes in Champagne, a region lying at the northern limit of European viticulture, struggle to ripen. Even when physiologically mature, they have a low level of sugar and a high degree of acidity. Just the opposite is true in sunny California, where grapes easily can get too ripe for sparkling wine. Only when winemakers began to use the Champagne model as a starting point rather than as an object of imitation did the quality of their wines improve noticeably.

Harry Osborne at Schramsberg, Greg Fowler at Mumm Napa, and Forrest Tancer at Iron Horse played pioneering roles in the rise of American sparkling wine, but the most inspiring wines were made by a Frenchman, Michel Salgues, at Roederer Estate. Salgues crafted what Robert Parker immediately hailed as "the best sparkling wine of all the French-American joint ventures," a nonvintage Brut that, while maintaining plenty of acidity, tasted rich, fruity, and delightfully toasty. It resembled Champagne, but was very much its own self. During the 1990s, more and more producers followed Salgues's lead, not necessarily making wine in his bold, rich style, but always taking care to respect the personality of the fruit they used. Today, sleek, elegant sparklers come from Domaine Carneros, Pacific Echo, and "J"; opulent, fruity wines from Gloria Ferrer and Mumm Napa; and toasty, nutty ones from Domaine Chandon, Iron Horse, and Schramsberg. Even beyond California, as exemplified by the wines coming from Fox Run in the Finger Lakes, Argyle in Oregon, L. Mawby in Michigan, and Gruet in New Mexico, quality has taken a quantum leap forward. Put simply, American sparkling wine became world class when it was no longer made solely in a foreign image—although, paradoxically, foreigners were the ones who showed the way.

The Champagne houses were the first large foreign companies to invest in American wine, but they were not the last. In 1979, the German firm of A. Racke purchased Buena Vista, Agoston Haraszthy's historic property in Sonoma. Racke devoted considerable resources to upgrading it, and today the winery makes upward of 200,000 cases of well-regarded, primarily Carneros table wine. In a similar move, the late Miguel Torres, the patriarch of one of Spain's leading wine-producing families, purchased vineyard land in Sonoma County's Green Valley appellation in 1983. His daughter, Marimar, took charge of the operation, which today produces award-winning Chardonnay and Pinot Noir. Not every foreign company investing in American wine was European. In 1988, Sanraku of Japan purchased the Markham Winery. Other Japanese purchases soon followed—for example, St. Clement by Sapporo and the Raymond Winery by Kirin. More recently, Southcorp, Australia's largest wine producer, formed a partnership with Paragon Vineyards on California's Central Coast to produce wines under the Seven Peaks label. For these companies, national boundaries proved irrelevant. All that mattered was the pursuit of quality and profit, both of which came from American vineyards.

As important as corporate investment was the individual initiative of vintners who came to the United States to start something new. Bernard Portet was one of the first. The son of the technical director at Château Lafite-Rothschild in Bordeaux, Portet visited California in 1970 on behalf of John Goelet, a New York businessman whose family had connections with the Bordeaux wine trade and who wanted to invest in the wine business. Portet traveled around the world on Goelet's behalf for more than a year, investigating possible vineyard sites in South Africa, South America, and Australia, but his arrival in the Napa Valley on a hot summer afternoon convinced him that this was the place. The specific place he had in mind was a plot of land in the Stags Leap district, where he noticed a dip in the temperature and a cooling breeze. Here the grapes would have the benefit of Napa sunshine without excessive heat. Goelet hired Portet to run the place, which they called Clos du Val. Portet made Clos du Val's first wines from purchased grapes in 1972, using mostly borrowed equipment. One of them, the Cabernet, was included in Stephen Spurrier's Paris tasting four years later. The ensuing publicity about a Frenchman, with ties to Château Lafite no less, making award-winning wine in California proved priceless.

Other foreign vintners soon followed. From Bordeaux came the De Wavrin family at Chateau Woltner and the Fourmeaux at Chateau Potelle; from the Languedoc via Paris, Robert Skalli at St. Supéry; from Alsace, Jacques Schlumberger at Michel-Schlumberger. And from Switzerland, Donald Hess at the Hess Collection; from Holland, Ben Pons at Bernardus; from Chile, Agustin Huneeus at Franciscan and then Quintessa; from England, Peter Michael at Peter Michael; from Australia, Robert Hill Smith at Voss and winemaking guru Daryl Groom at Geyser Peak. Founded in 1880, Geyser Peak had been a bulk wine producer before Prohibition. The property was revived in 1972 when the Schlitz Brewing Company purchased it, but the emphasis remained on low-end wines. (Geyser Peak in the Schlitz years had the dubious distinction of being the first winery to sell wine in cans.) When Schlitz

got out of the wine business, a local Sonoma County entrepreneur, Henry Trione, purchased Geyser Peak. In 1989, he
went into partnership with Penfolds, the popular Australian label, with part of the deal being that Penfolds would supply the
winemaker, who turned out to be Daryl Groom. For the previous five years, Groom had been responsible for Penfolds's
and Australia's greatest red wine, Grange Hermitage, and he
brought to Geyser Peak a degree of expertise it had not known
before. He has stayed in Sonoma ever since, through more
changes of ownership at Geyser Peak, all the while turning out
some of California's finest wines in their various price categories.

The most renowned foreign vintner in California was
probably Christian Moueix, the general manager of Château
Pétrus in Pomerol and the director of a veritable empire of estates in Bordeaux. In 1981, Robert Mondavi introduced
Moueix to Robin Lail and Marcia Smith, daughters of John
Daniel, the tragic, reticent steward of Inglenook. Mondavi,
flush with excitement over his recent partnership with Baron
Philippe de Rothschild at Opus One, suggested that Moueix,
Lail, and Smith consider a similar arrangement. They liked the
idea and so started a joint venture with the single goal of producing a world-class Napa Valley red wine. Moueix supervised
the winemaking, but the result was never designed to be a Bordeaux clone. For one thing, the soil was different. For another,
Pétrus was made almost entirely from Merlot, while the Napa
vines were predominantly Cabernet Sauvignon. Instead,
Moueix aimed for a powerful, intense New World wine. The
result, which he called Dominus, and which debuted in 1986,
was exactly that. "Prodigious," declared Robert Parker when he
surveyed Moueix's accomplishment. "This renowned French-

man and his Bordeaux-trained assistants have done something few others have managed to achieve in California — they have fashioned . . . a wine of historic significance that is simply more majestic than most others." Although the Moueix-Lail-Smith partnership disbanded in 1995, Dominus, now owned completely by Christian Moueix, continues to be one of America's benchmark wines.

A less famous but equally significant foreign-born vintner is Hermann Wiemer, who makes what are arguably America's finest Rieslings and Gewurztraminers at his eponymous winery on Seneca Lake, in the Finger Lakes region of New York. Born in Bernkastel, on the Mosel, and trained at the Geisenheim school of viticulture, Wiemer came to the United States in 1968 to be the winemaker for Walter Taylor at Bully Hill. He almost immediately began investigating the possibility of making wine with *vinifera* rather than hybrid grapes. His father had run Germany's largest nursery and supervised much of that country's vineyard replanting after World War II, and the young immigrant followed in those footsteps — starting a nursery devoted to clones of *vinifera* varieties and experimenting with techniques for growing them. In 1979, he bought an abandoned soybean farm and began planting vines. Progress came slowly, but by the 1990s his wines displayed true class. As important as the wines themselves is Wiemer's ever-growing nursery, which now supplies some 200,000 vines a year to winemakers and grape growers at home and abroad, including such prestigious California operations as Caymus and Kendall-Jackson. Back in 1908, U. P. Hedricks, then America's leading viticulturist, predicted that eastern grape growers "may now succeed" with European grapes. It took much longer than he thought, but his prediction did come true. Nowhere is that truth more evident than at Hermann Wiemer's nursery and winery on Seneca Lake, which sits about thirty miles away from the research station where Hedricks worked.

The foreign influence in the United States, much like the American influence abroad, brought the world of wine closer together. Old World vintners learned a great deal from the Americans—about technology, about research, and about their own customers' tastes and the emerging international style. At the same time, the Americans learned a great deal from the Europeans. They discovered that not every grape variety flourishes in every location; that excessive manipulation, particularly heavy-handed filtration, robs wines of nuance and charm; and most important, that quality originates in the vineyard, not the winery. Grape growers everywhere began to pay more attention to their vineyards, viewing them less as the source of a raw product to be manufactured than as the spring from which any wine's distinction and character flow. As a result, they began to fertilize less and to use fewer chemicals. Although many large-volume producers continued to harvest huge crops and to treat their wines industrially, and although more than a few upscale producers became preoccupied with glossy labels and fancy packaging, quality on the whole improved. There simply were more good wines from more places available to consumers than ever before. This was obvious in the United States, especially in the big East Coast markets like New York and Washington, D.C., where wine shops stocked the best from every continent. It became clear elsewhere too. In England, a market traditionally dominated by French wines, a new generation of consumers discovered wines from Australia, South America, South Africa, and, yes, the United States. British wine consumption increased dramatically. In Japan and other Asian countries, markets with no previous interest in wine, consumers began to experiment with it, at first as a status symbol, but then, helped immeasurably by reports of red wine's health benefits, as common practice. They too purchased wines from all over. The surging international interest in wine encouraged American producers to devote attention to these new markets, and in the 1990s exports increased 500 percent. American wine, long derided if not ignored abroad, had acquired new and deserved respect.

American wine's newfound renown comes from many things: the emergence of an international style that displays an uncanny California flair, the global dominance of the grape varieties that American consumers like best, and not least the sheer power of the U.S. dollar, which influences fashions throughout the world. Despite some critics' claims that regional distinctions are in danger of being lost, internationalization has not brought homogenization. Particularly in the last decade, American vintners have shown a new appreciation for *terroir*, a concept that they had long distrusted. It is an admittedly tricky notion. A French word for which there is no precise English translation, *terroir* means place, but in many different senses — geologically, including such things as soil structure, composition, and drainage; topographically, incorporating factors like exposure and altitude; meteorologically, meaning not just regional weather patterns but also local microclimates; and finally — this being the slipperiest part of all — culturally, the human history of the place. Human history has nothing to do with a vineyard's ecosystem. Yet it has everything to do with *terroir*, for without human history, that vineyard would not be a vineyard,

Vitis vinifera being a cultivated rather than a wild species. In Europe, where vineyards have been cultivated continuously for hundreds of years, this cultural aspect is all-important. But in America, it is virtually nonexistent, which helps explain why American wine growers for a long time took a dim view of the whole idea. Today, however, they are apt to embrace it—admittedly often just as the buzzword of the moment, but sometimes as the elusive key to genuine distinction.

Although he did not use the word back then, Paul Draper of Ridge Vineyards, in the Santa Cruz Mountains south of San Francisco, was the first prominent American winemaker to focus intensely on *terroir*. Beginning in the early 1970s, he pioneered wines that bespoke their vineyard origin in addition to any personal winemaking style, thus displaying the sort of balance that many of America's best vintners want to strike today. Draper came to Ridge in 1969, seven years after the winery had been founded by a group of scientists from the Stanford Research Institute. The scientists had purchased a plot of mountain land as a weekend retreat. It included a pre-Prohibition vineyard, and they hired Draper when they decided to expand their production. A native of Illinois, Draper was something of a vagabond. He had lived in California, New York, Europe, and South America, worked for U.S. Army intelligence and then for a development company promoting capital investment in Third World countries. One of his projects involved wine growing in Chile. It floundered, though, when Salvador Allende's socialist party gained power, and Draper was looking for a new job when he met Dave Bennion, the leader of the Ridge group, who took him to the vineyard above the clouds. There he found home.

Paul Draper has been at Ridge, as winemaker, part owner,

and now director (the winery having been purchased by a Japanese pharmaceutical firm in 1986), for more than thirty years. Much of the initial attraction came from the place itself —a fifty-acre plot of very mature vines, mostly Cabernet, on a ridge named Monte Bello, some 2,500 feet above what in a decade or so would become Silicon Valley. The site had a history, one that Draper insisted he could taste in the wine. He never considered blending those grapes with fruit from someplace else. But his job back then included expanding production, and since Monte Bello was the only vineyard Ridge owned, he had to look around for other sources of high-quality fruit. He quickly became fascinated by the differences in the character of the grapes from particular vineyards, no matter the varieties being grown there. So early on he decided to exploit those differences—to showcase the personality of individual vineyards, and to vinify, age, and bottle the wines from them separately. In other words, he decided to express *terroir*.

Draper's philosophy has never changed. "To take something from the earth, to carry it a step further through artisan ability, and make of it as sophisticated and complex a thing as fine wine"—that, he explains, is why he came to Ridge. If he had a model when he began winemaking, it was Bordeaux— specifically Château Latour, which he considered the first of the first growths. Yet he never aimed to fashion a Latour clone. He used American rather than French oak barrels, trucked grapes up the mountain from vineyards located far away, and devoted as much attention to Zinfandel and even Petite Sirah as to Cabernet. He made sure to keep the vineyard batches of these wines separate too, and then to market the resulting wines as individual personalities. His strategies all worked. Ridge's Petite Sirah from York Creek, and its Zinfandels from

Howell Mountain, Geyserville, and Lytton Springs, became darlings of consumers riding the new American wine wave. At the same time, the winery's Monte Bello Cabernet demonstrated to all who tasted it how rich, powerful, and site-specific an American red wine could be. Draper proudly identified his wines' *terroirs* on their labels. Ridge was far removed from the glamour of Napa or the rural chic of Sonoma. Its fame had nothing to do with lifestyle and everything to do with a distinctiveness derived from place.

In the years that followed, other winemakers would strive to express something similar. Slowly, gradually, *terroir* became a defining characteristic of the best California (and then American) wines. Award-winning Cabernets from Diamond Creek, Dunn Vineyards, and Heitz Cellars, as well as Chardonnays from Chateau St. Jean and Kistler, all vineyard-designated, helped lead the way. Today even Gallo, as part of its Sonoma operation, features varietal wines from single vineyards—the Frey, Laguna, and Stefani Ranches. And Robert Mondavi offers, in addition to his regular Napa line, a "district" series, wines identified by the specific appellation in which the grapes are grown—Stags Leap, Carneros, or Oakville. American wine's rise came initially in the guise of homage and emulation. Then it took the swaggering form of self-assertion. But the final and ongoing stage in that rise has come as vintners have begun to root their appreciation of their wines in native ground. Today, more and more American winemakers are trying to build a tradition of quality based on particular *terroirs* and distinctions of place.

The basic indicator of place with American wine is something called an American Viticultural Area (or AVA), created by the Bureau of Alcohol, Tobacco, and Firearms in 1978 as a means of certifying authenticity—so that, for example, a wine labeled "Napa Valley" must be made from grapes that actually grow in Napa (or, to be precise, 85 percent of the wine must come from there). The AVA system represents an important step in the history of American wine, as it was the first, and so far only, form of regulation having to do with geographical origin. The system is not, however, without flaws. Because the federal government refuses to become involved in matters of taste, the awarding of AVA status to a particular region is in no sense an indication of quality. Indeed, the official guidelines explicitly state that the "BATF approves a viticultural area by finding that the area is distinct from surrounding areas, but not better than other areas." As a result, AVAs tend to be created along political rather than geographical lines, and disputes concerning where to draw the boundaries almost inevitably get resolved in favor of expansion rather than constriction.

Some critics of the AVA system bemoan the absence of the sort of regulations that characterize the French *appellation contrôlée* system, in which a government organization delimits not only a region's borders but also what grapes can be grown there, how high the yields can be, and how the wines must be made. Such restrictions make little sense in America, however, where few regions have enough viticultural history to justify anyone's claims of sure knowledge concerning either viticulture or enology. (For that matter, they don't always make sense in France, especially in less prestigious areas where they can handcuff vintners by prohibiting experimentation and possible improvement.) In the United States, attention to place has to come through evolution, not mandate. And that is exactly what has been happening, as particular AVAs or parts of AVAs have begun to gain reputations for particular types of wine.

Nowhere has this evolution been more noticeable than in portions of California's Central Coast, where vintners first tried to grow just about everything, but then learned to specialize in grape varieties appropriate to their *terroirs*. This occurred with both large-scale producers and small, artisanal ventures. Monterey County's Salinas Valley witnessed an explosion of vineyard planting in the 1970s. Fueled by anticipated consumer demand, large corporations such as Coca-Cola and Prudential Insurance developed huge vineyards, Prudential's 8,500-acre San Bernabe Vineyard being the most massive. They planted the grape varieties that their market research indicated would sell best. The problem was that what sold well did not necessarily grow well, and many of these grapes, especially red varieties like Cabernet and Zinfandel, did not ripen fully in the relatively cool valley. The resulting wines tasted strongly vegetal. Development stopped, and not until the late 1980s was there any substantial reinvestment. By then, growers had learned their lesson. Existing vineyards were either replanted or grafted over to new varieties, especially Chardonnay, and new plots were devoted primarily to white grapes. Put simply, as Monterey changed color, both the quality and the reputation of its wines improved, all because the wines were better matched to the place.

Farther south, near the town of Paso Robles, where the climate is considerably warmer, a similar evolution occurred, albeit on a smaller scale. Growers who initially sought to profit from the demand for Chardonnay turned to red grapes—Cabernet, Zinfandel, and increasingly, Syrah. Today, some of the state's finest red wines come from there. Still farther south, in the paradoxically cooler Santa Maria and Santa Ynez Valleys (cooler because here the mountain ranges run west to east, rather than north to south, thus exposing the vineyards to a maritime influence), wine growing took off with a vengeance in the 1980s. Growers here emphasized Burgundian varieties, Chardonnay and Pinot Noir, and before long wineries such as Au Bon Climat, Babcock, Foxen, and Sanford developed something of a cult following. Large-volume producers from up north took note. Kendall-Jackson, Beringer Wine Estates, and Robert Mondavi all purchased land in Santa Maria, their rationale being clear—here the wines matched the place.

Jim Clendenen is one of the leaders of the Central Coast's rise to prominence. Something of a counterculture refugee, he started his winery in 1982, intent on fashioning vineyard-designated, *terroir*-specific wines, and so named it Au Bon Climat, or "of good site." (*Climat*, in French, means vineyard site, not climate, and so is synonymous with *terroir*.) Yet Clendenen does not own vineyard land. Instead, he purchases grapes from specific vineyards, even from specific parcels within vineyards, whose character he wishes to express. As a result, his wines tend to taste quite distinctive. At the same time, a stylistic thread ties them together. Fruit and varietal character are at the fore, with oak, spice, and mineral flavors playing a significant but clearly secondary role. In Robert Parker's words, they are "gorgeously fragrant, authoritatively flavored wines that combine complexity with decadence." That sense of decadence comes, no doubt, from Clendenen himself, who with his wild mane, unfettered enthusiasm, and strong opinions, appears to live life much as his wines taste—full throttle.

That is the final element in any great wine—the man or woman who makes it. *Terroir* surely is important, but if a vintner does not pay close attention to other factors, the taste of place in his or her wine will be rendered irrelevant. Great wine comes from great places, but also from great winemakers, and the United States today is blessed with an honor roll of them. Some work at small estates and others at large properties, just as some practice hands-off techniques while others are interventionists. The only common thread is that they all make wines that are true to both their *terroir* and their own visions. "That's the rule of the game," says Jim Clendenen, "to express the flavors indigenous to the vineyards . . . [along with] a consistency of winemaking style."

Greatness in American wine began to be realized on an unprecedented scale in the 1990s, compelling Robert Parker to declare that "only a knucklehead could ignore [it]." Unlike their predecessors twenty years earlier, the winemakers responsible for these wines no longer were following foreign models or trying to fool experts. Their goal instead was to declare independence with wines that would resemble time-honored classics but that also would have a personality of their own. In order to reach that goal, they had to redefine what constitutes true quality, making "great" a category of its own and not merely a modifier (as in "great Bordeaux" or even "great Cabernet"). At the same time, they had to rediscover the origin of their wines' character—the ground in which it took root. Not all American winemakers, even those with high ambitions, have reached that goal. But many have, and in the process American wine has become a world leader. It has risen to amazing heights in an amazingly short period of time.

BIBLIOGRAPHY
AND A NOTE ON SOURCES

The bibliography that follows identifies only those sources that I used directly when writing this book. For readers interested in pursuing the subject further, a few of these sources will prove especially valuable. Thomas Pinney's *History of Wine in America: From the Beginnings to Prohibition* is a magisterial work. It has not received the recognition it deserves from students of American cultural history, but no serious library is complete without it. An equally valuable resource for students of the post-Prohibition era is the series of oral histories compiled by Ruth Teiser for the Regional Oral History Office at the University of California. These chronicle the history of a struggling industry in the words of the men (and occasionally women) who lived it.

Two other sources, unfortunately now out of print, merit special recognition. Leon D. Adams's *Wines of America*, the third and final edition of which was published in 1985, is outdated when it comes to the state of wine production across the country, but remains an important source of historical and anecdotal information. And Ruth Teiser and Catherine Harroun's *Winemaking in California* is an excellent one-volume introduction to the history of wine in America's most important wine-growing state. Both of these need to be updated and re-released.

A number of libraries house impressive collections of material related to the history of American wine. These include the Library of Congress in Washington, D.C., the University of California Libraries at Berkeley and Davis, and the Napa Valley Wine Library in St. Helena. No library, however, provides a better working environment or has a more helpful staff than the Sonoma County Wine Library in Healdsburg. Bo Simons and his colleagues treat their collection as a resource rather than a treasure, making their public facility a wonderfully open place for anyone interested in wine to explore and learn.

Adams, Leon. *Revitalizing the California Wine Industry*, an oral history conducted in 1972 by Ruth Teiser, Regional Oral History Office, Bancroft Library, University of California, Berkeley, 1974.

Adams, Leon. *The Wines of America*. Third edition. New York, McGraw-Hill, 1985.

Adams, Leon. *California Wine Industry Affairs: Recollections and Opinions*, an oral history conducted in 1986 by Ruth Teiser, Regional Oral History Office, Bancroft Library, University of California, Berkeley, 1990.

"American Wine: There's Gold in Them Thar Grapes." *Time*, November 27, 1972.

Amerine, Maynard. *The University of California and the State's Wine Industry*, an oral history conducted by Ruth Teiser, Regional Oral History Office, Bancroft Library, University of California, Berkeley, 1972.

Amerine, Maynard. *Wine Bibliographies and Taste Perception Studies*, an oral history conducted by Ruth Teiser, Regional Oral History Office, Bancroft Library, University of California, Berkeley, 1988.

Amerine, Maynard, and Brian St. Pierre. "Grapes and Wine in the United States, 1600–1979." In *Agriculture in the West*, Edward and Frederick Schapsmeier, eds. Manhattan, Kan., Sunflower University Press, 1980.

Amerine, Maynard, Doris Muscatine, and Bob Thompson. *The University of California/Sotheby Book of California Wine*. Berkeley, University of California Press, 1984.

Asher, Gerald. *Vineyard Tales: Reflections on Wine*. San Franciso Chronicle Books, 1966.

Baxevanis, John. *The Wine Regions of America: Geographical Reflections and Appraisals*. Stroudsburg, Pa., privately printed, 1992.

Blocker, Jack, Jr. *American Temperance Movements: Cycles of Reform*. Boston, Twayne, 1989.

Brenner, Leslie. *American Appetite: The Coming of Age of a Cuisine*. New York, Avon Books, 1999.

Burck, Charles. "Happy Days for California Wine." *Fortune*, September 1971.

Burnham, John. *Bad Habits: Drinking, Smoking, Taking Drugs, Gambling, Sexual Misbehavior, and Swearing in American History*. New York, New York University Press, 1993.

California Wine Greats: Pioneers in Building the Wine Industry of California. M. Shanken Communications, Inc., 1984.

"Can Gallo Move Up?" *Forbes*, October 1, 1975.

Chazanof, William. *Welch's Grape Juice: From Corporation to Co-operative*. Syracuse, N.Y., Syracuse University Press, 1977.

Conaway, James. *Napa*. Boston, Houghton Mifflin, 1990.

Cooke, Phillip, ed. *The Second Symposium on American Cuisine.* New York, Van Nostrand Reinhold, 1983.

Crawford, Charles. *Recollections of a Career with the Gallo Winery and the Development of the California Wine Industry, 1942–1989,* an oral history conducted in 1989 by Ruth Teiser, Regional Oral History Office, Bancroft Library, University of California, Berkeley, 1990.

Cruess, William. *A Half Century in Food and Wine Technology,* an oral history conducted in 1967 by Ruth Teiser, Regional Oral History Office, Bancroft Library, University of California, Berkeley, 1967.

Dannenbaum, Jed. *Drink and Disorder: Temperance Reform in Cincinnati from the Washington Revival to the WCTU.* Urbana, University of Illinois Press, 1984.

Darlington, David. *Angels' Visits: An Inquiry into the Mystery of Zinfandel.* New York, Henry Holt, 1991.

Davies, Jack, and Jamie Peterman Davies. *Rebuilding Schramsberg: The Creation of a California Champagne House,* an oral history conducted in 1989 by Ruth Teiser and Lisa Jacobson, Regional Oral History Office, Bancroft Library, University of California, Berkeley, 1990.

De Chambrun, Clara Longworth. *The Making of Nicholas Longworth.* New York, Long & Smith, 1933.

De Villiers, Marq. *The Heartbreak Grape: A Journey in Search of the Perfect Pinot Noir.* Toronto, HarperCollins, 1993.

Dufur, Brett. *Exploring Missouri Wine Country.* Columbia, Mo., Pebble Publishing, 1997.

Flagg, William J. "Wine in America." *Harper's Magazine* 41 (June 1870): 106–14.

Forgione, Larry. *An American Place: Celebrating the Flavors of America.* New York, William Morrow, 1996.

Gabler, James. *Passions: The Wines and Travels of Thomas Jefferson.* Baltimore, Bacchus Press, 1995.

Gallo, Ernest, and Julio Gallo. *Our Story.* New York, Times Books, 1994.

Gomberg, Louis. *Analytical Perspectives on the California Wine Industry, 1935–1990,* an oral history conducted in 1990 by Ruth Teiser, Regional Oral History Office, Bancroft Library, University of California, Berkeley, 1992.

Grgich, Miljenko. *A Croatian-American Winemaker in the Napa Valley,* an oral history conducted in 1992 by Ruth Teiser, Regional Oral History Office, Bancroft Library, University of California, Berkeley, 1992.

Halliday, James. *Wine Atlas of California.* New York, Viking, 1993.

Hawkes, Ellen. *Blood and Wine: The Unauthorized Story of the Gallo Wine Empire.* New York, Simon & Schuster, 1993.

Hedrick, Ulysses Prentiss. *The Grapes of New York*. Albany, J. B. Lyon, 1908.

Hedrick, Ulysses Prentiss. *Grapes and Wines from Home Vineyards*. New York, Oxford University Press, 1945.

Hofstadter, Richard. *The Age of Reform: From Bryan to F.D.R.* New York, Alfred A. Knopf, 1955.

Husmann, George. *The Cultivation of the Native Grape, and Manufacture of American Wines*. New York, G. E. & F. W. Woodward, 1866.

Husmann, George. *Grape Culture and Wine-Making in California*. San Francisco, Payot, Upsham, 1888.

Husmann, George. *American Grape Growing and Wine Making*. New and enlarged edition, with several added chapters on the grape industries of California. New York, Orange Judd, 1896.

Hutchinson, Ralph. "The California Wine Industry." Ph.D. dissertation, UCLA, 1969.

Irvine, Ronald, with Walter Clore. *The Wine Project: Washington State's Winemaking History*. Vashon, Wash., Sketch Publications, 1997.

Johnson, Hugh. *Vintage: The Story of Wine*. New York, Simon & Schuster, 1989.

Kramer, Matt. *Making Sense of California Wine*. New York, William Morrow, 1992.

Lapsley, James. *Bottled Poetry: Napa Winemaking from Prohibition to the Modern Era*. Berkeley, University of California Press, 1996.

Lender, Mark, and James Martin. *Drinking in America: A History*. New York, Free Press, 1982.

Marx, Leo. *The Machine in the Garden: Technology and the Pastoral Ideal in America*. New York, Oxford University Press, 1964.

McCrea, Eleanor. *Stony Hill Vineyards: The Creation of a Napa Valley Estate Winery*, an oral history conducted in 1990 by Lisa Jacobson, Regional Oral History Office, Bancroft Library, University of California, Berkeley, 1990.

Melville, John. *A Guide to California Wines*. Second edition. San Carlos, Cal., Nourse Publishing, 1960.

Mendelson, Jack, and Nancy Mello. *Alcohol: Use and Abuse in America*. Boston, Little, Brown, 1985.

Mondavi, Peter. *Advances in Technology and Production at Charles Krug Winery, 1946–1988*, an oral history conducted in 1988 by Ruth Teiser, Regional Oral History Office, Bancroft Library, University of California, Berkeley, 1990.

Mondavi, Robert. *Creativity in the California Wine Industry*, an oral history conducted in 1984 by Ruth Teiser, Regional Oral History Office, Bancroft Library, University of California, Berkeley, 1985.

Mondavi, Robert. *Harvests of Joy: My Passion for Excellence.* New York, Harcourt Brace, 1998.

Ostrander, Gilman. *The Prohibition Movement in California, 1848–1933.* University of California Publications in History, vol. 57. Berkeley, University of California Press, 1957.

Ough, Cornelius. *Researches of an Enologist, University of California, Davis, 1950–1990,* an oral history conducted in 1989 and 1990 by Ruth Teiser, Regional Oral History Office, Bancroft Library, University of California, Berkeley, 1990.

Paul, Harry. *Science, Vine, and Wine in Modern France.* Cambridge, Eng., Cambridge University Press, 1996.

Peninou, Ernest, and Sidney Greenleaf. *Winemaking in California III: The California Wine Association.* San Francisco, Peregrine Press, 1954.

Peters, Gary. *American Winescapes: The Cultural Landscapes of America's Wine Country.* Boulder, Colo., Westview Press, 1997.

Pinney, Thomas. *A History of Wine in America: From the Beginnings to Prohibition.* Berkeley and Los Angeles, University of California Press, 1989.

Ray, Cyril. *Robert Mondavi of the Napa Valley.* New York, Warner Books, 1984.

Ray, Eleanor. *Vineyards in the Sky: The Life of Legendary Vintner Martin Ray.* Stockton, Cal., Heritage West Books, 1993.

Robinson, Jancis. *The Great Wine Book.* New York, William Morrow, 1982.

Robinson, Jancis. *Tasting Pleasure: Confessions of a Wine Lover.* New York, Viking, 1997.

Robinson, Jancis, ed. *The Oxford Companion to Wine.* New York, Oxford University Press, 1994.

Rorabaugh, W. J. *The Alcoholic Republic: An American Tradition.* New York, Oxford University Press, 1979.

Rossi, Edmund. *Italian Swiss Colony and the Wine Industry,* an oral history conducted in 1970 by Ruth Teiser, Regional Oral History Office, Bancroft Library, University of California, Berkeley, 1971.

Rossi, Edmund, Jr. *Italian Swiss Colony, 1949–1988: Recollections of a Third-Generation California Winemaker,* an oral history conducted in 1988 and 1989 by Ruth Teiser and Lisa Jacobson, Regional Oral History Office, Bancroft Library, University of California, Berkeley, 1990.

Sbarboro, Andrea. *The Fight for True Temperance: Practical Thoughts from a Practical Man.* San Francisco, privately printed, 1908.

Schoonmaker, Frank, and Tom Marvel. *American Wines.* New York, Duell, Sloan & Pearce, 1941.

Shaw, David. "He Sips and Spits, and the World Listens." *Los Angeles Times,* February 23 and 24, 1999.

Stevenson, Tom. *Christie's World Encyclopedia of Champagne and Sparkling Wine*. San Francisco, Wine Appreciation Guild, 1999.

Sullivan, Charles. *Napa Wine: A History from Mission Days to the Present*. San Francisco, Wine Appreciation Guild, 1994.

Sullivan, Charles. *A Companion to California Wine*. Berkeley, University of California Press, 1998.

Teiser, Ruth, and Catherine Harroun. *Winemaking in California*. New York, McGraw-Hill, 1983.

Thomas, Marguerite. *Wineries of the Eastern States*. Third edition. Lee, Mass., Berkshire House, 1999.

Toqueville, Alexis de. *Democracy in America*. 2 vols. Edited by Phillips Bradley. New York, Knopf, 1945.

Tyrell, Ian. *Sobering Up: From Temperance to Prohibition in Antebellum America, 1800–1860*. Westport, Conn., Greenwood Press, 1973.

Vine, Richard. *Wine Appreciation*. Second edition. New York, John Wiley & Sons, 1997.

Wagner, Philip. *American Wines and Wine-Making*, New York, Alfred A. Knopf, 1963.

Wagner, Philip. *Grapes Into Wine: A Guide to Winemaking in America*. New York, Alfred A. Knopf, 1976.

Wait, Frona Eunice. *Wines and Vines of California*. Facsimile of the 1889 edition. Berkeley, Cal., Howell-North Books, 1973.

Waters, Alice. *Chez Panisse Menu Cookbook*. New York, Random House, 1982.

Waters, Alice. *Chez Panisse Vegetables*. New York, HarperCollins, 1996.

Williams, Andrew. *Flying Winemakers: The New World of Wine*. Adelaide, Australia, Winetitles, 1995.

"Wine: Selling the New Mass Market." *Business Week*, February 23, 1974.

Winiarski, Warren. *Creating Classic Wines in the Napa Valley*, an oral history conducted in 1991 and 1993 by Ruth Teiser, Regional Oral History Office, Bancroft Library, University of California, Berkeley, 1994.

INDEX

A. Racke, 338
Académie du Vin, 2
Acampo, 142
Adams, Leon, 107–8, 116, 126, 217,
  251, 265, 316
Adlum, Maj. John, 21–22
Alexander, 20–21, 22
Alexander, James, 19–21
Alicante Bouschet, 100, 103, 117, 186
Allied Grape Growers, 113
Almadén, 163
American Center for Wine, Food, and
  the Arts, 167
*American Grape Growing and Wine-
  Making*, 69
American Place, An, 305
American Viticultural Area, 346–47
American Wine Growers, 254, 255,
  276
American Wines and Wine-Making,
  118
Amerine, Maynard, 171, 177–84,
  189–90, 191–92, 210, 279
Andrus, Gary, 284
"angelica," 62, 101
Annie Green Springs, 127
Antinori, Piero, 328
Anti-Saloon League, 32, 49–50, 96

appellation, 22, 124, 346–47
Argentina, 20, 195, 332, 333
Argyle, 337
Ariba, 115
Arizona, 285
Arkansas, 266
Arneis, 329
Arrowood, Richard, 239–40
Asher, Gerald, 290
Associated Vintners, 280–81
Asti, 100, 165
Asti Grape Products Company, 97,
  100–101
Au Bon Climat, 349
Auler, Susan and Ed, 285
Australia, 193, 194, 338, 340
AXR-1 rootstock, 184, 191

Babcock, 349
Baco Noir, 119
Baker, Purley, 49
Bale, Caroline, 67
Baltimore, Lord Charles, 18
Barbaresco, 328
Barboursville, 271–72, 332
barrels: oak, 122, 150, 157, 160, 166,
  198, 218, 240, 247; vs. oak chips,
  240; redwood, 157; topping of, 233

[*357*]